DAILY HOMILIES
FOR THE YEAR

By

Gerald P. Ruane

JOSEPH F. WAGNER, INC.

Publishers

NEW YORK, NEW YORK

Nihil Obstat:
John H. Koenig, S.T.L.
Censor Librorum

Imprimatur:
✠ Thomas A. Boland, S.T.D.
Archbishop of Newark

Preface

This is meant to be a practical book. It's aim is to help priests do one thing—preach short, simple homilies at Mass each feast day. It is limited in scope also, seeking to serve merely as a catalyst for each individual priest's thoughts.

I could not be happier if the reader disagreed with some of the ideas or their development. A good disagreement is often just what is needed to clear the air and get one's own ideas in order. If that happens, the homilist will be involved and thinking for himself.

At times a particular homily may seem irrelevant or "old hat." If this is so, the priest should use his own ideas and development—a much more effective approach. Why? He will be speaking for himself in his own words and getting his own ideas across. That's the best way for a priest to preach a homily.

The homilies as they are recorded in this book are not exactly as I prepared or preached them. Often I changed words and even ideas. There is a certain inspiration that comes at Mass; for while the priest proclaims the word of God, the Holy Spirit is at work. Such inspiration should not be refused. If the priest is inspired to switch the emphasis in his homily, or to change the whole thing and strike out in another direction, he should do so.

A Maryknoll priest who was on leave from his mission in

iii

Africa preached one Sunday in his home parish. He gave his prepared sermon at the first Mass but felt quite dissatisfied with it. He threw away the prepared talk and spoke from the heart about his work as a missionary in Africa. We priests should do the same if the lightning strikes us at Mass. However, no one should count upon the inspiration of the Holy Spirit at every Mass and refuse to prepare at all. *The Holy Spirit comes when and where He wills and not necessarily when and where we will.*

This is a book for the great majority of priests. It is not directed to the avant garde nor to the ultra-conservative. It is directed to the majority of priests who are open to the best of the present and are aware of the best in our tradition. Priests of the 20th century must be firmly convinced that many things in the past were right and should be kept. They must also realize that many things in the past were not right or suffered from misplaced emphases. Such areas must be improved. Without being radicals, priests will progress and grow with the Church. If this book fulfills the function of a prudent companion for a part of that endeavor, it will have been a good investment of the author's time and energy.

Two articles from *Worship* are given in the first section of the book by way of introduction. They exemplify the process of growth and development which I have undergone since I began the practice of a homily each day. The introductory chapters conclude with some notes on preparation of the homily and the impact of the Supplementary Weekday Lectionary on a daily homily.

In a section after the sanctoral cycle, longer homilies for six days in September are given. They show the possibility of development inherent in the shorter homilies. One kind critic remarked about the germinal quality of the homilies and suggested adding these examples.

In certain instances, more than one homily is presented for a feast which, it is hoped, will provide greater variety and suggest further development where necessary.

Of special importance and not often treated in such books

are the homilies given for the weekdays after Easter and Pentecost, two weeks of unusual depth and beauty in the Church's year of grace.

Most authors sternly warn their readers not to preach the homily exactly as it is written and never to read it to the people. I quite agree with such warnings in the ideal order but realize how far most of us are from such an existence. If a priest must choose between reading the homily or omitting it altogether, I would prefer that he read it *well*. I was converted to such a position because I have seen it done quite capably. Admittedly the presentation is not the best, but it is good and far better than nothing at all.

In conclusion I urge my brother-priests to preach a homily each day. Read the homily if you can do no more. Give your own if you have time, using the contents of this book for ideas or whatever else helps you in this most important priestly task.

Acknowledgments

Many persons helped and guided me in the preparation of this material. I would like to thank most especially the priests, sisters, and people of Our Lady of Lourdes parish in West Orange, New Jersey who listened to the homilies and encouraged me in the practice of giving a daily homily. I am also indebted to the sisters, novices, and postulants of Mt. St. Dominic Motherhouse, Caldwell, New Jersey who for the last few months have been the cheerful recipients of my homiletic efforts.

My family was a source of strength and encouragement in this undertaking. Their expressions of interest and enthusiasm were "just what the doctor ordered" when my parish and teaching duties almost forced a cessation of this effort.

I would like to acknowledge the wonderful typists, Susan Nolan, Margaret Meyer and Margaret Hendry who helped so substantially in the preparation of these homilies by their encouragement and their self-sacrificing dedication. Sister

Maura, O.P., Sister Rita Margaret, O.P., and Reverend Paul C. Perrotta, O.P. of Caldwell College graciously read the manuscripts and offered many worthwhile suggestions. Sister A. M. Gerardine, O.P., designed the jacket. Monsignor Theodore Bonelli of the Newark Chancery willingly gave of his time and talents and expedited matters a great deal.

I would also like to express my appreciation to His Excellency, Archbishop Thomas A. Boland, who encouraged me by his kind comments on the articles in *Worship* and by his praise of the practice of a daily homily.

GERALD P. RUANE

Contents

Preface iii

Introductory Materials

    Why Not a Homily at Mass Every Day? 1
    Further Thoughts on a Daily Homily 6
    The Preparation of the Daily Homily 16
    The Supplementary Weekday Lectionary 19

Daily Homilies for the Year 22

Six Longer Homilies by Way of Example 269

Homilies for Lent, Easter and Pentecost 280

Why Not a Homily at Mass Every Day?

VATICAN II in its *Constitution on the Sacred Liturgy,* Ch. 2, art. 52, encouraged the homily declaring "that it is to be highly esteemed as part of the Liturgy itself." In fact, the Council decreed "that at those Masses which are celebrated with the assistance of the people on Sundays and feasts of obligation, it (the homily) should not be omitted except for a serious reason." With these words, the Constitution restored the homily to its rightful place and laid to rest some fairly widespread abuses, e.g., 1. No preaching at first Mass because people are in a hurry; 2. No sermon during the summer because the people are too hot; 3. The first thing to go when pressed for time is the homily because no one listens to it anyway.

Even before the Council prescribed a homily at every Mass of obligation, and certainly since it issued its *Constitution on the Sacred Liturgy,* many priests have taken great pains to prepare and preach a worthwhile homily. Not a few of the brethren give a homily each day during Lent. I maintain that there should be a homily at every Mass when even a few people are present. Since December of 1964, I have tried to do just that each day and this practice has proved well worth the effort and time involved. Although I use the high praise that the Council has given the homily "as part of the Liturgy itself" to justify my practice, the reason I started was less spectacular. I simply "stole" a good idea from a fellow priest, which is rather a common clerical "failing."

In November of 1964 I met a Monsignor who mentioned that he had preached at almost every Mass for the last eight years. He was a well-balanced personality who had things to say to his people and used the daily homily to say them. As he explained his reasons for giving a daily homily, they seemed quite impressive to me and they still do.

There is one instance in my own personal experience which stands out as an example of how a few words said at daily Mass can do a great deal of good. When my younger brother's only child, a baby of ten months, died, I wanted to say many things to him and his wife but wasn't able to find the opportunity. At the Mass I offered for the family, I mentioned that I had been in the habit of giving a homily at every Mass and then proceeded to talk to them about heaven. It wasn't the time for emotion so I just listed some of the things theology tells us about heaven and drew one or two conclusions. The whole thing took approximately three or four minutes, which is more than twice the time I would normally give to a daily homily. Thank God it helped to reinforce the wonderful faith of my brother and his wife. It also had quite an impact on the others who assisted at the Mass.

Just a Minute or Two!

Right away let me emphasize that the daily homily should be very brief—perhaps a minute or two. The purpose is to give the people a thought and to hope that during the Mass they'll make it a part of their prayers. What good could just a few words possibly do? Is it worthwhile? Most assuredly, "yes!"

In the seminary on very warm Sundays, the Rector would preach perhaps the world's briefest homily. In a sentence or two he would say what he wanted to say. His homily was always to the point, was always thought-provoking and often-times left us with a question that we had to answer during the

2

Eucharistic celebration. His few words were definitely worthwhile. Any priest should be able to make a similar impact with just a little practice and some effort.

The preparation need not be long at all. Most of us just don't have the time. In fact, the preparation should be short—just enough to get a worthwhile thought to give to the people. This can be done with surprising ease—especially after a little trial and error, which are two of the best learning devices we people have.

Sources

The source material for such a talk is unlimited. Perhaps the greatest treasure trove is the Missal itself (the Bible Missal or the Maryknoll Missal, for instance). Just a casual reading of the Mass text is usually enough. The Collect of the Mass and the other prayers can always be the launching pad for a homily. The Epistle and Gospel are incomparable sources of information also. Don't overlook the Ordinary of the Mass either; many parts of it are not well understood by our people and they should be. There are many other source books, too, e.g., *The Year of Grace* by Pius Parsh.

Sunday Leftovers

When preparing a sermon for Sunday, there are often four or five different topics we would like to develop but time only permits us to develop one or at the most two of them. At Mass during the week, especially the ferial Masses, why not, in a very abbreviated form, develop these other thoughts? Why not take the leftovers from Sunday and use them during the week? Some housewives work wonders with "leftovers." Why can't we do likewise by adding a dash of ingenuity and a little effort?

We can always give a biographical sketch of the saint of the day. Aren't the saints given to us for our imitation? After a short summary of the person's life, we can usually point to one virtue or practice which explains why this person became a saint. It is a simple procedure to conclude by asking the people to offer their Mass so that they may gain that virtue.

If worse comes to worse and there is no time to prepare, I would suggest that this is one of those infrequent instances when you can cast your care upon the Holy Spirit and the *"Dabitur vobis."* If we read the Missal beforehand, especially now when we should be preparing the Epistle and Gospel, there will always be at least one thought to develop in the homily. The problem really isn't that priests talk too much or too often, the problem is that they do not talk enough about the right things and at the right time. In Mass there is a natural pause after the Gospel which almost cries out for a few words of instruction, encouragement or at least a directional sign for the people's own thoughts and devotions.

Growth for Preacher and Parishioner

The practice of giving a homily at every Mass has helped me in many ways. It has helped me to grow in the liturgical life and to understand better this wonderful year of grace which the Church gives us. It has made the Mass mean more to me chiefly because I am better prepared for the readings and the other parts of the Proper. I am also more conscious of the theme of each Mass which helps me to understand what the Church is trying to accomplish at this daily encounter with Christ Crucified and Risen.

Now I realize that each night I must get a thought—must read the Missal and, if possible, glance through one of the source books. Many times this reading is the only spiritual reading I manage during the day. In a way, it is the best possible spiritual reading because it makes Mass a more meaningful and more profitable experience. That is a boon to any priest.

In conclusion, may I offer an example of what I mean. On the Feast of St. Francis de Sales, January 29th, just a few words might be said about his gentleness, his culture and his great learning, all of which were used to serve Christ and to spread the Faith. Then encourage those at Mass to pray for the zeal to serve Christ and spread His faith. But, and it's a big "but," they must do it with the same gentleness and regard for others that St. Francis de Sales had.

Further Thoughts on a Daily Homily

As A result of my article in a recent issue of *Worship* suggesting a homily at Mass each day, I have received several letters from the U.S. as well as one each from India and New Zealand. The one from New Zealand summed up quite well the gist of most of them when it said: ". . . Certainly made a good point and one which we should not be afraid to follow up. I think such a practice would help our people considerably. Once again a jolly good thought-provoking article." A number of priests from the Archdiocese of Newark commented on the article at the annual retreat and wanted to know more about the basics of the practice. It was also surprising to discover the number of priests who give a homily every day and have done so for many years.

Whatever the reaction and, thank God, most of it was favorable, there were always questions of one kind or another. It is in hope of answering some of these questions that this article is written. Most of the questions were about what to say, how long it should be, what the source materials are, and if there is any book with homilies for every day. There was also some confusion about the necessity of permission for a daily homily.

As far as I can see there is no permission required other than that of the Ordinary. No justification for the practice is needed save that of the *Constitution on the Sacred Liturgy* which states that the homily is "to be highly esteemed as part of the Liturgy itself." [1] There are definite pastoral considerations which must be weighed, and these would urge one to consult his pastor. If there is initial opposition, it might be

[1] Ch. 2, art. 52.

broken down by references to the Constitution, the growing practice of delivering a homily every day in Lent, and the strongest possible stress on the brevity of such a talk. Many times it helps to mention an older priest who preaches each day, or at least lets his curates do so.

Most of the questions and difficulties can be met and answered by a reasonable application to one's own circumstances of the following principles:

a. *Be brief.* Several helpful reminders of the need for brevity will probably be standing [2] right in front of you, such as the men anxious to be on time for work and the women who must hurry home to get the children off to school. Take a cue from the Scripture readings themselves which are usually quite short. There is always the danger that a long homily will overwhelm the readings by mere weight of words.

A recipe for a daily homily might read as follows: "Capture a thought and then develop it briefly. Draw one concrete application and then conclude by repeating the thought. Also, if possible, make a definite connection between the homily and the sacrifice-banquet which is to follow."

As everyone knows, endings are quite important and should be prepared. There are certainly enough ways to conclude, but it is quite difficult if you don't know where you are going. One way to conclude is by urging a talk with Christ. For instance on the feast of St. James the Greater, encourage the people to say: "Lord, make me an Apostle. Teach me to be concerned with You and Your kingdom, to want to be near You in trial as well as in glory. Help me to drink the chalice which I must drink and to do it today at work with the boss and at home with the children."

As to an exact time limit, a minute or two seems ideal.[3] To confine oneself to such a limit demands a ruthlessness which

2 There is no reason why the people should be asked to sit for such a brief talk. There are enough spiritual calisthenics at Mass already.

3 Fr. F. McManus in *Worship,* Jan. '63 p. 127 remarks: "A weekday homily may be limited in many cases to 2 or 3 minutes; on more leisurely occasions a homily might be as long as 15 minutes." That particular type of leisurely occasion may languish under the burden of a 15 minute homily.

will cost much effort and even some grief. Most priests enjoy talking, and it may take them longer than a minute to "warm up" to their subject. However, if the priest is brief, the people will be interested because their attention span will be working in his favor. If he is not, they will not listen. The people have learned to shut preachers off just as they flip off the radio or TV. They may not follow the advice of a former assistant Secretary of Labor who suggested that they start walking out on rotten sermons, but as soon as the sermon starts, they'll mentally switch channels.

Some preachers may worry about the value of such a short homily and lean toward a longer one. They may be right. A longer homily (4 minutes or more) is good on special occasions and in the right circumstances. Nonetheless, if you talk that long, it becomes a full length sermon, and demands an interesting beginning, an even better ending plus a fairly well-developed body. The brief homily makes few of these demands mainly because of its shortness but also because of its simplicity.

After that admittedly lengthy dissertation on brevity, we come to the next guideline.

b. *Be simple in your exposition of the theme. Simplicity* must be the keynote.

We are no longer in the Seminary with the homiletic "prof" in the back taking notes, or our classmates sitting there waiting to be impressed. Most of us have a fear of sounding trite or pietistic which is laudable in due proportion, but which often drives us away from perfectly acceptable material. Many of our people lack background and so they do not need studies in depth. I am not counseling a superficial treatment or supporting the "parishioners-only-have-a-4th-grade-mentality" theory. I am just pointing out that there is a great deal of spade work which had to be done before we can talk to our people like an American Karl Rahner, and have them understand us.

What the people need is the expression of our heartfelt appreciation of Christ and His love as shown in the Mass of

8

the day. This should be a meditation on the Word of God in our own words and colored by our appreciation and sense of values. Naturally a priest's knowledge of his people's needs and circumstances will also come into play. A daily homily is just a conversation with God's people about the Mass. As has been said, such a talk needs a worthwhile thought and a good conclusion, and these basic elements can be handled quite expeditiously.

c. *Source material.*

As regards sources, I can only repeat what was said in the first chapter about the Missal being the primary reference and also a gold mine which many of us ignore. Some of the prayers of the Mass are quite good and contain an outline for an ideal daily homily. For instance, the Entrance Prayer from the feast of St. John Mary Vianncy (August 8th) mentions his admirable priestly zeal and his unflagging fervor in prayer and penitential works. Then it concludes: "May his intercession and example enable us to gain the souls of our brothers for Christ and with them attain to everlasting glory." How easy it is to mention these points and then tell the congregation: "Use the strength and grace which you gain here at Mass and Communion to win your brothers and sisters for Christ. In so doing you will be achieving your own salvation as well."

A practice which helps is to read the lessons from Matins just before retiring. There are often interesting highlights given in the third lessons, and on greater feasts the homilies of the Fathers usually suggest a profitable train of thought. At the very least such a reading and/or praying of that part of the breviary helps to collect one's thought for the morrow. It is almost too obvious to mention that a priest always has his own personal spiritual treasury to draw upon in developing such "leads." This is an invaluable asset, especially if he has kept up with the recent trends and changes.

As for books, besides Parsh and often in place of it, there are Emeric Lawrence's *Meditating the Gospels* and also his *Homilies for the Year* as well as *Days of the Lord* edited by William G. Storey. Unfortunately the last two only consider the Masses of the more important feasts. In fact there really is no book of daily homilies yet. Lawrence's *Meditating the Gospels* is only a partial solution. Thierry Maertens' *Guide for the Christian Assembly* is, as the sub-title signifies, a background book of the Mass day by day, but is rather a difficult book because of the superabundance of information which is offered. There are also articles in magazines and newspapers which may have a bearing on the Mass of the day.

d. *The liturgy of the day should be the launching pad for the homily.* Whatever the message which you seek to get across it should be tied in with the text or the theme of the Mass. Some people object rather vehemently to the "way out" devices which have been used to make the above-mentioned connection. The organic link which binds the homily to the Mass as a whole is most important and should be made obvious to the people. There need be no "way out" devices if one's thoughts are guided and inspired by the actual text. If the Missal is the primary source book, this suggestion will be implemented quite well and without any fear of artificiality.

The four recommendations explained above at some length should answer most of the questions aroused by the first chapter. However, there are a few other things which might be mentioned. The changes in the liturgy should be explained much more thoroughly than they have been, with great emphasis placed on the reasons behind the changes. The beauties of the liturgy have often escaped the people's notice because there was so little instruction given them. Their opportunities to grow and know were unfairly curtailed by our "get-it-the-first-time-or-else" approach.

Too often priests assume that their people will catch on with a minimum of instruction. When this does not happen some of the clergy have been loud in their accusations that "the people don't care." The people are guilty of no such offense. They are afraid to make a mistake. One instance stands out quite clearly in my own experience. Two regular church-goers participated in Mass offered by a priest in their

10

home. They were quite unsure of themselves and felt obliged to ask for detailed instructions on what to do.

Just recall what happens during Holy Week and on the Ember Days. These vivid and at times painful recollections point to the need for a deepening of the people's acquaintance with the theory and practice of the liturgy. They also should alert us to the need for constantly reviewing what has already been said and trying to find fresh ways of explaining such material. These points may have been explained at Sunday Masses and even in special parish workshops, but that is only a beginning. There must be constant review of these developments and applications made of them to actual worship life. This can be done by means of the daily homily in an unhurried atmosphere using the parts of the Mass to illustrate what is said.

English has not always been the panacea which some expected. Now many persons realize just how little some of the prayers (Gradual, Communion, etc.) mean in their present fragmented form. Here again there is material for a homily— one which explains the purpose of such prayers using the Mass of the day as an illustration. Even the minor responses warrant greater attention. Nearly everybody now replies "We have lifted them up to the Lord," when the priest says: "Lift up your hearts," but how many of them really do it? Father Clifford Howell had a fascinating series going in *Worship* from April '62 to July '63 on these responses and other Mass prayers also. This series is now available in paperback entitled: *Mean What You Say*. It provides a goodly supply of ammunition for homilies and meditations.

The practice of a daily homily is not fraught with difficulties, but there are some. Some Mass formularies are repeated any number of times in a year, perhaps even two or three times in a week, such as the Common of a Confessor not a Bishop.[4] Since there is an almost limitless variety of saints, it

4 The following chapter considers among other things the Supplementary Weekday Lectionary which was issued several months after the publication of this article.

11

should not be too arduous to figure diverse and interesting ways to handle such situations. One suggestion would be to use the theme of the Mass and show how it is realized in the Saint of the day. Certain key ideas may also be taken from the Epistle and Gospel and used to exemplify pertinent features of the Saint's life. Once again the prayer of the assembly or the other prayers of the Mass may be used. We should strive to give the people the "feeling" of the different parts of the Church's year of grace. Frequently a saint may be seen against the background of the liturgical year and even used as a flesh and blood realization of the season's meaning. Isn't it possible to relate a Saint to the theme or scripture readings of the previous Sunday's Mass? It would be a valuable pedagogical lesson since it would remind the listener of the primacy of the Sunday Mass.

One of the letters which I received made mention of a priest who preached a homily every day. The correspondent expressed his doubts whether the congregation profited from this since "he is no preacher at all—most dull and uninteresting; he is the type who knows how to make a short story long. It would be impossible for him to finish off in a minute or two." Granted that the description is an accurate one, the priest in question has a problem. However it is not an insurmountable one, and so he should not abandon the practice of a daily homily.

The solution to his problem is quite simple and may be of value to others. He must prepare himself to *write* out what he wants to say. That very effort will cut down on the verbiage, and the rest of the "fat" will show up at the first reading. Writing out a homily for each day is time-consuming but it is not a bad idea in the beginning and may be almost essential in special instances such as the one under discussion. The benefits which are reaped from the daily homily warrant such an expenditure of time and effort.

Most priests after a little practice and considerable doggedness in preparing will manage quite nicely with just an out-

line or a list of ideas, plus that always-elusive conclusion.[5]
Once again brevity is essential. It may not destroy dullness
altogether but it does a pretty good job of it, and certainly
makes talk more palpable.

It is unfortunate that several priests had the feeling that
this practice was all right for those who had a special gift, but
that they were definitely not among the "chosen few." If a
priest realizes that he is not the great all-American preacher
and will never cause Bishop Sheen any sleepless nights, there
is no reason to despair. He has plenty of company and may
well have more to offer to the congregation than he realizes.
His words, simple and hesitant though they be, may have a
powerful effect. He may well be able to show forth the love
of God in just the way that will inflame the people's hearts.
They may be better able to identify with his thoughts and
gropings than those of a more articulate and polished homilist.

As was said in the first chapter: "The problem really
isn't that priests talk too much or too often, the problem is
that they do not talk enough about the right things and at the
right time." It is hoped that the reader will realize that the
solutions given above to a particular problem are not so
"individualized" that they could not be easily adapted to any
priest's circumstances.

It is also a matter of no dispute that most of us tend to talk
longer as the practice develops. We find more to say and want
to make references to what we have said at other Masses. The
organic link which exists among certain Mass formularies and
also among certain groups of saints becomes clearer to us.
There is always the desire to have the congregation appreciate such a relationship also. This is a tendency which I have
noticed lately. It must be resisted quite ruthlessly where it
causes inconvenience for the parishioners, or the other priests.
However, it is advisable to make these relationships obvious

[5] This in no way denigrates the *dabitur vobis* or charism of spontaneous
homilizing but it is well to be prepared in case the former bolts of lightning
don't strike when and where desired.

to the people where possible because this is something which they do not realize or understand.

Many priests do not have the same Mass each day and so they are not able to establish any sense of continuity with the cengregation. This is a problem but need not be if one offers Mass at the same hour at least three or four times a week. Switching Masses may also be helpful in a week when the same Common occurs more than once: you will not have to vary your approach greatly because the congregation will vary. This would also be beneficial when a number of ferials occurs during the week.

The first chapter closed by listing some of the "extras" which come from the daily homily habit. Here are a few more, most of which are based on the adage that "a good thought goes a long way and bears some repetition." The Mass homily often makes an excellent Novena sermon in slightly expanded form. Many times what had to be left out at Mass because of the time limit can easily be said at the Novena. It is good for the people at Novena to be reminded of the Mass and its unquestionable preference to any form of private devotion. It is a subtle yet quite effective restatement of what comes first.

It also relieves the busy priest of the necessity of finding a subject for such a talk. Mass and its scriptural passages are the topics, and who could ask for better ones? Even should the same group attend both the Mass and the Novena, the homily could easily be expanded by some biographical details plus graphic descriptions of time and place, etc. If the Novena crowd is not noted for participating at Mass, they might just decide to give it a try.

Some young adults have been heard to complain about the "assembly-line" attitude of certain priests in confession. Such an attitude can easily foster a spirit of indifference with regard to this sacrament. The main thought of the morning's homily might serve as the basis for a confessional exhortation. At such times it is possible to make a more telling and personal connection with the actual circumstances of the indi-

14

vidual's life and problem. Once again there is the opportunity of highlighting the very strong link between the Sacrament of Penance and the Sacrifice-Sacrament of the Eucharist.

Last in our list of "extras" is the beneficial effect such a practice has on Sunday preaching. Sunday preaching may very well improve because of the stringent time limit which one imposes on himself during the week. Another factor working for such an improvement is the effort exerted daily to produce a hard-hitting concise exposé of the Mass theme. If a priest addresses the people only on Sundays or only once every few Sundays, there is a tendency to go "overboard" and dump everything upon the poor heads of his unsuspecting parishioners. The daily homily is good therapy for such an impulse. It provides an opening to say what must be said but in more digestible doses.

Some may object that there are too few persons in church at daily Mass to make any such talk truly effective. Although there are only a few parishioners at daily Mass, if something worth quoting is said, it will be quoted far and wide. Just remember the story of the priest who got up one extremely warm Sunday and preached perhaps the shortest homily on record. He said: "If you think it's hot here, remember that there is a much hotter place. Make sure you stay away from it." That story and its main theme have been used innumerable times and with invariably good results. It just goes to prove what a few well-chosen words can accomplish. That really is the burden of this whole apostolate.

The Preparation of the Daily Homily

THE HOMILY outlines in this book are divided into three parts; theme, exposition, and application. This division was chosen because it was orderly and would be more easily retained by *the busy parish priest,* (and make no doubt about it, that is the person for whom this book is written), so that he will be able to read the outline, check back on certain key ideas, and rest assured that he has the substantial part of his daily homily well in hand.

The priest might read through the homily outline the day before he is to preach it. If possible, he should think about the ideas and their development during the day when he has a few minutes to spare—perhaps when he is driving, or waiting to go down for meals or whenever there is a lull between appointments. Special consideration should be given to the examples and the conclusion. If there is no time to read the outline earlier, then he should read through it at night just before retiring or before Mass.

It is essential, and this cannot be stressed too often, that the homily at daily Mass should be *short* and *to the point.* Such precision comes only with preparation. Some priests write out the complete text of a homily or an outline of ideas; others jot down a few thoughts, and some happy few never prepare claiming that they are able to preach at the drop of a hat. In some of the older churches there are clips on the back of pews which obviously were put there so that no hats would ever drop. Perhaps this is the wisdom of the ages showing a certain practicality which we do not often attribute to it *and underlining for all that preparation is essential for worthwhile preaching.*

In preparing the outline, the priest must be selective. He must pick and choose what he can use. He may omit some of the biographical details or expand them at will. They are the accordion-type part of the outline. His own homiletic sense will lead him to a happy medium with regard to such facts and their relative importance. The purpose of the examples is to offer ideas and a certain development. *He should feel free or rather compelled to go his own way and develop his own approach.*

One priest from a suburban, metropolitan area cannot make applications suitable for the whole country. The priest-reader must accept, reject, or adapt the applications contained in the outline. Either way, in some degree he must change them and apply them to his own area. He might utilize the theme and exposition; and make his own application with reference to a religious, social, political or economic event which is current in the newspapers or on TV. In fact, the ideal application is the one which is as up to date as yesterday's or even today's newspaper. If a flood or a riot has occurred recently in his area, the application might have some connection with the flood or the riot.

When the Newark riots broke out in the summer of 1967, the Sunday that fell during the five days of rioting contained the Gospel of Jesus weeping over Jerusalem. Many preachers drew a comparison between what was going on in Newark at that time and our Lord's reaction to the City of Jerusalem. The people in the Newark metropolitan area had failed to involve themselves in the problems of their colored brothers and the slums because they had not taken the message of Christ to heart and lived it. Drawing a comparison between Newark and Jerusalem and Jesus' reaction to both cities made the Gospel of Christ *relevant to that day, to that hour* and *to that particular riot.*

17

The applications that are made daily cannot be as startling and up-to-the-minute as the news reports on the television, but they can and must be relevant. Our Lord did not bat 1.000 in His preaching, in His teaching, in His missionary work or even in His training of the Apostles. The servant is not greater than the master. We have to accept the fact that at tmes the application will be the "old stuff" but that doesn't mean that it is the bad stuff. Sometimes the application will not be as relevant as we might like. Nevertheless, if we are trying and if we are aware of the necessity of making a connection with the spiritual condition of our congregation and with the news of the day, then our batting average on the whole will be good.

Certain outlines are open-ended. The application is not too well developed. In such cases it is up to the priest to fill in what is missing. Here again he should exert himself to make the application as relevant as possible to the people of his congregation.

The Supplementary Weekday Lectionary

EARLY IN 1967, the National Conference of Catholic Bishops received permission from the Holy See to use the *Supplementary Weekday Lectionary* [1] at Mass. This Lectionary is intended as a partial and a provisional step toward the goal expressed by the Second Vatican Council when it said: "The treasures of the Bible are to be opened up more lavishly in the most sacred mystery of the Eucharist so that richer fare may be provided at the table of God's words" (*Constitution on the Sacred Liturgy*, Article 51).

The S.W.L. provides semi-continuous selections from the Biblical books for weekday Masses whenever no proper passages have been assigned. This avoids the frequent repetition of readings from the Common of the Saints, or the use of the Sunday readings on several days of the week. It is only a provisional arrangement and will be replaced by the reformed Roman Lectionary.

Archbishop Hallinan, in his preface to the S.W.L., says: "It is especially hoped that the provision of these readings may encourage the preaching of daily homilies on the sacred text— 'The proclamation of God's wonderful work in the history of salvation, that is, the mystery of Christ, which is ever made present and active within us, especially in the celebration of the liturgy (*ibid.* 35, 2; cf. 52) as an integral part of the week-

1 Referred to as S.W.L. during the rest of the chapter.

19

day Masses, wedding and funeral Masses and Masses for Children and young people."

Archbishop Hallinan's high praise for the daily homily will do much to encourage the practice of preaching a homily each day. He clearly states that the homily each day should be based on the sacred text. No one would deny Archbishop Hallinan's contention that the homily *should be based* on the Sacred Scriptures. If this is so, what role, if any, do the saints have in a daily homily? *The sanctoral cycle is being downgraded, but it is not being eliminated.* There will always be feasts of the saints. Even now the S.W.L. is not allowed on certain feasts and their vigils. There are no selections for the few days after Christmas, the week after Easter and all of Lent.

Since there are quite a few days when the S.W.L. may not be used, some homilies on saints will be needed. Even the saints of lesser importance are with us for a while, perhaps a long while. They have a *message for us*. They are flesh and blood models for us to imitate. They have found their place in God's plan and lived it to the fullest.

There need be no conflict between the readings from the S.W.L. and the less important saints of the Church's calendar. It is possible to forge the two into a hard-hitting and impressive homily. First read the lesson and try to straighten out any fuzzy points. Not all of us are exegetically geared to a competent explanation of the scriptural passages, especially the first readings of the Lectionary. At times even a competent exegesis will not be homiletically sound nor particularly relevant.

If the S.W.L. does not yield any thought-provoking ideas, one can always fall back upon the saint of the day. If the S.W.L. readings do yield an idea, check the homily outline to see if there is any connection between the two. The idea from Sacred Scripture might be amplified by the life of the saint, and then referred to the Eucharistic celebration which follows.

Many times there is a natural connection between the Scripture selection and the saint of the day. I have done the

20

above and found it possible and profitable. In 1967 on the feast of St. Leo I, the S.W.L. reading was from the first Epistle of St. Peter. There was an obvious and intimate connection between the two which formed a succinct daily homily.

The Gospel selection from the S.W.L. and a few of the selections for the first readings are at times too short to form the basis for a homily. The message may be so obvious that the celebrant will be forced to look for something to add depth and meaning. The life of the saint is a "natural" ally in such an effort. Certain passages from the Gospels have been over-exposed and the people no longer listen to the "same old story." Once again, some details about the saint of the day might add a note of interest and variety.

Not every priest will use the S.W.L. and so might be overjoyed at the "change of pace" from repeated readings offered by the daily homily. However, there is little likelihood of such a reaction. A priest who does not use the S.W.L. will probably not bother to give a homily each day.

Priests who do use the Lectionary, if they do not already preach a homily each day, will slowly but surely gravitate toward that practice. They will soon realize that they must prepare or face the possibility of reading the Scriptures poorly. If they use a translation other than the Confraternity, they will discover almost immediately that the wording has been changed.

If the first or second reading in the S.W.L. for the day provides an idea that can be developed and related to the Eucharist, the priest may decide not to use the outline for that feast. Nonetheless, there will be occasions when he will look for something more. Perhaps the outline will provide an idea which he can develop and connect with the reading. There are good reasons for this. Many times in preaching I have noticed a heightened sense of interest in the congregation, a sudden silencing of coughs and shuffles when a saint is mentioned. People seem to enjoy hearing how one weak human being like themselves lived the topic under discussion.

21

Daily Homilies for the Year

November 30—St. Andrew, Apostle

THEME

Christ calls every person to help Him in His great work of saving souls.

EXPOSITION

Andrew, first follower of Christ along with John the Evangelist, was directed to Christ by John the Baptist with the words: "Behold the Lamb of God." When Andrew had followed and talked to Christ, he went to Peter, his brother, and said: "We have found the Messiah." Then Andrew introduced Peter to Christ. Andrew was later called by Christ to be one of the chosen Twelve. His answer meant constant companionship with Christ. It meant years of toil as an outstanding preacher and a ruler in the Church. It meant suffering, persecution and martyrdom. Andrew's love of the cross and his desire to share it with Christ is well known. The cross had an almost hypnotic effect on him.

22

APPLICATION

It is good to meet Andrew as we begin a new liturgical year of grace. He teaches us what it means to say "yes" to Christ's invitation to "come and see." All of us have been called to share Christ's work of saving souls. We may not be martyrs, but certainly we can be witnesses to Christ. Andrew shows us the way.

At this Mass, we hear Christ's invitation: "Come follow me." At every Mass this invitation is repeated in the liturgy of the Word and in the Eucharistic sacrifice. Every time Christ calls, please answer him as Andrew and all the Apostles did.

December 2—St. Bibiana (died c. 363), Virgin and Martyr

THEME I

Today's saint spurs us to a greater union with God in love.

EXPOSITION

Saint Bibiana's voice echoes through the Entrance Hymn as we cry out: "Sinners wait to destroy me but I pay heed to your decrees, O Lord." Bibiana came from a family of martyrs. Both her mother and her father endured death rather than deny Christ. Christ did not abandon Bibiana in her time of trouble—"in the midst of storms and dangers." United in love to her Lord and Savior, she endured her persecutors' threats, their efforts to corrupt her and their tortures to the death.

APPLICATION

The Entrance Prayer asks God "to unite our souls to you by love through the intercession of this saint so that we may be

23

shielded from all danger and obtain eternal rewards." What better gift could we ask today's saint to win for us than such a union of love? What better setting for such a request than this liturgical celebration where we should express our oneness in love with God and all His people?

Seek to enter more fully into the spirit of love which permeates the Mass. By this love grow more intimate with Christ, your Savior. By this love grow more considerate of and agreeable to your neighbors and co-workers. If you cannot love the latter, then you don't love Christ!

Theme II

On this day in 1942 the first self-contained nuclear reaction took place in Chicago amidst great secrecy. From that experiment came the atomic bombs which destroyed 170,000 lives in two Japanese cities. Pray that the horror of those first and second atomic bombings will remain so vivid to the conscience of mankind that there will never be a third atomic bombing of any city.

December 3—St. Francis Xavier (1506–1552), Confessor

Theme I

Our apostolic zeal must find its dynamism in our love-union with Christ and in our continuous spirit of prayer.

Exposition

The life of St. Francis is an almost exact realization in the flesh of Christ's missionary appeal in Mt. 16:15-18. Francis is the patron of the missions. He was one of the first Jesuits and was sent to the missions by St. Ignatius, his superior. He

24

worked in India and Japan for ten years, dying on an island off the coast of China as he was about to sail to evangelize that land.

He went "into the whole world and proclaimed the good news to the whole of creation." Wondrous signs accompanied his efforts for Christ. Some of these signs were even more wondrous than those promised by Christ.

APPLICATION

Today, when we think of the distance Francis traveled, the lands he visited, and the people to whom he proclaimed the good news of Christ, we gasp in amazement. Could any man, even in our jet age, equal his apostolic efforts?

Yet, even though he was an outstanding example of a man of action, what struck his contemporaries most of all was his fervent interior life—his almost continuous spirit of prayer. Ask St. Francis through this Mass and Communion for the grace to live in constant union with Christ. Let all your activities spring from the love-relationship which you initiate and deepen during this eucharistic act. If you are giving yourself to Christ by making life a little better for the poor and oppressed, you may not have much time to steal away and pray. Don't worry—make the most of what you have. Let this Eucharist help you to see every action as an act of worship of God in Christ Jesus whom you are serving in those you help.

THEME II

Each of us is called to be a missionary in the tradition of Francis Xavier. Our missionary activity must center principally in our home, office, factory, or wherever we are. These places need a missionary of the good news of Christ. Often these places need such a missionary desperately. Are you willing to fill the vacancy?

25

Pius Parsh calls Francis the Advent preacher to many pagans (volume 1, page 152). He was Christ's precursor to India and Japan—the John the Baptist of the Far East. We are called to be Advent preachers also—to follow in the footsteps of John the Baptist and Francis Xavier.

December 4—St. Peter Chrysologus (died c. 450), Bishop and Doctor of the Church

THEME

Respect for the Word of God as presented, explained, and applied by the priest at Mass.

EXPOSITION

Peter was Archbishop of Ravenna from 433 to 450. He earned the title Chrysologus (man of golden speech or golden-worded) because of his brilliant oratory. The people of his church were deeply moved by his forceful and fervent preaching. Today's saint could rightly claim that "In the midst of the assembly he opened his mouth and the Lord filled him with the spirit of wisdom and understanding" (Entrance Hymn). He preached the glory of God in a marvelously effective way.

APPLICATION

Each homily which we hear at Mass demands our respectful attention and consideration. The priest may be far from "a man of golden speech" but his words enjoy a special efficacy. They are set in the surroundings of God's inspired word.

They are often the priest's sincere meditations on the readings of the Mass. Listen carefully to what is said.

Most often the priest will tie his thoughts into the sacred action which is soon to happen. Even if he does not, you should always make the connection with the Eucharistic sacrifice-banquet. Don't hesitate to do that because you think it's Father's Mass. It isn't my Mass or your Mass. It's the Church's Mass and we who are here represent all the Church. Let's do the best we can as representatives of all God's people.

December 6—St. Nicholas (died c. 324), Bishop and Confessor

THEME

Our Advent-preparation for Christmas, if it is to be worthwhile, demands love for our neighbor.

EXPOSITION

Today's saint is a familiar one to us, at least by name. We know very little about his life except that he was Archbishop of Myra in Asia Minor. He died in the year 324. Legend has it that he was a man of great Christlike charity and extraordinary miracles.

APPLICATION

Advent is a time of preparation for Christmas. It is a time when we should be absorbed in Christ Who became Man and was born at Bethlehem because of love . . . love of the Father Whose will He did . . . love of all mankind whose salvation He sought.

Nicholas became a saint because of the love that he had for God and for his fellow man. The example of today's Saint helps us to prepare for Christmas in the right way. At Mass and in your prayers during the day and in the ordinary course of your work and recreation, catch the spirit of St. Nicholas. He believed in giving gifts. How about you? Give the gifts that really count . . . kindness, love, Christlike gentleness and consideration. You have these gifts waiting for you at Mass, in Christ Who is its Priest and Victim.

December 7—St. Ambrose (died 397), Bishop and Doctor of the Church

THEME

God works in strange yet wonderful ways to achieve His purposes.

EXPOSITION

Ambrose was a great preacher and defender of the Faith. Perhaps we know him best as the convert-maker who, by his preaching, led St. Augustine back to Christ's Church. Ambrose also had the distinction of being elected by the people of Milan to be their Bishop even before his baptism. He proved to be a magnificently apt choice for bishop.

APPLICATION

God certainly works in strange yet wonderful ways when He wants to get something done. Who would have thought such an unlikely candidate as Ambrose would become one of the Church's greatest bishops? Who could have predicted his influence on Augustine? Augustine heard Ambrose preach and, influenced by his words, turned to Christ once again.

You know, all of us are in a certain sense very unlikely candidates to be followers of Christ. Yet, we are just that. We can also lead others to Christ just as Ambrose led St. Augustine if we are willing to live our Christian lives to the full.

28

In the intimate union which we share with Christ and one another at this Eucharistic celebration, pray for the grace to place yourself completely at Christ's disposal. Try to lead others to Him as Ambrose did. It's the best way to save your soul and the best way to please Christ.

December 8—The Immaculate Conception

THEME

The vision of Mary's grace-filled soul beckons us to a life of holiness which will be expressed in apostolic activity.

EXPOSITION

The words of the angel still echo in our ears: "Hail, full of grace, the Lord is with you, blessed are you among women." The Gospel ends abruptly yet on a positive note with the angel affirming the greatness of Mary's gift of grace. Today we celebrate her Immaculate Conception—God Almighty gave her the privilege of being conceived with the fullness of grace in her soul.

APPLICATION

The vision of Mary's grace-filled soul calls us to a life of holiness no matter how burdened we are with sin and its effects. Such a life will not be a static existence but one vibrant with apostolic action. Mary was destined to be wed to the Holy Spirit, to bear Christ and to bring Him into the world. She did this as a lay person, while fulfilling the ordinary duties of any village woman of her time. Yet hers was a true, a complete apostolate.

What does this word "apostolate" mean? It means to re-

29

ceive Christ into our hearts, to grow in union with Him, and then to share Him with others. Isn't this a perfect description of Mary's role?

It must be your role; for you also have an apostolate to fulfill. Mary as your Mother is only too interested in helping you to find and to fulfill your apostolic role. Ask, she will give it to you. Seek, she will help you find it. Knock, she will open the doors of her Son's heart to you through this Mass and through your daily life.

December 11—St. Damasus (4th Century), Pope and Confessor

THEME

Damasus gives us an example of how interested we should be in the Sacred Scriptures . . . how much we should love to read the Bible and hear it read.

EXPOSITION

Damasus, a Spaniard who was Pope from 366 to 384, defended the Church against the attacks of those within and those without the Church who were attempting to destroy it. He is most famous because he commissioned St. Jerome to prepare the Vulgate translation of the New Testament.

APPLICATION

The treasures of Sacred Scripture are being uncovered more and more. The Second Vatican Council has called Sacred Scripture the soul of theology. It is the soul of more than theology; it is the soul of all our Christian living. We, in the spirit of Vatican II, should learn to love and to appreciate Sacred Scripture. The Mass is so filled with scriptural readings and prayers that we can begin at this Mass. Ask St. Damasus and St. Jerome for the grace to love the Sacred Scripture in the Mass. Love it and then let its message direct your life.

December 12—Our Lady of Guadalupe

THEME

Devotion to Our Lady of Guadalupe makes us realize that no matter where in the Americas we live we are all Mary's children and form one family.

EXPOSITION

Mary's visit to Elizabeth brought joy to all Zachary's house. In the same way her visit to Juan Diego, a poor Aztec Indian convert, brought joy into his life on that December morning in 1531. Her wish to have a church built on the site was fulfilled. This church of Our Lady of Guadalupe has never been closed, even during the many periods of persecution. The shrine has become a symbol of hope and unity for all of Mexico, in fact for all of the Americas.

APPLICATION

The fever of nationalism is still sweeping our land and its neighbors. Our Lady of Guadalupe can be the source as well as the symbol of our unity as children of God. Ask God "Who has placed us under the special patronage of the Blessed Virgin Mary" to continue His shower of endless blessings through her intercession.

Offer Mass today for the intention that all Americans may recognize Mary as their Mother, and one another as fellow-

31

members of God's holy people. As the first step in achieving such a goal, start doing it yourself.

December 13—St. Lucy (died c. 304), Virgin and Martyr

THEME

Love of Christ and faithfulness to His plan for us is the hidden treasure, the one really valuable pearl for which we search.

EXPOSITION

St. Lucy should be familiar to us. Each day after the Consecration of the Mass we mention her as one of the martyrs whose company we wish to join. She is the patron of Sicily. She could cry out as we will in the Communion hymn: "Princes persecute me without cause, but my heart stands in awe of Your word. I rejoiced at Your promise as one who has found rich spoil."

Strengthened by her love for Christ and seeking His holy will, she met and defeated her persecutors' attempts to separate her from her Lord. She died realizing full well that she had found the treasure—the really valuable pearl of this earthly life.

APPLICATION

Each day at Mass as you mention her name, reaffirm once again your desire to search always for the treasure hidden in this great sacrifice. Realize that the one really valuable treasure for which you search is Christ . . . to love Christ in and through this Mass so that you will be able to love Him in and through your neighbor and yourself.

32

December 16—St. Eusebius (died 371), Bishop and Martyr

THEME

Community spirit—What is it? How does it affect us at Mass?

EXPOSITION

Eusebius, the Bishop of Vercelli, Italy, earned the title martyr because of the harsh treatment he endured while in exile for defending the divinity of Christ against the Arians. He was the first Bishop in the West to introduce the practice of community life among the secular clergy. The reason for the change was quite simple. He wanted his priests to form a community so that the liturgy could be celebrated more perfectly.

APPLICATION

It's the fashion nowadays to speak of those at Mass as a community of love, a family at worship, brothers and sisters united around the Lord's table. Although we talk about this community aspect of the Mass, we have not yet understood its ramifications. Most of us are only now beginning to inch our way very hesitatingly toward the full realization of that goal. *The Constitution on the Sacred Liturgy* of Vatican II and all liturgical reforms seek to help us achieve a community awareness at worship.

How are we doing here in our parish? How are you doing as an individual? When you come to Mass are you determined to stay aloof from the others and remain safely ensconced in your own side pew toward the rear of church?

When you come to Mass, God wants you to be a member of His family—to think and act like one of His children; and His family prays and sings together, worships and stays to-

33

gether. How about it? Are you willing to give up your individualistic isolation and enter into this family worship?

Ember Wednesday in Winter

THEME

Come, let us walk in the light and the love of the Lord, our God.

EXPOSITION

These Ember Days just before Christmas give us the opportunity to look back over the last three months and to prepare ourselves for the coming of Christ at Christmas. Please don't miss the opportunity the Church offers you. Reassess your commitment to Christ during the last three months, make amends for the wrongs done, and offer thanks for the blessings you have not only received but used. When this is done, turn from the past and look to the great feast which is coming. Prepare well.

APPLICATION

Christmas is so close yet it is easy to miss the real meaning of Christ's coming. Has the peace among nations prophesied in the first reading come to our world yet? No, indeed! There is no such peace now. There will be no such peace until we take to heart the concluding words of the first lesson: "Come, let us walk in the light of the Lord, our God." Is that an impossible dream? No! It isn't. It just seems that way because we—all of us who supposedly follow Christ—don't try hard enough.

Christ, the Priest and Victim of this sacrifice, asks us to walk in His light—to live in His love. Are you going to say

34

"Yes" or "No"? If you say "Yes" make sure your family and the poor feel Christ's light and love through you. If they don't, your "Yes" won't mean much.

Ember Friday in Winter

THEME

Service to others must be the keynote of our lives as it was of Mary's.

EXPOSITION

Mary, the Mother of God, the Queen of Heaven and Earth, goes to visit Elizabeth to be of service. Mary does not doubt God's messenger; what he said, she believes. She acts upon her belief; love moves her to be where she is needed, and so she goes to her cousin. She is greeted with the words: "Blessed are you among women and blessed is the fruit of your womb." She responds with the beautiful prayer: "My soul magnifies the Lord, my spirit rejoices in God my Savior."

APPLICATION

Service to others was the keynote of Mary's life. Vatican II has told us that service to others is really the keynote of the Church's life. Such selfless service must be our way of life. All of us are anxious to welcome Christ at Christmas. Let's do it with love! Through this Mass and your prayers, learn how to love Christ. Realize that you show his love best when you serve Him as He lives in your neighbor. He lives in all your neighbors but try to see and love Him in the people you like the least. It'll be a good test of your Christmas spirit!

35

Ember Saturday in Winter

THEME

Repentance for our past sinfulness is an appropriate way to prepare for Christmas.

EXPOSITION

On this last of the Ember Days before Christmas the Church sets before us her favorite Advent preacher, John the Baptist. "He went into the whole region of the Jordan preaching a baptism of repentance leading to remission of sin." Today John the Baptist speaks to us about the necessity of being sorry for our sins. Repentance for our past sinfulness is an appropriate way to prepare for Christ's coming.

APPLICATION

What a magnificent man John the Baptist was! How he gripped the imagination of the people of his day! Let this man and his call to repentance stir your heart and help you to prepare well for Christ's birth and manifestations.

The Prayer after Communion says: "O Lord, our God, may we be healed now and forever by these sacred rites which were instituted to protect us in our life of grace." Our life of grace is our life with Christ. These sacred rites we offer together as a family should protect that life.

Now that you realize the purpose of this Eucharistic celebration, always offer it in the best possible way. If you do, then the new birth of God's only begotten Son which we now await will free us from the heavy bondage and yoke of sin. (Second Prayer of Mass) We will live in the freedom of those who follow Christ with a love that speaks heart to heart.

36

December 21—St. Thomas, Apostle

THEME

Believe as Thomas believed after he saw the Risen Christ.

EXPOSITION

Thomas appears quite prominently twice in the Gospel. He is the one who urged the other apostles to follow Christ to Jerusalem where torture and death awaited Him: "Let us go too, that we may die with Him" (Jn. 14:2-6).

These fine sentiments did not survive the shock of Christ's humiliating death on the Cross. Thomas was not going to believe so easily after Calvary. When told of Christ's Resurrection, he said, "I'll never believe . . ." as we just heard in the Gospel. Doubting Thomas, the original "man from Missouri," had to be shown that Christ was truly risen from the dead. Christ loved Thomas enough to meet his conditions. Then Thomas believed.

APPLICATION

Christmas is so near. It is good to celebrate the feast of St. Thomas at this time of the year. Thomas' doubt and his demand for proof strengthen our faith in Christ. Thomas teaches us that we have to believe many things that our senses cannot fathom. He is urging us today to realize that the true spirit of Christmas must include the humble and sincere admission: "I believe that Christ is both God and Man even though He came to us as a Babe in the manger."

Thomas urges us to listen attentively to the words of Christ: "Happy are you who have not seen but have believed." Believe as Thomas believed after he saw the Risen

37

Christ. Believe that in this Mass you come into closer contact with Christ than Thomas did when he touched Our Lord's wounds. Believe enough so that at the Consecration you can *say* and *mean:* "My Lord and my God."

December 26—St. Stephen, the First Martyr

THEME

Stephen's example of forgiving and loving his murderers is a perfect realization of the true Christmas spirit.

EXPOSITION

Stephen, the first martyr, was chosen by the Apostles to help them in their work. As we read in the Acts of the Apostles, he was a "man full of the Holy Spirit"—a man filled with grace and power who worked great wonders and signs among the people.

In the midst of his work for the poor of the Church, some Jewish people engaged him in a debate. They were no match for the wisdom and spirit with which he spoke. In their rage at his words and at the vision he had of Christ standing at the right hand of God, these people stoned him to death. Even as the stones crashed down upon his head, he prayed: "Lord, do not hold this sin against them."

APPLICATION

Stephen's example of forgiving and loving his murderers is a perfect realization of the spirit of Christmas. Christ became incarnate because He loved each individual. By His birth, life and death He teaches us how to love each person as He does. In the Entrance Prayer we asked Our Lord that "by imitating St. Stephen we may learn to love even our enemies for he prayed for his persecutors. . . ."

Stephen gave us a wonderful example when he forgave those who were murdering him—when he loved them to the end. Let's not allow his good example to go unimitated. We must learn to love our neighbors in the true spirit of Christmas. Why can't we begin here at Mass and branch out to the other areas of our life?

December 27—St. John, Apostle and Evangelist

THEME

St. John, the disciple whom Jesus loved, deepens our understanding of the true meaning of Christmas.

EXPOSITION

Among the disciples one stands out as being closest to Christ—St. John the Evangelist. He of all the Apostles was chosen to be the guardian of the Mother of God, to be her support and comfort as she stood beneath the Cross. He witnessed Our Lord's Transfiguration and His agony in the garden.

St. John in his writings and in his sermons stressed one thing repeatedly—the love of God for us and the love we must have for one another. When he was a very old man and could hardly speak, he was content to sum up the message of Christ in the words, "Little children, love one another." John caught the true spirit of Christ which is the true meaning of Christmas—love for one another.

APPLICATION

John above all people knew the heart of Christ. We who are children of love must follow the example of the disciple of love and learn the true meaning of Christmas.

As we unite around this altar, we must realize that we are a family offering sacrifice to God and sharing a meal in an atmosphere of love. In the intimate union which we establish with Christ and God's family at this Mass, we will find the means whereby we can "love one another."

If Mass doesn't mean these things to you, ask St. John to help you understand its family aspect. Perhaps he will show you how Mass must possess that warmth and love which was so apparent two days ago when families gathered to share their Christmas dinner.

December 28—Feast of the Holy Innocents, Martyrs

THEME

The Holy Innocents bore witness to Christ not by words but by dying for Him.

EXPOSITION

In the eyes of twentieth century people, Herod may not seem to have been such a bad person. We have become so used to men and nations who murder on a large scale. Compared to them, Herod was a small-time operator.

These martyred Holy Innocents were the first of many who would die for the sake of Christ. They gave testimony by their blood. We must give testimony by our lives. By freeing ourselves from the evils of sin, we must bear witness to our faith in Christ. Ours must be a faith expressed in actions as well as in words.

APPLICATION

Chances are you've heard that before any number of times. Chances are that you readily agreed with such sentiments.

Vague generalities and pious clichés go down very easily. Be a little more specific today. See if you have been limiting the true spirit of Christmas to your friends and other "nice" people. There are other people around you at home and at work who are desperately in need of a dose of Christ's love. If the last three days have meant anything to you, you will have some love to spare and share. How about it?

December 31—Year's End

THEME

Look both ways before you cross into the new year.

EXPOSITION

Mary, as we are told in the Gospel, had the habit of treasuring all things and turning them over in her heart. We have to do the same thing with the gifts that God has given us during the past year. As we gather round the altar on this last day of the old year, it is a good thing to look back and to see whether we have grown. It is a good thing to be able to say that we have grown in knowledge and love of God and of our neighbor.

APPLICATION

I sincerely hope that all of us can look back over the past year with joy and satisfaction. I will remember all of you and your families at this Mass so that you will have a sane and safe New Year's Eve. Please offer your Mass for every member of our parish-family so that next year may be for us a year when we grow to love God and neighbor more than ever. May it be a year of peace and prosperity. May it be a year in which all of us learn how to live like brothers and sisters in Christ—loving children of a loving Father. Before you cross into the new year, look both ways. Look back to see whether you have grown; look ahead and resolve that you will grow even more in Christ next year.

January 6—The Feast of the Epiphany

(Several outlines are given for this feast because its Mass-formulary is repeated so often.)

THEME I

May our lives be an Epiphany—a manifestation of Christ to the world.

EXPOSITION

The word "Epiphany" means manifestation. We celebrate today the manifestation of Christ to the Gentile nations of the world. The Magi, wise men from the East, represent the millions of people who are non-Jewish. As Christ was manifested to the world so many years ago on the feast of the Epiphany, we today in our lives must be a manifestation of Christ to our world. All Christians must realize this responsibility to be reflections of Christ to their world.

APPLICATION

Christ manifests Himself to us at this Eucharistic sacrifice under the appearance of bread and wine. It takes great faith to recognize Christ in the Host which we receive in Communion. But that faith we have.

Ask Christ at this Mass to help you realize and believe that you are Christ also—that you must manifest Christ to each individual you meet. Do not be surprised at the honor which is yours! You are more worthy to be Christ than bread and wine.

THEME II

At Mass Christ is manifested to all of us.

EXPOSITION

The Divine Office for today's feast proclaims repeatedly "Your light has come, Jerusalem, and the glory of the Lord has risen upon you; nations shall walk by your light, Alleluia." The priest will also say "Begotten before the daystar and before the ages, the Lord, our Savior, has appeared this day to the world."

Today we celebrate the manifestation of Christ to all the nations of the world. The Magi, wise men from the East, represent all the non-Jewish peoples of the world. The Magi brought their gifts of gold, frankincense and myrrh. They adored the Child and paid homage to Him as King of Heaven. Perhaps they had expected a King of earthly glory but they did not reject the One they found.

APPLICATION

In the Prayer over the gifts, we ask God: "Look with favor upon the gifts offered by Your Church. It is not gold, frankincense and myrrh that is offered now. The King, God and Savior, Who was signified by these gifts is Himself our sacrifice and our Food, Jesus, Your Son, our Lord." How wonderful is the Mass we offer! It's too bad that so few Christians appreciate it. It's too bad that so many millions of people know nothing at all about it.

At this Mass, as you join with your brothers and sisters in

Christ to offer His sacrifice and yours also, ask Almighty God to provide those vocations which are needed so that all nations may realize Who Christ is and how much He loves them. In your own lives be anxious to know and love Christ.

THEME III

Epiphany Preface.

On days when the Preface of the Epiphany is used, a short homily might be given on the two natures of Christ—Divine and human. This Preface speaks of the light of Christ's immortality being enclosed in His mortal nature. These thoughts could be developed and the people at Mass asked to make an act of faith in Christ as God and Man.

Themes for the Mass of the Holy Family when it is repeated during the week with its proper readings.

THEME I

We should never stop marveling at this Christ whom we follow.

EXPOSITION

The Gospel for the feast of the Holy Family lends itself to a consideration of Christ's two natures. Christ is the Son of God Who has to be about His Father's business. This was and is His primary concern. Mary and Joseph did not realize the implications of Christ's words or of His actions—at least, not at the time.

Christ is also man. He was subject to Mary and Joseph. He grew and made progress in wisdom, age and grace before God and man. He wasn't play-acting at being a man. He was

44

like us in all things except for sin. Too often when people hear Christ called a perfect man, they only hear the "perfect" and forget about the "man." He had a complete human nature and knows what it means to live through joy and sorrow, pain, temptation and disappointment.

APPLICATION

At Mass we offer Christ as both God and man to the Father. Christ is our sacrificial victim and our priest. At Communion we receive Christ as God's gift to us. This is a union that should be most dear to us—one that we should never neglect. In it we find the way, the truth and the life which help us to be better men and women and better sons and daughters of God our Father.

THEME II

During the New Year let us become more aware of Christ's Mystical Body.

EXPOSITION

The Epistle speaks of the Mystical Body of Christ. The New Year must be one in which we become more aware of the Mystical Body—more aware of the union of love which unites us as members of this Body of Christ. Christ pours forth His love upon the members of His Body and He wants them to share willingly with one another His love which they have received so undeservedly.

APPLICATION

Do you take care of your spouse, your family, your parents and relatives as Christ takes care of His Church? Do you love them as He loves His Mystical Body? Even if you must *spend* your life for them, even if you must endure great privations

45

and inconveniences, do not refuse to do so. If you suffer all these things, you have not yet done as much as Christ did. Learn the depths of His love at this Mass.

January 13—Commemoration of the Baptism of Our Lord

THEME

We must appreciate how completely baptism has dedicated us to Christ.

EXPOSITION

Today we commemorate the baptism of Our Lord in the River Jordan. It must have been a wonderful experience for John to see the Spirit descend on Christ, indicating that this "is the One Who is to baptize with the Holy Spirit." Meeting Christ and seeing such a manifestation of God's favor drew from John the statement: "This is God's Chosen One." John baptized with water. Christ baptized with water and the Holy Spirit. This is the baptism we have received.

APPLICATION

St. John the Baptist at the River Jordan gave testimony to Christ's unique role. We have to do the same in our daily lives. Our baptism gives us the right and the duty to proclaim to our age: "Christ is God's Chosen One."

We prayed in the Entrance Prayer: "May He who outwardly was like us *change* us *interiorly*." The change we ask for today at Mass is a renewal of our baptismal dedication. If we only appreciated how completely baptism dedicated us to Christ, we would strive mightily to be worthy of the honor.

As we offer this Mass today in memory of Christ's baptism,

let us remember what happened to us at our own baptism. Baptism was not a spiritual drycleaning to remove some stains from our souls. It made us God's children, members of His Holy People, the Church. We live and love with the life and love of God. We follow in the footsteps of Christ our Brother. We are completely His in life and in death. May this feast help us to realize and to live our dedication to Christ. It started when we were baptized and should have grown since then.

January 14—St. Hilary (c. 315–367), Bishop and Doctor of the Church

THEME

The saints guide us on our way to eternal salvation.

EXPOSITION

Today we move away from the celebration of the great events in Christ's life: His birth, His manifestation to the Gentiles, and finally the beginning of His public ministry at the River Jordan. We turn once again to the feasts of the saints.

Today's saint, Hilary, is a good example of what a saint is supposed to represent for us Christians of Vatican II. He is called the champion of the Divinity of Christ. Although he fought and hated heresy, he loved his opponents with the charity of Christ. Because of his logic and his undying dedication to truth, but most of all because of his Christlike charity, he converted many heretics.

APPLICATION

In the Entrance Prayer we praise God Who has "given us Blessed Hilary as a guide on our way to eternal salvation" and we beg God to let "him who once instructed the faithful on earth now intercede for us in heaven." This is the role of all the saints. They are to instruct us and guide us on our way to eternal salvation.

In the Prayer after Communion we ask the Lord that this sacrifice may bring us closer to our salvation through the intercession of the blessed Bishop and illustrious Doctor Hilary. Offer this sacrifice for that purpose. If you do that, then your Mass will produce the fruits that Christ wants it to produce.

January 15—St. Paul (died c. 341), the First Hermit

THEME

We Christians of Vatican II do not have to seek Christ in the wilderness, but in our own urban civilization.

EXPOSITION

St. Paul, the first hermit, followed the example of Christ Who often went into the desert to pray. St. Paul gave up the world and went into the desert to spend his whole life in solitude so that he would be able to pray and be close to God.

APPLICATION

It is a wonderful thing to be able to do what St. Paul did. I do not want to minimize in the slightest way what he did. However, a 20th century Christian cannot cut himself off from all contact with the world. In the spirit of Vatican II we must embrace the world—we must bring the world to Christ and Christ to the world.

If St. Paul the Hermit were alive today, I have an idea that he might find his work amid all the hustle and bustle of the

48

20th century. He would probably be in the midst of all the efforts made to achieve racial and community peace, slum clearance, fair-housing practice, better schools and better family life, etc.

Even if he would take off for the desert, don't you go along for the ride. Stay where you are and make the world better. Make this Mass your source of strength, your personal "launching pad" so that you will be able to Christianize or "Christ-ize" that world which is your world.

January 16—St. Marcellus (Early 4th Century), Martyr

THEME

We need greater loyalty to Christ and His Church.

EXPOSITION

Today's Martyr was a man who took his responsibility seriously. He knew that if he succeeded in shepherding the flock of Christ, an unfading crown of glory would be his. When he was free from prison he took care of his flock personally. When he was imprisoned, he did so by letters. He died worn out from the hardships and the persecutions he suffered because of his determination to be Christ's good shepherd.

St. Marcellus may seem like a distant figure to Catholics of this century. The Church, realizing this possibility, directs our thoughts not so much to the saint as to the Church. She prays to God at the offering of the gifts that: "your light graciously shine upon your Church so that this flock may everywhere prosper and its pastors under your guidance be truly pleasing to you."

In the Prayer after Communion we ask that the Lord will govern the Church which He has been pleased to enrich with

the heavenly food. We continue: "guide her by your powerful direction that she may enjoy greater freedom and remain
unshaken in the fullness of faith."

APPLICATION

Our loyalty is to Christ and to His Church. St. Marcellus was
loyal. He sets before us a much-needed example of tenacity
in doing Christ's work; of loyalty to the end. He teaches us,
during the Eucharistic celebration, how we can be loyal.
Let's try to learn this lesson well.

January 17—St. Anthony (died c. 356), Abbot

THEME

The secret of Christian sanctity lies in our love of God and
of neighbor, especially our fellow Christians.

EXPOSITION

Anthony, called the patron of all monks, lived at the end of
the third century. When his parents died, he went into the
desert to seek in solitude perfect union with Christ. Anthony
was famous for the severe penances and mortifications that he
inflicted upon himself. However, as the Maryknoll Missal
points out, he realized that the secret of Christian sanctity
does not lie in bodily mortification but in love of God and of
neighbor.

APPLICATION

Holiness means loving God and our neighbor, especially our
fellow Christians. Tomorrow we start the Week of Prayer for

Christian Unity. In this era of the Church's life we are called to the task of promoting Christian unity. I urge all of you to participate in this Week of Prayer and to offer your Masses and Communions for Church Unity. Pray during this week "that all may be one" as Christ prayed at the Last Supper.

Prayer is not the only means that we have at our disposal. Brotherly love is the other. We must have a double-barreled approach to this problem—prayer and brotherly love. In your Masses seek the grace to follow the example of Christ Who loves and treats us all as brothers. Remember that every Catholic must be a true crusader for unity, and must manifest in his daily life the love of Christ for all mankind. May we find this love of Christ at Mass today through the intercession of St. Anthony.

January 18 and 19

Where possible, the Mass for Church Unity should be offered. The homily could be drawn from the booklet sponsored jointly by the Graymoor Friars and the National Council of Churches.

January 20—Sts. Fabian (died c. 250) and Sebastian (died 288), Popes and Martyrs

THEME

Are you willing to be a martyr for the cause of Christian Unity?

51

EXPOSITION

Today and tomorrow we will offer Mass in memory of several martyrs of the Church. Today's saints were full-grown men who were well-equipped to meet and defeat the enemy. Tomorrow's saint was at most a teenager. Fabian as Pope was very much interested in bringing Christ to other people. He may have been responsible for sending St. Dionysius and other missionaries to Gaul.

Sebastian was a Christian Roman, an officer of the Imperial Guard in the 4th century. His influence was such that he was able to protect his fellow Christians and even convert some of his fellow officers to Christ. He rebuked the Emperor for persecuting the Church and fearlessly pleaded with him to cease. He died a martyr for this act.

APPLICATION

Today's saints were loyal to Christ in their own centuries. We must be loyal to Christ in our day. Pray today for the Church and the fulfillment of the work of the Second Vatican Council.

Would to God that all of us were willing to be martyrs for that cause. Not martyrs who shed their blood for Christ—red martyrs—but dry martyrs. We must be willing to sacrifice ourselves for the fulfillment of the dream of Pope John when he called the Council. Ask Fabian and Sebastian for some of their courage and loyalty to Christ.

We have to give our time and energy to the painful task of acknowledging and atoning for past wrongs. We must learn more about our own beliefs and then study what our separated brothers in Christ believe. And throughout this whole process of study, dialogue and active cooperation, we must pray constantly for God's blessings and guidance in this, His work. Ask Fabian and Sebastian for some of their courage and determination to serve Christ before all others. You'll need it and, what is even better, you'll get it.

January 21—St. Agnes (died c. 300), Virgin and Martyr

THEME

God chooses the weak things of this world to achieve His purposes.

EXPOSITION

Today we celebrate the feast of St. Agnes, a virgin-martyr of the Church. She was probably only a young girl when she gave up her life for Christ. We prayed just a little while ago: ". . . God, Who chooses the weak things of the world to confound the strong, may your blessed virgin martyr, Agnes, intercede for us who celebrate her feast." Agnes was one of the weak things of the world but God used her to confound the strong.

APPLICATION

We are weak also in many ways. Our weakness is rarely more apparent than during this Week of Prayer for Christian Unity. Yet God will take our weakness and use it if we give it to Him. We might pray today for the Orthodox and Oriental Churches, the Anglican Communions and the Old Catholic Church, that they may find the unity of Christ's true Church.

If such unity is achieved, it will be because God accepted all the sacrifices and prayers of the weak things of the world to achieve His wonderful purpose. Offer your Mass and your prayers today for this purpose. Ask St. Agnes to help you to be completely loyal to Christ in these efforts for unity, even as she was completely loyal to Christ back in the 4th century.

January 22—St. Vincent and St. Anastasius, Martyrs

THEME

East and West together—that's a goal to work for with everything we have.

EXPOSITION

Vincent is a martyr of the Roman Church and Anastasius is a martyr of the Eastern Church. It is fitting that during the Week of Prayer for Christian Unity we celebrate a feast which links together martyrs of the Western and Eastern Churches.

We pray in this Mass that the honor we pay to God's saints may please Him and "that the reception of this Bread of Heaven may strengthen us against all adversity through the intercession of Your Martyrs, Vincent and Anastasius."

APPLICATION

We must pray for the unity of the great Catholic and Orthodox traditions during this Week of Prayer for Christian Unity. We should also pray for Protestant denominations. It will take the courage and love of North, East, South and West to achieve Christian Unity. Don't you be the weak link in this effort.

Beg God through Vincent and Anastasius to form all Protestant denominations and the great Churches of the Catholic and Orthodox traditions into His family. Beg as you've never begged before and pray just as hard because the time is right if we are ready to move.

January 23—St. Raymond of Peñafort (1175–1275), Confessor

THEME

We will reach the harbor of our eternal salvation by loving all men and especially the Jews.

EXPOSITION

For a hundred years St. Raymond prepared himself to meet his Master. He was known as an outstanding director of souls and is revered as a patron saint of confessors.

In the Entrance Prayer we mention that God "chose Blessed Raymond to be a true minister of the sacrament of penance and marked his life by the miraculous trip across the sea." The Church chooses two things from the life of St. Raymond and applies them to us. "May his intercession help us to prove our repentance by our deeds and reach the harbor of our eternal salvation."

APPLICATION

We should love the sacrament of penance and all of Christ's sacraments. We should prove our sorrow by our deeds so that we will be able to weather the voyage of life and to reach the safe harbor of eternal salvation.

One of the intentions of the Week of Prayer for Christian Unity is for peace between Jews and Christians. St. Raymond converted many Moors, Jews and heretics during his lifetime by his love and understanding.

At Mass today try to learn how to appreciate the sacrament of penance and to reach the harbor of eternal salvation. Remember also the intentions of Unity Week and pray fervently and often for peace between Jews and Christians.

January 24—St. Timothy, Bishop and Martyr

THEME

Every Christian must be a missionary after the example of Paul and Timothy.

EXPOSITION

Timothy gave a splendid profession of faith in Christ as St. Paul urged him to do in the first reading of this Mass. Timothy was a missionary-companion of St. Paul. He was appointed by Paul as Bishop of Ephesus, where he met his death.

It is fitting during this Week of Prayer for Christian Unity, that we pray for the missionary endeavors of all Churches and of all Christians and for united Christian missions. Timothy, faithful companion and beloved spiritual son of St. Paul, is interested in this intention and will use his authority and his power before the throne of God to make sure that our petitions are heard.

APPLICATION

Paul was a missionary; Timothy was a missionary. Every Christian of the early centuries knew that he or she had to be a missionary. You are missionaries also. The Second Vatican Council emphasized that the whole Church is missionary and that the work of preaching Christ is a basic duty of the People of God. The Council reminded bishops of their special responsibility in this effort and pointed out that they are consecrated not just for one diocese but for the salvation of the entire world.

Our baptism and confirmation placed somewhat the same responsibility on us. We must work for the salvation of the world personally by our prayers and interest, and through others whom we support and encourage by our loving concern and our financial help. Discover in the Mass the strength and determination you need to be a true missionary who follows in the footsteps of Christ, Paul and Timothy.

January 25—Conversion of St. Paul

THEME

Paul teaches us to be completely converted to Christ. Ananias teaches us to say to every other Christian, "My brother."

EXPOSITION

Today we celebrate the world's most famous "about face." Saul was a violent hater of Christ and all Christians, a confirmed persecutor of "the New Way." Paul, after Christ had appeared to him, was filled with an equally fervent love of Christ and of His message. Christ made Paul His great missionary to the Gentiles and said, "I will teach him how much he will have to suffer for My Name." Paul was a chosen vessel of Christ for this great work of spreading His Name, and of suffering for Him.

APPLICATION

Paul was completely converted to Christ. We are not so lucky. Our conversion is a slow process which began when we were baptized into the Family of God. There is still much in us that has not been given completely to Christ. The process of conversion goes on. Today, be inspired by the example of St. Paul to give yourself more completely to Christ and to His message.

On this last day of the Week of Prayer for Christian Unity, the example of Ananias is especially worth noting. Ananias was ordered by the Lord to go to Saul, the Church's violent persecutor. Ananias tried to tell Christ who this man was, and received in reply a glimpse into Paul's mission and greatness. Ananias finally went to Paul with the Lord pushing just a little bit. He went in and, inspired by the Holy Spirit, said to this former enemy: "Saul, my brother."

You may for one reason or another still distrust Protestants and Orthodox believers. If you can bring yourself to see Christ in them and to treat them with the same respect that Ananias showed Paul, then the cause of Christian unity will have moved a little closer to realization. Remember at this Mass to give yourself completely to Christ. Ask for the strength and grace to love Him in all Christians and to say to every man: "My brother."

January 26—St. Polycarp (died c. 156), Bishop and Martyr

THEME

We are proud of our apostolic ancestors in the faith such as Polycarp. Are they proud of us?

EXPOSITION

Polycarp, the disciple of St. John the Evangelist, ordained by him and made Bishop of Smyrna, links us with Christ through his Apostles. We can be proud of the type of man Polycarp was. He proclaimed the message of Christ in broad daylight and from the housetops. He knew Christ's words, "Whoever acknowledges Me before men, I will acknowledge before my heavenly Father." Today's saint not only knew these words; he acted on them.

When he was being persecuted, the authorities tried in every way to get him to deny Christ. He refused even to consider the possibility and said: "For 86 years I have served Him. How can I blaspheme my Savior and my King?" He died as he lived—a man of true apostolic zeal.

APPLICATION

We can be proud of St. Polycarp and our other apostolic ancestors in the Faith. Can they be proud of us? They can be and are proud of us if we know that we are Christ's apostles, if we think, speak, and especially act like His apostles. At Mass today, you will be united with the source of all apostolic strength and zeal, Christ the Lord. Discover in this union the grace that you will need to walk in the footsteps of Polycarp and of all those who followed Christ.

January 27—St. John Chrysostom (died 407), Bishop and Doctor of the Church

THEME

When was the last time you asked the Holy Spirit to inspire a preacher's words?

EXPOSITION

John Chrysostom, eloquent Patriarch of Constantinople was the glory of his age. He was a Bishop, a Doctor of the Church, a martyr and the most famous preacher of his day. So great was his eloquence and consummate skill as a preacher that he was called "Chrysostom—golden-mouthed." Pope St. Pius X officially proclaimed him the patron of preachers. He was no less a writer than a preacher and both his writings and sermons are well worth reading today.

APPLICATION

I mean no dishonor to St. John when I focus on just one facet of his brilliant career—his preaching. He knew and loved the holy Scriptures as few men have. The Bible was always the basis for his sermons. Wouldn't it be nice to have a John Chrysostom around these days? So often our preaching leaves a lot to be desired. We priests must study more, prepare harder, practice often, and love God's holy Scriptures.

What are you going to do to help? When was the last time you asked the Holy Spirit to inspire a preacher? Your prayers can mean a great deal! Next time you get hit with a boring sermon, don't sit there and groan. Whisper or shout a prayer to God to make the priest aware of his deficiencies—and to make him willing to overcome them, and eager to explain the message of Christ.

Ask St. John Chrysostom to help a brother-priest in need. And when you find a homily enjoyable, interesting and profitable, don't keep it a secret. Be as loud and clear in your praise as some people are with their complaints.

January 28—St. Peter Nolasco (1189–1256) Confessor

THEME

A Christ-like person will find ways to show his love no matter when or where he lives.

St. Peter Nolasco was a Christ-like person who found a way to love Christ in his fellow Christians. He sold his inheritance to ransom Christians enslaved by the Moors. He did more. With St. Raymond of Peñafort, he founded the religious order of the Mercedarians whose chief apostolic work was to purchase the freedom of Christian captives from their Moorish masters.

APPLICATION

In Peter's time it was a definite apostolic work to ransom the Christians enslaved by pagans. In our time the need is different. It may be civil rights; it may be local or national politics; it may be working with the poor in the inner-city or in Appalachia or in other anti-poverty programs. It may be any number of things, but there is a need, and it will respond to Christ-like love.

Ask today's saint through this Mass for the courage to respond to the need that faces you right now. Work hard to solve it both as an individual and a member of a larger team. Seek in your daily contact with Christ at Mass the love which will help you to solve today's problems.

January 29—St. Francis de Sales (1567–1622), Bishop and Doctor of the Church

THEME

The Church of Vatican II desperately needs gentle and holy apostles like St. Francis de Sales.

Francis was a leader of the Catholic Reformation—a movement which was not always marked by its gentleness or by its rational approach to a problem. He converted many of his opponents by his kindness. He was a man of action. He was a founder of the Order of the Visitation.

Francis was a writer of great Christian classics, works that stressed the holiness and the apostolate of the laity before this was a generally accepted notion. Above all and in everything he did, he was a true Christian gentleman, a holy and gentle apostle who was able to achieve a balance between the demands of his work for Christ and the demands of his gentlemanly nature.

APPLICATION

Today we are in an era of reform within the Church. Many of the notions that St. Francis stressed are coming to the fore. Among all the activities and changes of the Church of Vatican II, there is a danger that we can lose the ideal of what it means to be true Christian gentlemen and women.

Ask St. Francis through this Mass for the grace to be gentle and holy as he was. Model yourself on him who modeled himself so faithfully upon the gentle, humble and holy Christ.

January 30—St. Martina (died c. 228), Virgin and Martyr

THEME

Those whom we so foolishly call the weaker sex often show us an example of courage that puts us to shame.

Martina, the virgin-martyr whose feast we celebrate today, was not afraid to face persecution and even death for Christ. She certainly had caught the theme of the first lesson of today's Mass. She was convinced that God would rescue her "from the grasp of the pagan nations"; that in every danger she could count on Christ.

APPLICATION

Every Christian owes a great debt to those women who died martyrs for Christ. These people whom we designate as the weaker sex gave us an example of courage, fortitude, and determination in the face of persecution that should inspire us. In many ways it should also make us feel ashamed. Ashamed that we do so very little for Christ.

We might pray today at Mass as the Church does that St. Martina will draw us all closer to Christ. Make it your business to learn from her how to live for Christ. If you know how to live for Christ and with Christ, don't ever wonder if you'll have the courage to die for Him if the occasion arises. You, like St. Martina, will die the way you lived.

January 31—St. John Bosco (1815–1888), Confessor

THEME

O God, enkindle in us a fire of love to seek after souls and serve You alone.

EXPOSITION

"Come children, hear me. I will teach you the fear of the Lord." These words which form the Offertory Hymn could

have been the motto of St. John Bosco. He spent his life leading young people to Christ. He founded two religious orders,
under the protection of the Virgin Mary, to take care of boys
and girls who needed help. His ideal was to become as a little
child himself. He considered himself of little account and
welcomed the little children for the sake of Christ, realizing
that by so doing he would be welcoming Christ.

APPLICATION

The prayers of the Mass set before us what we should be seeking through this sacrifice. We want Almighty God to enkindle
in us a fire of love to seek after souls and to serve Him alone.
In the Prayer over the Gifts we say: "Accept O Lord, the
offering of this life-giving sacrifice. May we love you in all
things and above all things so that our lives may praise and
glorify you."

Our names are not John Bosco. We are not confronted by
the same circumstances that he was, but there is much that we
can learn from him. The secret of his success was that he
loved others for Christ; he loved Christ in others.

Through this Mass learn his secret of success. After this
Mass and because of its grace put his secret to work in your
lives.

February 1—St. Ignatius (died 107), Bishop and Martyr

THEME I

Nothing can separate us from the love of Christ except the
love of self.

EXPOSITION

"Unless the grain of wheat falls into the earth and dies, it remains just a grain of wheat; but if it dies, it bears much fruit" (Jn. 12:24). St. Ignatius, successor of Peter in the See of Antioch and its second Bishop, not only knew, followed, and loved Christ, but even thought and spoke as the Master did. As Ignatius was being brought to Rome to be thrown to the lions, he cried out: "I am the wheat of Christ. May I be ground by the teeth of beasts that I may be found pure bread!" These words form the Communion Hymn.

APPLICATION

In a while we will offer bread and wine to God as our gift at Mass. The statement of St. Ignatius, "I am the wheat of Christ," should make us realize that we also are the wheat of Christ. We are ground into the pure bread of Christ not by the teeth of beasts but by the daily cares that each of us must endure. Not many of us seem to realize that fact.

Realize today that you are a grain of wheat which must fall into the ground and die in order to produce much fruit. You must have your incarnation as Christ had His. Ask Almighty God for the grace to be "the wheat of Christ" and to accept your daily crosses as the providential means to attain that goal.

THEME II

"Who will separate us from the love of Christ?"

EXPOSITION

In his epistle this morning, St. Paul seems so certain that nothing can separate him from the love of God that comes in Christ Jesus, our Lord. Ignatius felt the same certainty. They were caught up in God's love and would not let anything divorce them from it.

65

It seem as if many things separate us from the love of Christ. They're not really big things—not death and life things—but often relatively minor things. At this Mass, in the union of love which you share with God through Christ, seek to be rooted ever more firmly in love. Then you will be able to live as Paul and Ignatius lived. You will be able to say with them: "I am certain that nothing will be able to separate us from the love of God that comes to us in Christ Jesus, our Lord."

February 2—The Purification of the Blessed Virgin Mary

THEME

Our modern world will be torn apart unless we have respect for law.

EXPOSITION

The Gospel explains the meaning of today's feast. Mary goes to the temple to be purified according to the Law of Moses. Joseph and she bring Jesus to present Him to the Lord because it is written in the law: "Every first-born male shall be consecrated to the Lord."

Jesus, the author of the law, did not have to obey it. However, for a Jewish person, the way to perfection was obedience to the law of God; and Jesus, true man and true Jew, followed this way. Nor did Mary His Mother have to submit to the purification rites, but she too obeyed the law because she loved the God who gave the law.

Some of our contemporaries have a unique attitude toward the law. They think that it is an unreasonable restraint upon their freedom. They take great glee in getting around the law and ignoring it. The concept of law that we have set before us in the Gospel today is far different from that. Jesus and Mary willingly, lovingly submit to the law because they know that it is the will of God for them. Especially today when riots and quasi-revolutions are not unknown even in our cities, we desperately need respect for law. Why not be as humble as Jesus and Mary and imitate their attitude toward the law?

You may never have taken part in a riot, broken into a store, looted it, set it afire, but that does not say that you have always respected and followed the law. On this feast day promise Jesus and Mary that you will follow their example. Seek at this Mass and Communion for the grace that you need to fulfill this pledge.

February 4—St. Andrew Corsini (died 1373), Bishop and Confessor

THEME

Thank God for a saint who found it hard to live his life of dedication to God.

EXPOSITION

Andrew Corsini was a saint of the 14th century; but, before he was a saint, he was a wayward youth—which is not an unusual beginning for a life of holiness. His mother's grief, and the fact that he had been dedicated to the Blessed Virgin at birth made him realize that he was meant for better things. He entered the Carmelite Order and eventually became a Bishop. The interesting thing to note about St. Andrew is the fact that even though he dedicated himself to God, he was persistently tempted and assailed by the devil. He did not find it easy to live his life of dedication. Although he did not find it easy, he did live it.

APPLICATION

Thank God for saints like Andrew Corsini. Sometimes we think about the saints only as they were in the fullness of their union with God. At this point they seem almost completely removed from the realities of our life. It is good to realize that the saints had problems too. Andrew found it difficult to live his life of dedication. Through Mass, the sacraments and his great pastoral work for souls he found the means to overcome the temptations and to live his life of dedication.

The moral of the story for us is simple. If you're tempted, overcome the temptation by loving and serving God in your neighbor. Even if you fall, don't be discouraged. Many people fall, but they get up. That's what you have to do. Ask God through every Mass and Communion, through every prayer that you say and every good work that you do to help you to live your life of dedication. Andrew was able to do it. Go and do likewise.

February 5—St. Agatha (died c. 251), Virgin and Martyr

THEME

Do we love God's gifts more than we love the God who gave them?

68

Agatha is the last of the four virgin-martyrs mentioned in the Canon of the Mass. She was a very beautiful girl, and the Roman Governor was attracted to her. When his advances were rejected, he demanded that she sacrifice to the pagan gods. She refused and he in his anger—his love now turned to the deepest hate—ordered that she be tortured until she sacrificed to the gods. She was stronger than he thought, even stronger than she was beautiful, and she resisted to the end and died a martyr.

APPLICATION

Legend has embellished the story of Agatha. However, we can be sure of the few facts we have mentioned and from them learn a valuable lesson. God gave her great beauty which was not only a blessing but a liability. She used God's gifts well, always realizing that He was the important person and the gifts He gave were secondary.

Let's consider the gifts God has given us. Do we value them for themselves or do we value them because of the One Who gave them? Many good people give in to the temptation of loving God's gifts to the point where they no longer love the God who gave them. Examine yourself and see how you're doing in this regard. Make sure you love the God who gave the gift and not just the gift.

February 6—St. Titus (1st century), Confessor and Bishop

THEME

Newspaper advertisement: A busy, hardworking Savior seeks apostolic helpers.

EXPOSITION

"The harvest is plentiful but the laborers are scarce, so pray to the owner of the harvest to send out laborers to reap it." Titus was a convert to Christ from paganism, an ardent follower of St. Paul, and finally the Apostle-Bishop of Crete. He found a plentiful harvest of souls waiting for his apostolic reaping. You will, too, if you look around you.

APPLICATION

Look around you today as you race through your busy schedule. No matter where you are or what you are doing, there are souls to be saved. Be an apostle. Answer Christ's advertisement: "Busy, hardworking Savior seeks apostolic helpers." At this Mass pray earnestly and perseveringly to the owner of the harvest to send laborers to reap it. Why not roll up your sleeves and pitch in yourself? It's not bad work and the rewards are outstanding, especially the retirement plan.

February 7—St. Romuald (c. 951–1027), Abbot

THEME

"Lord, what are we going to possess?"

EXPOSITION

Our first Pope was not the type to beat around the bush. He got right to the point even with Christ. The Apostles "had given up everything to follow Christ" and wanted to know what rewards to expect in return. Peter asked the question that was in the minds and on the lips of all the Apostles. "Lord, what are we going to possess?" Our Lord promised

70

them the highest places in heaven. He included in the twofold promise of eternal life and the hundredfold reward everyone who would give up loved ones or possessions to follow Him.

How true are Peter's words in our case? Have we "given up everything to follow Christ?" Hardly! Most of us try to perform a little juggling act, holding on to some of the things of the world even as we seek to follow the Lord. During the season of Lent which starts soon try to make Christ and His work a more intimate part of your lives.

Start with your family. Let them feel the kindness and love of Christ through you. Give at least a few hours a week to serve Christ in C.C.D. work, in the apostolate to the sick, the aged, the poor, or the young. Ask Christ the same question Peter asked: "Lord, what are we going to possess?" He may give you the same answer He gave Peter. Or He may just answer: "Me, in this Mass and in the work we do together afterward."

February 8—St. John of Matha (1160–1213), Confessor

THEME

Christ commands us to love our neighbor as He has loved us.

EXPOSITION

As a young priest St. John realized that his vocation was to minister to the Christians captured by the Saracens. With St. Felix of Valois he founded the Order of the Most Holy Trinity for the ransoming of captive Christians. He gave of

71

himself unsparingly to do this work of God. Christ's command to love others not as much as we love ourselves but as much as He loves us was heard and obeyed by today's saint.

APPLICATION

It is hard for us to love others as we love ourselves. We have so little in common with many of the people we meet. If this is so, how are we ever going to love others as Christ has loved us? With our own puny powers of loving, we will never be able to achieve such a lofty goal. But there is a way. We must love others with the love of Christ. That love is ours through the sacrificial meeting with Christ which is ours at Mass today.

Be prepared to relinquish your selfish and unloving ways. Be ready to love without restriction the Christ Who lives in your neighbor. Why not begin today? If you do decide to begin today, remember that there is only one place to begin—where you are now. Take a small step first, and then go on from there.

February 9—St. Cyril of Alexandria (died 444), Bishop and Doctor of the Church

THEME

Love of the truth demands a willingness to defend it.

EXPOSITION

Cyril, the Patriarch of Alexandria, is called the Doctor of the Incarnation and the Defender of the Motherhood of Mary. He took a fearless stand against the heresy of Nestorius and presided over the Third Council of the Church held at

72

Ephesus in 431. Thanks to his efforts the Council decreed that Christ is both God and Man, and that the Blessed Virgin Mary is truly the Mother of God. It wasn't easy for Cyril to fight the heresy of Nestorius, but there was no choice. If anyone could pick and choose what he wanted to believe of the teachings of Christ, Christianity would become a mockery.

APPLICATION

The prayers of this morning's Mass deal with the fact that Mary is truly the Mother of God and also that Jesus Christ is co-eternal with God in glory. These are two of the most cherished truths of our faith. We should love these truths and realize that we must understand them, be able to explain them and defend them. Through this Mass we come into intimate contact with Christ, Who is co-eternal with the Father, and with Mary, the Mother of God. Ask Cyril for the grace to realize the intimacy of your contact with Jesus and Mary at Mass. Following in the footsteps of a man like Cyril, seek to love and to defend the truths of your religion.

February 10—St. Scholastica (480–547), Virgin

THEME

The innocence of the Virgin Scholastica should inspire us to seek Christlike innocence no matter what our state in life.

EXPOSITION

Scholastica, the twin sister of St. Benedict, is noted for her innocence of life as well as for the great devotion she had to her brother and to his work. Inspired by his teachings, she devoted her whole life to serving God. The story is told that Benedict spent the whole night discussing spiritual things with his sister and then went back to his monastery. A few days later he saw her soul going to heaven in the form of a dove.

APPLICATION

Please don't get the idea that today's saint has anything in common with TV's flying nun. Scholastica had her feet firmly planted on the ground. She worked alongside her brother in his efforts to bring Christ to people. She is a model of innocence not because she flew around in space completely divorced from earthly demands but because she was able to see Christ in the most menial tasks and in the lowliest person. She had a Christlike outlook on life. Are you interested in such an outlook? At Mass, ask her to let you see things in a Christ-tinted way.

February 11—Apparition of Our Lady of Lourdes (1858)

THEME

The greatest miracle of Lourdes is that many people leave there physically uncured, yet spiritually contented with their sufferings.

EXPOSITION

Today we celebrate the apparition of Our Lady at Lourdes in France. Who of us has not heard of Our Lady of Lourdes and St. Bernadette? Who of us has not wanted to visit that Shrine? But I wonder if we realize that this is not just a feast

74

to honor the appearance of Our Lady. It is a celebration of the joyful fact that she was conceived with the fullness of grace in her soul. The words of Our Lady to Bernadette at Lourdes contain the essence of today's feast: "I am the Immaculate Conception. . . ."

APPLICATION

If you ever do visit Lourdes, you may see a miracle, a physical miracle . . . a man or woman cured of a disease that was incurable. If you go to Lourdes, you will definitely see many miracles . . . the miracles that take place with people who go there suffering terribly and come away from the Shrine suffering still. The greatest miracle of Lourdes is that so many leave there physically uncured, yet spiritually content to suffer with Christ . . . not just content but anxious to follow in the footsteps of their Crucified Savior.

During Mass today we can have the essence of a pilgrimage to Lourdes. The essence is Christ and His Mother teaching us to accept our life and its difficulties, its sorrows and its pain. Yes, they teach us to accept and even to love these things because we thereby become more like the crucified Christ.

February 12—The Seven Founders of the Servite Order (13th Century), Confessors

THEME

At Mass today we ask Christ and His Mother Mary to help us share in the effects of His redeeming sacrifice.

EXPOSITION

Today we have set before us the example of seven young citizens of Florence who became hermits dedicated to meditating on the Passion of Christ and the Sorrows of Mary at the foot of the Cross. They did this to atone for the sins of their fellow citizens of Florence and to beg God for peace. Mary used these seven to start the Order of the Servants of Mary, which we call the Servites.

APPLICATION

These seven holy men are our ancestors in the faith along with the Apostles and all the Saints. They are related to us in Christ. Their example of meditating on the Passion of Christ and the Sorrows of Mary at the foot of the Cross should inspire us. At Mass today we join with them and with the Sorrowful Mother of Christ here at Calvary.

We will pray in the Prayer after Communion: "Refreshed by the Sacrament of heaven, O Lord, may we follow the example of these saints and stand steadfast beneath the Cross of Jesus with Mary, His Mother in order that we may also share in the effects of His redeeming sacrifice." Today may we share even more intimately in the effects of Christ's redeeming sacrifice. In one of his sermons, Cardinal Newman spoke of the Cross of Christ as the measure of the world. Use the Cross of Christ to measure your life with all that it contains and see how things look! It might be quite a revelation to some of us to see how far we miss our mark.

22

The feast of the Chair of Peter recalls Peter's authority as the head of the apostles, as well as the authority of all those who succeed Peter. The term "Chair of Peter" is a theological expression that signifies the authority—especially the teaching authority— of the pope. In early Christian times, bishops had official chairs on which they sat as they preached and taught their people. Over time, the chair of a bishop came to be viewed as a symbol of his authority and has been regarded with respect.

Jesus told Peter that he was the "rock" upon which he would build his church and that Peter would be given "the keys of the kingdom of heaven" (Matthew 16:18-19). Consequently, to Peter and his successors is accorded a kind of primacy over the church, and so the chair of St. Peter has come to represent the pope's special calling to teach and serve the people of God.

Following the example of his master, Peter ultimately became the servant of the servants of God. As a fellow elder in the primitive church, he exhorted the other leaders and led them by his example. Now, as Peter's successors, our popes are called upon to tend the flock of God willingly and humbly as imitators of Christ in their own right. How vital it is that we pray for them and intercede on their behalf!

Let us pray for our pope and for all the bishops of the church as well as for the countless others who serve God in any capacity. Let us pray that God will lead us all in

> "Goodness and mercy will follow me all the days of my life."
>
> —Psalm 23:6

humility as we take up our calling. Most especially, let us pray that he will continue to guide the church by his Spirit. The pope has been called into the humility and love of Jesus, the Good Shepherd. He is responsible for shepherding all of us. He is called to lead us and show us how to care for the lowly and the lost. As Jesus prayed for Peter, let us pray for our pope.

"Lord, help and comfort those you have appointed to serve you, especially the pope. Through his ministry, bring all your people together as one. May we all clothe ourselves in humility as we follow your call."

▶ **Psalm 23:1-6; Matthew 16:13-19**

February 22—St. Peter's Chair

THEME

Union with the Pope is for us a sure sign of union with Christ.

EXPOSITION

Today's feast is called that of St. Peter's Chair. This Chair is a symbol of the authority and power of St. Peter and his successors. Christ's promise and His later bestowal of power on Peter was not meant for him alone; it was bestowed upon his successors also. Today we honor Peter and the long line of Popes who have succeeded him in his Chair of authority and power.

APPLICATION

Union with the Pope is for us a sure sign of union with Christ. Every sincere Catholic must seek to unite with the Holy Father in professing Faith in Christ both by word and deed. We Catholics of today are called to an ever-deepening union with the Pope in the service of mankind and in spreading the Church.

In this Eucharistic sacrifice you will find the strength to do your part in helping the Pope spread Christ's teachings. In this Eucharist you will be united with Christ Who is the unifying principle which binds together the Pope and all baptized persons. Make good use of this opportunity.

February 23—St. Peter Damian (1007–1072), Bishop and Doctor of the Church

THEME

Our age needs apostolic reformers just as much as St. Peter Damian's era did.

EXPOSITION

The Church has her "ups and downs." She has her periods of great fervor as well as times when the fires of love seem almost to go out. Some centuries witness the fullness of Christian love and activity; others experience the near triumph of evil. St. Peter came along just as the Church was emerging from one of her "downs." He was a great apostle of reform and aided many of the Popes in their efforts to restore the Church to her ancient purity and zeal.

APPLICATION

The Church in our century has experienced a great growth in holiness. Nonetheless, as Vatican II showed, there is much that we Catholics have to do if the Church is to become everything Christ wants her to be. Study the blueprints for renewal that Vatican II provided and work with your bishop and the rest of God's people to build a better Church. Don't daydream about the glorious things you would have done if you had lived when St. Peter Damian did. Our age needs apostolic reformers just as much as his era did, so why not volunteer for one of the openings? Learn from St. Peter Damian what it means to be an apostle of reform. Learn from this Mass how you can be "the salt of *this* earth" and the "light of *our* world."

78

February 24—St. Matthias, Apostle

THEME

Every Christian has been chosen to take the place of an Apostle, to do the work of those Christians who have gone before him.

EXPOSITION

Today's First Lesson provides us with the story of how Matthias was chosen to take the place of Judas. Matthias, as we have heard, was one of those who shared the company of the Apostles all the while the Lord Jesus moved among them. He would become a witness with the Apostles to the resurrection of Christ.

APPLICATION

Matthias was chosen to take the place of an Apostle who failed. We Christians are chosen to take the place of Apostles who did not fail. They spent themselves working for Christ. All but one of them died martyrs because they would not stop preaching the Good News of Christ. We are called to be their successors. Are we?

At Mass today renew your dedication as an apostle of Christ. Find the strength in this sacrifice-banquet to be truly an apostle to your family, to the place in which you work, and to the community and state in which you dwell. That is your calling as a follower of Christ. Don't be a Judas-Apostle; be a real Apostle.

February 27—St. Gabriel of Our Lady of Sorrows (1838–62), Confessor

THEME

Gabriel shows young and old alike that youth can achieve great holiness.

EXPOSITION

The young man in the Gospel who wanted to know what he had to do to become perfect did not accept Christ's invitation to come and follow Him. He had great wealth which he did not want to surrender, and so he passed up the chance of a lifetime.

Today's saint is one of the many who took up the challenge that the young man in the Gospel refused. He gave up what he had and followed Christ as a member of the Passionist Order. He died after only six years in the religious life, but they were six years of intense growth in Christlike love and holiness.

As we say in the Entrance Prayer, God taught Gabriel "to meditate constantly on the sorrows of Mary and exalted him by his virtues and miracles." Pope Leo XIII said that Gabriel of Our Lady of Sorrows was so devoted to the sorrows of Mary that he deserved to take his place beside St. John at the foot of the Cross.

APPLICATION

Youth today faces many challenges. The greatest challenge is to decide what they will do with their lives. Gabriel shows them and us how one young man decided to follow Christ. No one can tell us exactly how we as particular individuals must follow Christ. That's our decision, and only we can make it.

Today's Saint gave us quite an example to follow. Imitate Gabriel in his many virtues. Ask him to help you take your place at the foot of Christ's Cross close to his mother Mary, warmed by her love and guidance.

March 4—St. Casmir (1459–1484), Confessor

THEME

It was just too good an offer to resist.

EXPOSITION

Today the Church sets before us the patron of Poland, a very young man who was able to live his commitment to Christ even though surrounded by the trappings of royalty and great worldly pleasures. He was offered the throne of Hungary, and much to the displeasure of his father, the Polish King, he refused it. He had better things to do for he had to help the needy, to make peace, and to practice what he believed.

APPLICATION

I wonder how today's saint would have felt in our modern society where so many shady deals are overlooked as long as they help a person get ahead in his work. The rationalization is often heard: "It was just too good an offer to resist. There were some shady aspects to it, but it was a good move on my part; it helped me get ahead." We Christians have to fight against this attitude because it is so prevalent and attractive.

St. Casmir was a young man but he had learned this lesson well. He knew that he could not divorce any part of his life from his commitment to Christ. Have we learned that lesson yet or are we still trying to keep Christ in church and out of our stores, factories, and homes? Let's hope that we learn this lesson well so that we will realize what it means to follow Christ.

March 6—Sts. Perpetua and Felicity (died c. 203), Martyrs

THEME

Devotion greater than even a mother's love.

EXPOSITION

A slave and her mistress make up the combination of saints whose feast we celebrate today. Perpetua was a young mother and wife of noble birth. Felicity was her slave. Felicity followed her mistress because their relationship was greater and deeper than any that could exist between a slave and a mistress. They were followers of Christ and knew the equality that true Christians possess with one another. Perpetua was allowed to keep her nursing child with her in prison; Felicity gave birth to a child just three days before her martyrdom. Both these mothers willingly gave themselves to Christ. They loved their children but they loved them enough to realize that they could not deny Christ and still be good mothers.

APPLICATION

The relationship that existed between Perpetua and Felicity speaks volumes for our times. We could talk about how these valiant women proved that the weaker sex is strong when the chips are down. We could talk about many things, but in these times it is good to highlight a relationship that tran-

March 19
St. Joseph (1st century)
Spouse of Mary, Foster Father of Jesus,
Patron of the Universal Church

Scripture records not a single word spoken by St. Joseph. The little we know of him portrays him as a man of great faith, prudence and obedience, "a just man."

As protector of Mary's honor in becoming legal father of Jesus, he was entrusted with the duty of providing for the Mother of God and God's Son. What a privileged position! Yet Joseph went about his daily labors as a carpenter in a quiet, unassuming manner, eager to be of service to his family and neighbors. Because he was the divinely appointed head of the Holy Family, Pope Pius IX solemnly proclaimed him Patron of the Universal Church (1870). As such he is the guardian and protector of the family of the Church and all Christian families.

Let us pray to him with confidence for all our needs, to be faithful to the duties of our call in life, and finally for the grace of a holy and peaceful death.

— **Sister Lorraine Dennehy, C.S.J.**

TODAY: Remember, there is no higher praise of a man than saying he is just.

March 20
St. Cuthbert (d. 687)

scended social barriers. A noble woman was as far removed from a slave girl in Roman times as the highest echelon of our most wealthy classes is from the poorest sharecropper or Negro worker.

Between Perpetua and Felicity Christianity built a bridge of love, respect and dedication. We need the same type of Christianity today which will ignore social classes and barriers and build a bridge person to person. Let Our Lord and today's saints help you to realize that true Christianity builds such a bridge of love and respect among people, or it isn't Christianity. If it's true Christianity, it is worth any sacrifice. Are you ready to make such sacrifices?

March 19—St. Joseph

THEME

A life of complete dedication to God.

EXPOSITION

St. Joseph is the strong silent type of the New Testament. His strength is shown in many ways. He was strong enough to do the heavy work of a small town carpenter, to travel many miles into a strange land and to protect his family on the journey. The Gospels record not one single word that he spoke. He was the silent type who spoke volumes by his actions.

St. Joseph, the just and upright man, was unwilling in any way to hurt the reputation of the Blessed Virgin Mary. The scene in this morning's Gospel gives a clue to his character. There would be no scene or vehement public denunciation of Mary. He would divorce her quietly. He knew that Mary was pregnant and it was not his child. When God spoke, Joseph put away all doubts and took Mary as his wife.

When he became the husband of Mary and the guardian of Jesus, he won lasting fame. However, his greatest claim to fame and the essence of his holiness was his complete dedication to God's will. Even if he had lived his life as an unknown village carpenter his complete dedication to God would have assured him a high place in heaven.

APPLICATION

If there is one message that Joseph gives us during this season of Lent, it is: "Dedicate yourself completely to doing God's will. Don't waste your words talking about doing His will; do it!" Some people never are quite sure what God wants them to do. They spend most of their time considering the problems and their possible solutions. By the time they decide what to do, it's too late!

God tells us what He wants us to do in many ways. Our state in life and position of employment, the example of Christ, the teachings and directions of the Church, and our bishops, the dictates of our well-formed and factual conscience—all these show us what God expects of us. Joseph thought it was God's will to divorce Mary quietly. When God told him something different, he never hesitated.

We must do our best to discover God's will and then do it. If we find that we have made a mistake, fine, then we'll do it the right way. It is not as easy as it sounds, but it can be done. Let St. Joseph help you to be dedicated completely to God's will. "Lord, help us to obtain through the influence of St. Joseph the grace to know and to accomplish Your will."

84

March 25—The Annunciation of the Blessed Virgin Mary

THEME

Mary's example of humble submission to God's will points the way for all of us.

EXPOSITION

Mary hears the words of the angel telling her that she is to be the mother of God. She hears and believes these highly flattering and yet seemingly improbable words. St. Ambrose points out that Mary does not form any high opinion of herself despite the unexpected promise. She who is chosen to be the Lord's mother proclaims herself His handmaid: "Behold the handmaid of the Lord; be it done to me according to Your word."

APPLICATION

Mary's words will be faithfully echoed by her Son in the Garden of Gethsemane when He cries out: "Not My will but Yours be done." Jesus and Mary beckon us to follow their example and to submit humbly and completely to God's will in all things.

Every Christian ought to follow this example; but we, who offer this sacrifice to God, should most of all feel compelled to submit to His will. At Mass and several other times today, make Our Lady's words your own and say: "Be it done to me according to your word." Live your day and your Lent as she lived her life—in humble submission to God's will.

April 4—St. Isidore (c. 560–636), Bishop and Doctor of the Church

THEME

A faith so strong that it prepared people for centuries of persecution.

EXPOSITION

Isidore, the Archbishop of Seville, was the greatest churchman of his time in Spain. He was a man of the people. He possessed an advanced liturgical sense and knew that the liturgy should teach people not only how to worship but also how to live. To him belongs the credit for the restoration of the faith in Spain after the Visigoth kingdom was converted. He was the one who presided over the most important Council of the Spanish Church. He did his work so well that when the Moors conquered Spain in 711, people did not give up their religion, but rather they held on to it even more strongly.

APPLICATION

Isidore was a man of his age. We have to be men and women of our age. Isidore teaches us how important faith is. In our own lives we must constantly pray for an increase in faith and we must study to understand better the teachings of God. We have to take great care that we hand this priceless possession to our children and to our families and to our students in the right way. We must give them an appreciation for their Christian faith.

If only we could hand the faith on to others as Isidore did. He did his job so well that centuries of persecutions could not tear it from the hearts of the people. With the help of this Mass and of everything we do for God and His people, we will be able to possess and to give our children a faith strong enough to meet the needs of our century.

April 5—St. Vincent Ferrer (1350–1419), Confessor

THEME

Preach Christ in your own words, not in a preachy manner.

EXPOSITION

Vincent Ferrer was one of the most effective preachers of the Dominican Order. He shows us that when the liturgy is lived to its fullest, it is not sterile but promotes every Christian virtue, especially a deeper love for God and neighbor. He found in Mass, the Office, and the sacraments the strength to live in practice what he preached by word. Since he preached almost constantly, there was an ever-present danger that he would become "as sounding brass or a cymbal clashing." The liturgy, alive, lived and dynamic, helped him to avoid what is an altogether too common pitfall for preachers.

He preached innumerable sermons and thereby converted many people to Christ. He had such influence because he used the power that God had given him to spread the word of God and not the word of Vincent.

APPLICATION

How many times a day do we talk about God? How many people have we ever led to a closer relationship with Christ? We cannot all convert thousands of people to Christ as Vincent did, but we can do our part. We must do our part.

Ask St. Vincent through the power of God to take the shackles off your vocal cords, and help you to talk about Christ and what it means to follow such a leader. Preach Christ in your own words, not in a preachy manner. Speak from the heart, and not with a stained-glass window voice. If your belief in Christ has blossomed into love, if the liturgy is helping you achieve a greater harmony between what you say and what you do, you will be preaching the most effective sermon possible.

April 11—St. Leo I (reigned 440–461), Pope and Doctor of the Church

THEME

How strong is an ideal? How powerful is a man of ideals?

EXPOSITION

Many people know Pope Leo the Great for only one thing. He stopped Attila dead in his tracks and prevented the sack of Rome. He was a great man in other respects. However, let us stick with that famous meeting of the Pope and Attila. It teaches us a great deal about a man with ideals.

What a conflict that must have been! Attila the Hun was a man of brute strength before whom all the world seemed to quiver in fear. Leo was fearless and in control of himself. He was a man whose ideals were so strong that he could face the barbarian leader. The Pope not only faced him, but in some way he touched Attila's heart and was able to convince him to spare the city of Rome.

Today's saint teaches us a much needed lesson. There is an atom bomb and a hydrogen bomb and there will soon be bigger and more destructive bombs. We have all the weapons we will ever need to destroy our world. Do we have the strength to control such weapons? Strength and brute force are two different things which are often equated in our minds.

The greatest strength that we have as human beings is the strength of an ideal. We Christians have the greatest ideal the world has ever known—an ideal of love and of charity, of peace and of kindness. We have this ideal in the flesh—Christ the Lord. With such an ideal no one can stand against us. Pope Leo had such an ideal and look what he did to Attila. How strong are our ideals? How Christian are our ideals?

April 13—St. Hermenegild (died 585), Martyr

THEME

Every earthly possession fades before the priceless joy of possessing Christ.

EXPOSITION

"None of you who does not renounce all his possessions can be My disciple" (Lk. 14:33). "One who does not carry his cross and follow Me cannot be My disciple" (Lk. 14:27). Christ does not mince words when He talks about His followers. If they chose Him, then He must take first place in their lives. St. Hermenegild realized this, and he had a lot more to lose than most of us. Hermenegild gave his life for Christ, accepting death rather than deny the Savior.

Christ must come first in our lives. We know this, but it's difficult to reduce it to practice. During Mass each day we should reaffirm our allegiance to God. It's easy to see how Christ is the most important person in our lives when we are here at Mass, but afterwards we forget. Today don't forget. Use the graces of your loving encounter with Christ and His holy people to help you keep first things first and first persons first.

April 14—St. Justin (died 165), Martyr

THEME

Christian faith is a reasonable and reasoned response to Christ.

EXPOSITION

Justin became a Christian because he was impressed by the courage and fortitude of Christian martyrs. He had a natural bent for teaching so he established the first school of Christian philosophy. He realized how vital reason and philosophy could be to the Church, and was determined to bolster his faith with every possible natural defense. When the time came for him to die, he faced the Emperor's fury and suffered martyrdom absolutely convinced that what he did was demanded by his reasonable and reasoned faith in Christ.

APPLICATION

Justin died a happy man. He, like St. Paul, had "preached Christ crucified. . . . Christ the power of God and the wisdom of God" (1 Cor. 1:23-4). He counted "everything loss, because of the excelling knowledge of Jesus Christ . . ." (Alleluia Hymn).

Some modern people are confused because their faith tells them one thing and their reason another. They are greatly disturbed by this conflict which colors their whole existence. If you feel such a conflict, make sure your faith is the true one and your reasoning is correct. Once you have checked out those two items, examine yourself.

The problem may not be with faith or reason but with you. Are you trying to live as an adult with a grade school understanding of your religion? Are you caught in a habit of sin and seeking for a convenient exit from the conflict between the sinful habit and your religious beliefs? Give yourself a good spiritual, moral and mental "check-up." Talk over your problems with Christ right now at Mass. Ask Him for the humility to love the truth and follow it.

Realize that there is need for study as well as prayer in this undertaking. Read and study the documents of Vatican II, as well as current books and magazines on faith and reason. You might consider joining a study group or a discussion group. Our Christian faith is a reasonable and reasoned response to Christ. It demands reasonable and reasoned effort on our part.

April 21—St. Anselm (c. 1033–1109), Bishop and Doctor of the Church

THEME

A true reformer starts his work at home before looking for others to help.

91

Exposition

Anselm is an example of many virtues. He exemplifies self-denial because he gave up his family, his country and his possessions to enter the Benedictine monastery of Bec in France. He made this monastery the center of true reform in Normandy and England.

He was devoted to the Church, staunch in defending the liberties and rights of the Church against the King, even to the extent of losing all his worldly goods and being exiled from his archbishopric of Canterbury. In his many writings and in his part in the Council of Bari, he showed once again the zeal of a man intensely interested in helping the Church and her members grow in holiness.

Application

Anselm was a true reformer. He reformed himself by strict discipline and mortification; then, and only then did he try to reform the Church and others. Vatican II in its *Decree on Ecumenism,* Article 6, says: "Christ summons the Church as she goes her pilgrim way to that continual reformation of which she always has need insofar as she is an institution of men here on earth."

The Church has to be reformed because we, her members, are ever in need of reform. A true reformer starts his work at home before looking for others to help. Is there anything in your life which needs to be reformed? Don't give a hasty answer! Think about the question during Mass and discuss it with the Eucharistic Christ.

April 22—Sts. Soter (died 175) and Caius (died 296), Popes and Martyrs

THEME

When a Christian says "yes" to Christ, he says "yes" to Christ's Cross.

EXPOSITION

Soter and Caius were successors of Peter as Bishop of Rome. Soter was Pope in the second century and Caius in the third century. They were rulers of the Church and leaders of God's people. They were men who gave everything for God and His people. They accepted Christ for what He was and they realized that when they accepted Christ as their leader, they accepted the Cross of Christ into their lives also.

APPLICATION

Each Christian when he accepts Christ must also accept the Cross of Christ into his life. Too many Christians try to separate Christ from His Cross because He has become socially acceptable, but His Cross has not. Such people become half-baked Christians—the type, as the saying goes, who come to church only "to be hatched, matched and dispatched."

Christians must be willing to accept the Cross that Christ sends them. So often people worry about what it will be. Will I be strong enough to accept it? Don't worry about such things. The God Who loves you will not let you be tried beyond your strength. So like Soter and Caius do your best to fulfill your duty as a Christian and accept the Cross Christ sends.

Realize that with the Cross comes Christ Who will help you to carry it. We are here at Mass today where the sacrifice first enacted on the Cross at Calvary will be re-enacted. Study it well and ask Christ in Communion to help you say "yes" to Him and His Cross in your life.

April 24—St. Fidelis of Sigmaringen (1577–1622), Martyr

THEME

Fidelity in God's service until death.

EXPOSITION

St. Fidelis was born in Southern Germany and became a brilliant lawyer. He felt called to a more apostolic life so he entered the Capuchin Order and was sent as a missionary to Switzerland. Here by his eloquence he brought many of the Swiss back into the Catholic Church. He often begged God for the grace of sacrificing his life in defense of his faith. God granted this wish. A group of bandits knifed him and as he died he said, "Lord, forgive my enemies."

APPLICATION

Fidelis means faithful. Today's saint was faithful in life and in death. We just asked God to make us strong in faith and love through the prayers and merits of St. Fidelis. Why? So that with God's help we can be faithful in His service until death.

The service of God is a demanding, time-consuming service. We must give our all, not just an hour on Sunday or a half-hour each day of the week. All our time means just that— every moment we have. May we be faithful in God's service now and until death. Stress the "now" in that last sentence. We want to know God now, to love Him and our neighbor now, and to serve both of them now.

April 25—St. Mark the Evangelist

THEME

When was the last time you of your own accord picked up the Gospel and read it?

EXPOSITION

The young man called John Mark appears first as one of the companions of St. Paul and St. Barnabas in their work of evangelizing the Island of Cyprus. Later he became the trusted companion and secretary of St. Peter. He set down in writing Peter's sermons about Jesus and His message. This is what we call the Gospel according to St. Mark. It is a Gospel which is picturesque and to the point. It must be very close to the actual words of the fisherman of Galilee, our first Pope.

APPLICATION

Many of us, if we were told that we would be able to hear St. Peter speak, would travel almost any distance to be in that place at the right time. In the Gospel according to St. Mark we have Peter speaking to us about his beloved Lord Jesus Christ. Why is it that so few of us ever take the time to read Mark's Gospel, or any of the other Gospels for that matter?

Vatican II believed that familiarity with the word of God would make all of us better followers and stronger members of Christ. In the *Dogmatic Constitution on Divine Revelation* (art. 26) the Council declared: "Just as the life of the Church grows through persistent participation in the Eucharistic mystery, so we may hope for a new surge of spiritual vitality from intensified veneration for God's words which last forever."

Make the Council's dream your reality. Grow stronger through your participation in the Eucharistic mystery. Grow stronger by your daily contacts with God's word of life in the Scriptures.

April 26—Sts. Cletus (1st Century) and Marcellinus (died, 304), Popes and Martyrs

THEME

Did you ever think that you, by your Christlike life, could prevent the Church from being persecuted here in America?

EXPOSITION

Only a few days ago we celebrated the feast of two other Popes and Martyrs, Soter and Caius. Today we honor Cletus and Marcellinus. Cletus was the second successor of Peter in the See of Rome, and Marcellinus was Pope in the early years of the fourth century. Both died martyrs for Christ. Marcellinus wisely decreed that there should be large rooms in the Catacombs for liturgical use during the persecutions. Although Mass could only be offered infrequently in such places, the liturgy was a great source of strength and comfort at such times.

APPLICATION

Even in our day there are countries where it is a violation of law to celebrate the Mass. There are other countries where the Church is hampered by petty laws. In America the Church is free. We need no catacombs and unless things change radically, our faith will not be tested as was the faith of Cletus and Marcellinus. Nonetheless, we should share their enthusiasm and their willingness to die for Christ.

No one but God knows the future, and we most assuredly cannot be certain that our day and age will never see a persecution. By our prayers and sacrifices we must prepare ourselves for whatever comes. By our lives and example we must bring others to Christ. Perhaps we will influence those who, if it were not for our example, might have become the persecutors of the Church. I admit that it's only a possibility, but let's not miss any opportunity to save Christ's Church and ourselves from a bloodbath.

April 27—St. Peter Canisius (1521–1597), Confessor and Doctor of the Church

THEME

There is a crying need today for dedicated apostles in the catechetical mission of the Church. Are you one of the apostles the Church needs so much?

EXPOSITION

St. Peter Canisius is known as the second apostle of Germany. After Peter became a Jesuit, he realized that there was much that he could do to help Catholics who had no clear knowledge of their religion. He wrote and preached as a leader in the Catholic counter-reformation. He was a pioneer of the Catholic press and founded many colleges in Germany, Austria and Bohemia. He is most famous for his catechism, a work that has influenced catechetical instruction to the present day.

In his catechism, St. Peter tried to sum up in a simple format the teachings of Christ and of His Church. He succeeded. In our day we are witnessing a similar revolution in catechetical instruction. We have been tied to the catechetical methods of St. Peter Canisius and those who followed him for too long a time. We do not deny the value of his efforts; but if he were living today, he would definitely want to change his approach and revitalize catechetical teaching.

In the spirit of St. Peter Canisius, we can do two things. We ourselves should try to learn more about our religion and to learn it in such a way that it influences our daily lives. Then we can teach what we know to others, adults as well as children. In the spirit of St. Peter Canisius take up this work; volunteer to teach if you are qualified or to help in the CCD schools in your parish. If you are already doing so, for God's sake and in the spirit of St. Peter stick to your teaching apostolate. Don't be a one-year man or woman, but give of your time and of yourself in this wonderful work of Christian education.

May St. Peter Canisius strengthen your faith and help you to bear witness to Jesus Christ in your life and work, and especially in your parish religious education school.

April 28—St. Paul of the Cross (1694–1775), Confessor

THEME

Devotion to the Cross of Christ is just as necessary for us as it was for St. Paul of the Cross.

In the Mass so far have you noticed that the Church has emphasized the word *Cross?* She does so because today's saint was so devoted to the Cross of Christ that he earned the title, St. Paul of the Cross. He echoed the words of Paul the Apostle: "With Christ I am nailed to the Cross. . . . I live in the faith of the Son of God Who loved me and gave Himself for me" (Entrance Hymn). "The message of the Cross, it is true, is foolishness to those who are perishing but to those who will be saved, to us, it is the power of God" (1 Cor. 1:18). Today's saint is known for the wonderful conversions he worked by his sermons on the Passion. He established the religious Order of the Passion whose members are popularly called Passionists.

APPLICATION

We have just asked St. Paul to make us always mindful of Christ's Passion so that we may share in its reward in heaven. The liturgy itself is the greatest and most excellent means of venerating Christ's sacred Passion, for here at Mass we are brought into contact with the Savior who redeemed us by His sufferings at Calvary.

We, as true Christians, must love the Cross and Christ crucified. It's not hard to do so here at Mass, but the Mass cannot be the end. It is always a beginning. The Cross must influence our lives so much that our friends and neighbors can put "of the Cross" after our names. So often nowadays they just say: "He's a cross." What are your chances of changing their minds?

April 29—St. Peter of Verona (1205–1252), Martyr

THEME

It is a good idea to take a fresh look at familiar things.

EXPOSITION

Peter of Verona, a Dominican Priest of the 13th century, by his eloquence and his miracles was able to bring many "stray sheep" back to the faith. He did his work well but in his capacity as Papal inquisitor he made enemies. Two of these waylaid him as he was returning to Milan and stabbed him to death. It is said that as he was dying, Peter wrote the word "Credo," "I believe," on the ground with his blood.

APPLICATION

The story about Peter writing the first word of the Creed with his blood as he was dying shows that this profession of faith must have held a special place in his life. The Creed is familiar to us too. We say the Nicene Creed at Mass. We pray the Apostles Creed at baptism and during the rosary. Whichever Creed we use, it is good to say it slowly, to think about the truths of the faith we proclaim.

It is a good idea to take a fresh look at something which is so familiar to us. Peter wrote the Creed in his own blood as he was dying. I wonder if possibly we could write the Creed in our lives by our actions. If we are not doing it, we should be. Why not ask St. Peter through this Mass to help you stamp on your actions the words, "I believe"?

April 30—St. Catherine of Siena (1347–1380), Virgin

THEME

The Church of Vatican II needs women like Catherine of Siena.

EXPOSITION

For the second day in a row we turn our eyes to a saint of the Dominican Order. Catherine of Siena, the youngest of 25 children, decided at an early age that she would consecrate herself to Christ. At the age of 15, after overcoming much parental resistance, she entered the Third Order of St. Dominic.

Her fame soon spread so that thousands came to see her and to be comforted by her. Her influence was such that she was able to restore peace among kings and worldly princes. Her greatest achievement came when she persuaded Pope Gregory VII to return to Rome from Avignon. She died at the age of 33. In this short period of time she accomplished an amazing amount of work for God and for His Church.

APPLICATION

For her own century Catherine of Siena was a marvel and a thoroughly modern person. The Church of Vatican II needs women who can do the same for our age. They must be thoroughly modern women devoted to Christ and to His Church, seeking to carry out the reforms of the Council.

If Catherine were alive today I imagine she would be right in the midst of things working to make people better, the world more peaceful and the Church more Christlike. She isn't here, but you women are. Why not ask her for the grace to do for our time what she did for hers? Catherine drew support through the Eucharistic Food of heaven for her earthly life. Why don't we do the same? We can, you know.

May 1—St. Joseph the Worker

THEME

It isn't so much what you do as how you do it that matters to God.

EXPOSITION

The first of May is the feast day of St. Joseph the Worker. We gather to honor the man entrusted by God with the care of His only begotten Son and the Blessed Virgin Mary. Today, however, we honor Joseph as the model for every worker. May Day, as you know, is famous among the Communists as their special feast day. The Church tries to capitalize, if I may use that word, on this situation by honoring St. Joseph the Worker.

St. Joseph was not a very successful businessman. He did not reap tremendous material rewards from his work. His work was dull and monotonous. Most of us know that type of work well. And yet, Joseph took the dullness and monotony and turned it into something wonderful because he did it all for God. Whatever he did in word or in work he did it in the name of the Lord Jesus giving thanks to God the Father through Him. St. Joseph perfectly fulfilled these words of St. Paul even before they were written.

APPLICATION

If you work with a computer, a typewriter, an adding machine, electric dishwasher or a vacuum cleaner, you may feel

102

far removed from the time of St. Joseph. ~~You are, as far as machines go.~~ But please don't be far removed from the spirit that made his work so acceptable to God. Catch the spirit of St. Joseph the Worker—the spirit that takes the dullness and monotony of labor and offers them to God.

Joseph worked with a full heart; full of love for God, for Jesus and Mary, full of joy that he could fashion things with his hands. We need to have a similar joy and sense of fulfillment in our work. Can St. Joseph show us the way? Do you think he's interested in such things any more? The Church does! How about you?

May 2—St. Athanasius (c. 297–373), Bishop and Doctor of the Church

THEME

Defending the faith of Christ has not gone out of style. Today we must be willing to fight for Christ's faith more than ever before.

EXPOSITION

Athanasius was a witness to the great Council of Nicea. He attended the Council as a deacon and took part in its deliberations. This Council defined the true doctrine concerning the Divinity of Christ, and condemned Arius. Athanasius was a marked man for the rest of his life and had to endure severe persecutions because of the part he played at the Council, but he never wavered from the profession of faith made by the Nicene Fathers. The persecutions and the exiles that he underwent tempered his faith and made it stronger. By his writings, his sermons and his example, he testified to his

103

belief in Christ's divinity—to the great truths of the Council of his day.

We live in an era which is dominated by another Council. Vatican II and the *aggiornamento* that it brought upon the Church have not changed anything at all of the essentials of our religion. Everything in the Creed of Nicea is applicable to the Church today. What Vatican II has done is to give us a new sense of direction.

The Church of Christ is under attack right now. The faith has to be defended today, but make sure it is the true faith. As your way of honoring St. Athanasius, dedicate yourself to the great cause of making your life a heroic profession of faith in Vatican II. The Church is on the move today. Are you moving with her?

May 4—St. Monica (died 387), Wife, Mother and Widow

THEME

Evil wins no permanent victories when it faces the power of a mother's love.

EXPOSITION

Monica is known to all the world as a determined mother. By her prayers and good example she converted her pagan husband to the true religion. Her son, Augustine, provided a greater test to her powers of prayer and perseverance. He possessed a brilliant intellect but was drawn to the pleasures of the flesh. He quickly fell into the morass of sinful pleasures and philosophical systems which encouraged such excesses. But Monica never gave up. By her prayers and her tears of many years she won the grace from God to see her son a true Christian. He followed her saintly examples and became a priest, a bishop and a saint.

APPLICATION

Monica won no small victory by her years of prayer and suffering. To give Christ's Church an Augustine was to provide the Church with one of the greatest theologians and philosophers who ever lived. St. Monica teaches us the power of a mother's love and the efficacy of constant prayer. Through the contact that you have with her and the source of all her strength at this Mass, realize that you too can do the wonderful things that she did if you persevere in prayer.

The powers of evil gained no victory over the maternal love and determination of today's saint. Can you love even in the face of apparent failure as she did? Can you pray when everything seems lost? St. Monica shows you the way. Will you follow?

May 5—St. Pius V (1504–72), Pope and Confessor

THEME

Today's saint shows us the power of persevering prayer and action.

EXPOSITION

St. Pius V, a famous member of the Order of Preachers, was a reforming Bishop of the Church in an era when reform was badly needed. Because of his strict life and his desire to reform his diocese and the Church, no one expected that he would be elected Pope. As Pope he reformed the Church by his prayers and by his actions. As Pope he convinced the Christian princes to unite against the Turks and their Sultan. It is said that the Turks were defeated at the battle of Lepanto more by his prayers than by the military forces of the Christian princes.

APPLICATION

Today's saint shows us that it is not enough to pray; we have to act also. The two have to be coupled—persevering prayer and firm Christian action. Together they are unbeatable. Too often we pray like saints on Sunday at Mass, and act like heathens during the rest of the week at work and in our communities. Isn't it about time we Christians began to talk and to act like Christ's followers all week long, every place we go? Ask St. Pius V to help you to pray as if everything depended upon your prayers, and to act as if everything depended upon your actions.

May 7—St. Stanislaus (died 1079), Bishop and Martyr

THEME

What a privilege it is to live for Christ in the strength of our daily Mass.

EXPOSITION

Stanislaus was the Bishop of Cracow in Poland. The King at that time was a famous warrior, but a man of lust and cruelty. Stanislaus the Bishop, realizing his duty to preach Christ to everyone, rebuked the King for his conduct and tried to bring him back to the Church. The rebuke failed and only antagonized the King, who went to the Chapel where the Bishop was saying Mass and murdered him at the altar.

APPLICATION

It is a great privilege to die for Christ while offering His sacrifice. It is also a great privilege to live for Christ in the strength of our daily Mass. At Mass we should offer ourselves completely to God our Father in Christ our Lord. When we leave Mass strengthened by the Eucharistic union with Christ and all other Christians, we must try to live for Christ and our brothers. Stanislaus did this and he paid for it. Are we willing to do it no matter what the price? Please don't answer that question now. Think about it and ask Christ at Mass for the grace you need to give the right answer.

Sometimes it seems easier to die for Christ than to live for Him.

May 9—St. Gregory Nazianzen (c. 325–390), Bishop and Doctor of the Church

THEME

In God's plan, no man is indispensable.

EXPOSITION

Gregory was a great theologian. In fact, so profound was his theological knowledge that he was called "The Theologian." He was Bishop of the town of Nazianzcs when he was called to be the Patriarch of Constantinople. Once there he drove out the heretics, and brought the city back to the purity of its ancient faith. In achieving his goal he stirred up a storm

107

of protest. Realizing that the Faith was now safe and that his continued presence only endangered it, he resigned as Patriarch and returned to his native land. There, in prayer and in writing, he spent the rest of his life.

APPLICATION

Gregory teaches one lesson we all need to learn. He knew that he was not indispensable. God could get along without him. Gregory saw that much of the opposition to his reforms centered on his presence and personality, so he resigned. He was not a coward but a farsighted man who realized that, right or wrong, his very presence prevented the complete realization of his reforms. He had the courage to step aside.

We need the courage to give ourselves completely to every task. We also need the courage to admit that we are not indispensable. When and if the time comes that we are an obstacle to Christ's work with an individual or community, let us imitate St. Gregory's act of selfless courage. Until such time, let us imitate his enthusiasm for reform and renewal in our lives and in that of the Church.

May 10—St. Antoninus (1389–1459), Bishop and Confessor

THEME

Nothing can come close to the joy of completely giving oneself to God.

EXPOSITION

Today's saint was christened Anthony but was called Antoninus, the diminutive of his given name. This was partly because of his small stature, but mainly because he was a very lovable person and people expressed their affection by using the diminutive. He may have been small in stature but everything else about him was "giant size." As a Dominican Friar he showed exceptional talents and was chosen to become Archbishop of Florence against his will. He quickly earned the title "Father of the Poor."

When I talk of Antoninus, I think of a little Sister of Charity. What a joy it was to meet her in school or around the Church! She completely and joyfully gave of herself during her years of active service. Nothing in her manner changed even during the final years of her life when she could no longer teach Christ's people but merely suffer for Him and them. Antoninus must have been made from the same mold.

APPLICATION

A saint like Antoninus, who lived centuries ago, can still inspire us to imitate him. A teaching or nursing Sister can also inspire us, perhaps even more so because of her physical presence, to give our all for Christ. At Mass today, ask Our Lord for the grace to follow in the footsteps of Antoninus. You also may know some lay persons, sisters or priests who resemble Antoninus. Learn from them how to serve God in his people joyfully and completely. We must try very hard to realize that good health is not essential for our apostolate. Good will and true love is.

May 11—St. Philip and St. James, Apostles and Martyrs

THEME

No Christian is an "assembly line" product, but a specially made priceless work of God.

The Apostles did not always understand what Christ was saying but they did listen and were never afraid to ask questions. They interrupted Jesus at will and asked Him to explain a little more thoroughly what He meant. They were on such close terms with Christ that the dialogue flowed freely.

St. Philip, one of the principals in this morning's account, was a man of great simplicity. Christ loved Philip's naiveté and took great delight in teasing him. St. James was one of Christ's own relatives. He was a man of serious nature, almost the complete opposite of Philip. Notice the individual characteristics of these two Apostles. Our Lord loved both of them because of what they were. He never tried to change their personalities. He wanted them to use their special talents, and they were willing. That's why He chose them to become his Apostles.

If we are to be apostles of Christ, which we are all called to be, then we must be on intimate terms with Christ. Perhaps that is the best way to explain what we are doing here at this sacrifice-banquet. We are sharing with Christ the greatest act of His whole life. Today and every day seek apostolic strength and fortitude as you offer the Mass and receive Communion. Learn the delights of intimacy with Christ.

APPLICATION

Each of us is different. Each has his own personality, talents and characteristics. God made us that way and He wants us to use such individuating features in serving Him and His people. He doesn't want us to destroy them. Unfortunately some Christians, maybe some of us, are convinced that being a follower of Christ means conforming to a set pattern or forcing ourselves into a mold.

Throw away that notion and be yourself. There is only one pattern. Christ is our pattern and He is big enough to include every individual quality and feature. Ask Him to show you how to be yourself, your Christ-self—your best self. You did not come off any assembly line. You are a specially made, priceless individual in God's eyes. Don't underestimate your own value!

May 12—Sts. Nereus, Achilleus, Domitilla, Virgin (all died, end of 1st Century), and Pancras (died 304), Martyrs

THEME

We must be men and women of our promise.

EXPOSITION

Today we honor four saints. Nereus and Achilleus were officials of the Roman Emperor's court who were converted by St. Domitilla. They were baptized, and soon afterwards suffered martyrdom for their belief in Christ. Domitilla was a cousin of the Emperor, a woman born to wealth and position, who turned her back on these things. She preferred Christ before everything else. Pancras was a noble young boy of 14 who was converted and baptized by the Pope. When he was given the option of worshiping the false gods or of dying for Christ, he preferred to remain loyal to his baptismal promises of allegiance to Christ.

APPLICATION

The four saints whose feasts we celebrate today made no firmer promises to Christ than we did when we were baptized. They realized how deeply they were committed to Christ and to His cause. Do we? Our words can never fully answer that

111

question. Only our lives can prove conclusively whether or not we are observing our baptismal commitment to Christ.

Lent spoke to us of our duties and privileges as baptized members of Christ. The renewal of the baptismal promises during the Easter Vigil service was the culmination of that phrase of the Lenten message. The Masses of Easter and the week that followed it deepened our understanding of baptism and its effects. There is no law forbidding us from renewing our baptismal promises at other times.

Today realize the depth of your commitment to Christ and the loyalty you should have to Him. Find in this sacrifice the strength that you need to fulfill your baptismal promises. Why not begin by renewing them right now?

May 13—St. Robert Bellarmine (1542–1621), Bishop and Doctor of the Church

THEME

Today's Christian needs a burning love for the Church which will inspire ceaseless service to her.

EXPOSITION

The great Italian Jesuit, Robert Bellarmine, is an outstanding example of what a true Christian should be. He opposed in every way possible the Protestant enemies of the Church. By his works, his writings and his sermons he fought against what he considered to be an attack against the unity of the Church. In our day and age we have turned from this in-fighting among Christians to a search for a greater perception of what binds us together in the Lord.

Although we approach Protestants in a different way now and have turned our backs on some of the methods of St. Robert Bellarmine, we do not disown the saint. We can imitate his ardent love for Christ and the Church, his ceaseless service of the Church. In our day and age these are virtues which are dearly needed. Ask St. Robert for the grace to love the Church today as he did in his time.

On May 13, 1967, Pope Paul traveled to Fatima to pray for peace. Let us today repeat his plea for peace to our Lady and ask St. Robert to add his voice to our prayer.

May 15—St. John Baptist de la Salle (1651–1719), Confessor

THEME

The Church must become more adult-centered without neglecting young people in any way.

EXPOSITION

John Baptist de la Salle, a tremendously talented man, gave up what would have been a brilliant secular career to become a priest. He founded the Brothers of the Christian Schools, a congregation which has spread to all parts of the world and is devoted to the education of young people. As the Entrance Prayer stated, St. John was inspired by God to teach the poor and to lead the young in the path of truth.

APPLICATION

Today many Christians insist that the Church must become more adult-centered. We are beginning to realize that too much of the Church's energies have been concentrated on children. Not enough has been done for adults, and especially for family life. It is good that we are achieving this sense of balance.

A man like St. John Baptist de la Salle reminds us, however, that we can never forget the young people. We do not want to go from one extreme to another. We must hold the middle ground, updating our apostolate to the adult world without neglecting the young. Ask St. John on his feast day to help the Church maintain its balance in this apostolate. His intercession and example should help us to do our share in forging such a balanced apostolate for the Church.

THEME II

St. John de la Salle would definitely encourage Head Start schools, tutorial and cultural programs which feature person-to-person relationships, and other apostolic and humanitarian service projects for deprived children.

May 16—St. Ubald (died 1160), Bishop and Confessor

THEME

If you do your job in life to the best of your ability, you will never need to apologize to anyone.

EXPOSITION

Today's saint was an outstanding Bishop who watched over his flock willingly as God would have it and became an example of Christlike virtue to his people. St. Ubald was Bishop for more than 30 years of a town in Italy called Gubbio. He was a father in Christ to all the townspeople. He was a peacemaker who not only preached peace but did something about it. When two groups of townspeople were fighting, he threw himself between them and restored the peace. During another time of strife, he was able to convince the Emperor to spare the city from destruction.

We could say other things about today's saint but I think we say it all when we say he was an excellent Bishop and father to his people. He did his job to the best of his ability. Each of us has a job to do on earth. Each of us has a position to fill. If we do that one job well, if we fill that one position to the best of our ability, then there is no need to apologize to anyone.

Ask today's saint through this Mass for the grace to learn this lesson well. Then you won't go running off in a hundred and one directions at the same time trying to do everything at once. Do well what God wants you to do; don't worry about the rest.

May 17—St. Paschal Baylon (1540–92), Confessor

THEME

Ask St. Paschal to help you participate more actively at Mass and to be more fervent in receiving Holy Communion.

EXPOSITION

St. Paschal was a Franciscan lay brother whose greatest source of strength was Christ in the Eucharist. This very undistinguished person has been named the patron of all Eucharistic confraternities and congresses and all Eucharistic works. The

Entrance Prayer mentions how God filled Paschal with a wondrous love of the sacred mysteries of Christ's Body and Blood.

The Entrance Prayer continues: "May we draw from this divine banquet the same spiritual riches he received." The riches which we seek from this sacrifice are more active participation in the Mass and greater fervor in receiving Communion.

Because we offer Mass so often, it can become a routine thing. We must fight against this. If you ever attend a Eucharistic Congress on a regional, a national or an international level, you will see how the Eucharist becomes the center of everyone's life for a few days. Don't wait for a Eucharistic congress. Make the Eucharist the center of your life now and not merely for a few days.

If you think of yourself as a poor, simple soul with not much to distinguish you from other people, then consider St. Paschal. He was a poor, uneducated man; but he won great distinction because of his devotion to the Eucharist. Perhaps that is the path we should follow.

May 18—St. Venantius (235–250), Martyr

THEME

How strong is your faith?

EXPOSITION

When Venantius was 15 years old, he faced the biggest decision of his life. He was arrested because he was a Christian.

His faith was strong, but he was young. The Roman judge must have smiled to himself and chuckled: "This one is going to be easy. He'll need only a little torture, and he'll sacrifice to our gods." Nothing could have been farther from the truth.

Venantius knew that if he persevered in following Christ, he would have to die. He was ready to die for Christ. To live for Christ was wonderful; to live after denying Christ was hell. The Roman judge reacted violently to Venantius' faith and courage. The boy was tortured terribly and finally beheaded. In this young boy Christ had won again. Venantius may have been only 15 years old but he was a *man* in his allegiance and devotion to Christ.

APPLICATION

"If he could do it, why can't we?" We can do it! We can and we will grow in strength and courage because of our meeting with Christ here today at Mass and Communion. The challenge to our faith may not be as spectacular as the challenge to his faith, but it is there. It is more insidious because it is less apparent.

Few of us will ever be tortured to give up our faith. There are other inducements, however, such as social, business, or personal ambition, resentment at a priest's or nun's attitude toward us, problems with loving one's neighbor, with purity or birth control. Our faith in Christ should be bigger than these problems and should help us solve them. Ask today's saint to help you imitate his resolute faith. Don't let a fifteen year old boy show you up!

May 19—St. Peter Celestine (1221–1296), Pope

THEME

How many of us have the brains to know that we are not qualified to hold a certain position and the courage to act upon this knowledge?

EXPOSITION

Peter Celestine spent most of his life in solitude as a hermit. His way of life attracted others to follow him, so he devised a rule and founded a religious order. When he was a very old man, he was chosen to be Pope. It did not take him long to realize that he was incapable of fulfilling the duties of his high office. He had the supreme humility to resign.

APPLICATION

How many of us, when placed in a situation we can't handle, have the honesty to act likewise? So often we deceive ourselves and try to keep going, saying that we will do better if only we try harder. There is no disgrace in recognizing that the position we now fill was not meant for us.

If you are happy in your position in life and are doing a good job, then be satisfied. If you realize that your present occupation is not for you, have the courage to act upon that knowledge. If circumstances permit, try another sphere of activity. If you cannot do that, at least try a new approach to your present occupation.

God has called you to serve Him in a very special way. Don't waste your time in the wrong field of activity. Find the right one and find it fast.

May 20—St. Bernardine of Siena (1380–1444), Confessor

THEME

Nominal Christians would not be half bad if they realized exactly what their name meant.

EXPOSITION

Today's saint is called the Apostle of the Holy Name. One Pope called him the second St. Paul because of his powerful and eloquent preaching. St. Bernardine was born in Siena, Italy, and became a priest in the Franciscan Order. He traveled throughout all of Italy spreading devotion to the Name of Jesus and urging a moral reform. In the Entrance Prayer the Church mentions his remarkable love for the Holy Name of Jesus. Through this Name he worked many wonders and converted many people to Christ.

APPLICATION

We are called Christians. It is a great distinction to bear the Name of Jesus Christ Our Lord. Sometimes we talk about nominal Christians. By that we mean people who are Christians in name only. Did you ever think what would happen if everyone who was called a Christian realized what his name meant and followed out its implications in his life? What a wonderful thought that is! Do you think it will ever come true? Can you do anything to help it come true?

Ask today's saint to help you love the Name of Jesus Christ. Ask him for even more—that you will always be proud of the name you bear, and that you will always act as a Christ should act. Never, never disgrace the Name of Jesus Christ which is really your name!

May 25—St. Gregory VII (c. 1020–1085), Pope and Confessor

THEME

Our century needs to rediscover the effectiveness of moral weapons.

EXPOSITION

Any student of Church History knows of Gregory VII. As the Benedictine monk Hildebrand, he was for 25 years an active assistant to several popes in their efforts to reform the Church. Finally, in 1073, he was elected Pope. He was a strong man with a remarkable personality. He spent his whole life trying to reform the Church, fighting against the evils of his time— evils which were slowly but surely weakening the Church. Because he loved the Church so much that he was willing to fight for her, he ran into great opposition. He finally was forced to flee Rome to die in exile. He died unaware that he had succeeded in reforming Christ's Church.

APPLICATION

We have to admire this man of courage. We have to admire even more the fact that he was able to overcome such great difficulties with moral weapons alone. Protestants as well as pagans look upon Gregory as a great man. One of them has said that the monk who won without weapons has a right to be admired more than Alexander, Caesar or Napoleon.

In the 1960's when we think about weapons, we think about weapons that Gregory never even dreamed of, so horrible have they become. Nonetheless the best weapon we have is the same weapon that he had—a moral weapon—our belief in God and our love for Him and our neighbor. Ask Gregory today to help you be convinced of the effectiveness of such a weapon. Be convinced of it and use it.

If you think that all this talk about moral weapons is a lot of nonsense, review the facts about St. Gregory VII. Learn a little bit about him and you will see that it is a good story—a good story which is made even better because it is true.

May 26—St. Philip Neri (1515–1595), Confessor

THEME

If you want to start doing something for Christ, start where you are now.

EXPOSITION

Philip Neri, the humorous saint who by his gay, joyful spirit was able to touch the hearts of all he met, has been called the Apostle of Rome. For fifty years he devoted himself to renewing the religious and the ecclesiastical life of the Eternal City. He did wonderful things for the City of Rome and its people. He founded a religious congregation, the Religious of the Oratory.

All of this might never have been done if the ambition of his youth—to be a missionary in foreign lands—had been realized. A Benedictine friend told him that his work was in Rome. He listened to the advice, stayed in Rome, and did wonders there.

APPLICATION

Don't we often think along the same lines as St. Philip Neri? If we want to do something wonderful for Christ, we believe that we have to go away from our home, factory, school or club. We think about going to the foreign missions to do something for Christ.

If we are ever going to do anything worthwhile for Christ, it has to begin where we are right now. Start here and work for Christ. You will be surprised at the task to be done. Ask St. Philip Neri to help you be a little humorous and joyful about the whole thing. Sad-faced saints are a contradiction in terms. In the Entrance Prayer at the Mass we say that we joyfully celebrate St. Philip's feast day. How about joyfully imitating him in our lives?

May 27—St. Bede the Venerable (673–735), Confessor and Doctor

THEME

Don't ignore the opportunities that are yours at Mass to grow in appreciation of the Bible.

EXPOSITION

Bede, confessor and a doctor of the Church, was the first English historian and a Benedictine monk. He was a man of great learning, and in fact has been called a bridge between the Germanic cultures which had just been converted to Christ and the Greco-Roman cultures. Above all he was a true Benedictine whose life revolved around prayer and his work. Of all the things that stand out in his life, his love for the Bible and his desire to explain it are predominant.

APPLICATION

We of the English-speaking world have a special tie with St. Bede the Venerable. He is one of our ancestors in the faith.

Today as we celebrate the feast of this man who so often and so beautifully explained the meaning of the Sacred Scriptures, let us dedicate ourselves to a greater love for the Bible.

Why not follow his example of explaining it to others? Of course, before we can explain it to others, we have to know it ourselves. Here at Mass we listen to the readings from the Bible, we have them explained by the priest in the homily, and we apply them to ourselves during the sacrifice.

Don't ignore the opportunities that the Mass offers to come closer to the Scriptures. Resolve that each day you will read and study the Bible and thus follow in the footsteps of men such as St. Bede the Venerable.

May 28—St. Augustine of Canterbury (died 604), Bishop and Confessor

THEME

May St. Augustine help all English-speaking Christians to reunite as one body around the center of unity—Christ the Lord.

EXPOSITION

Every missionary who has been true to his vocation has echoed the words of St. Paul in his first letter to the Thessalonians (2:8): "So solicitous were we for you in fact that we wanted to share with you not only the Gospel of God but even our very life, so beloved had you become to us." Augustine and his companions felt this love. Because of such love and the respect they had for the people to whom they were sent, they were able to lead many of the English to Christ.

APPLICATION

Augustine would be sad today if he were to see how the people to whom he handed the faith had been torn to a large extent from the Church which he respected, the Church of Rome. He reminds us that we have a tradition in common that cries out for unity. Our present disunity itself is a plea to return to union.

May this great saint through our Eucharistic offering win for all English-speaking Christians the grace of reunion once more around the center of all life—Christ the Lord. Repeat the sentiments of the Entrance Prayer during the sacrifice and often today: "May his (St. Augustine) prayers convert the hearts of those who have strayed away so that they may find their way back to the unity of truth, and may we ourselves always be united in doing Your (God's) will.

May 29—St. Mary Magdalene of Pazzi (1566–1607), Virgin

THEME

The Eucharist should be the source of the love and purity which must characterize our lives.

EXPOSITION

St. Mary Magdalene came from a famous family in Florence and at an early age entered the Carmelite Order. She is known for her devotion to the Holy Eucharist, for her great love of God and neighbor, and for the purity of her life. She found in her daily contacts with her Eucharistic Lord the strength to walk in the paths of love and purity.

124

The Church tells us exactly what we should seek from this Mass. She does so in the Prayer of the Mass in which she praises God Who enkindled in the heart of the Blessed Mary Magdalene a divine love and blessed her with heavenly gifts. The prayer concludes: "May we who celebrate her feast imitate her purity and her love."

These two virtues, purity and love, are the goal of our sacrifice. Our sacrifice will be the source of these virtues if we offer this Eucharistic celebration in the correct manner. How do we do that? The answer is simple. We must offer this Mass as God's people united around the Lord's banquet table. It's an easy answer, isn't it? Putting it into practice is another story. Do your best and depend on the Lord and today's saint to do the rest.

May 30—Memorial Day

THEME

May the dead rest in peace; and may we, the living, learn to live in peace.

EXPOSITION

Today is what is called a ferial day in the Church's year. On such a day we usually say the Mass of the preceding Sunday, a votive Mass, or the daily Mass for the dead. Because it is Memorial Day, it seems only natural that we should be offering together the votive Mass for peace—asking Almighty God that the words of Christ, "Peace be with you," may be realized in our own time.

Christ did not give His peace as the world gives it. So often what the world calls peace is an ephemeral thing—a thing of appearances only. Christ gives true peace—peace of heart and mind.

APPLICATION

Memorial Day for these many years past has been declared a day of prayer by the President. It is a day on which we remember those who have died for our country fighting to preserve the freedom and peace which we so cherish in these United States.

As we gather here we are fulfilling the President's request to pray for peace on this day. We are doing something concrete to bring that peace about. Offer the Mass today for the intention that the dead may truly rest in the peace of Christ the Lord and that we, the living, may learn to live in the peace of Christ our Lord.

May 31—Mary, Our Queen

THEME

It is our glorious destiny to reign with Christ in heaven and it is just as much our destiny to spread His Kingdom on earth.

EXPOSITION

We close the month of May, the month of Our Lady, with this feast of Her Queenship. Pius XII, during the Marian Year of 1954, established this feast. He proclaimed that Jesus Christ is King in the full literal and absolute sense of the word because He is true God and Man. Mary shares in His royal prerogatives. Mary reigns as Queen beside Christ the King because she stood beside Him in His suffering. The Alleluia hymn sums it up: "Blessed are you, Oh Virgin Mary, who stood beneath the Cross of the Lord. Now with Him you reign forever."

APPLICATION

There used to be a philosophy of life which told Christians to grin and bear it on earth so that they could earn the glory of heaven. Such a way of life made it seem as if nothing on earth was really worthwhile, except as a cross to be borne. Such an outlook on life is an insult to God's love. The earth is good and everything human is good because Christ became Man and sanctified everything that we do.

Mary teaches us by her life that we must work to our fullest to better ourselves, those around us and the whole world. Only then can we appreciate and achieve the glory of heaven. Ask Our Lady today from her throne in heaven to help you appreciate the work you are to do here on earth. You will get to heaven much faster and enjoy it a great deal more if you don't turn your back on God's people and God's world.

June 1—St. Angela Merici (c. 1470–1540), Virgin

THEME

St. Angela used worldly goods for her apostolate. They never possessed her. How about us?

EXPOSITION

Angela Merici started her religious life as a Franciscan Tertiary and later dedicated herself to educating poor children in her native town. From this humble beginning she went on to organize schools in other towns and gathered around herself a group of women to teach in her schools. Finally she organized them into an institute and then into a formally erected religious congregation, the Ursulines, the first order of teaching women in the Church.

APPLICATION

The Church urges us today to think about St. Angela and her virtues, urging us to renounce earthly things for the sake of everlasting happiness. She is really telling us that the things of the earth are not lasting. They are not to be held tightly but rather lightly so that we will be able to give them up when, and if, it is necessary to do so.

Ask St. Angela today for the virtues that so dominated her life—the virtues of detachment from and renunciation of worldly things. She did not despise the world and its goods. In fact she used them to fulfill her apostolic labors. She used them. They never possessed her. Could we make the same statement?

June 4—St. Francis Caracciolo (1564–1608), Confessor

THEME

Christians need special zeal for prayer and mortification if they are to be what their name signifies.

EXPOSITION

St. Francis, the founder of a religious order, was characterized by a special zeal for prayer and a love of penance. The Church mentions these virtues and urges us to imitate his example so that "by prayer and the restraint of evil inclinations in our bodies" we Christians may be made worthy of heaven.

128

A life of prayer and mortification has always been a sign of Christ's followers. It is never an easy thing to lead a life of prayer. Especially in our century it is not easy to have a love for penance and mortification. We have become so accustomed to the luxuries of the world that we think they are necessary for our happiness. Nonetheless, the Church insists that we imitate St. Francis in his love of prayer and mortification.

The liturgy provides us with the needed assistance to do so. It gives us the example of St. Francis; it gives us the sacred word of God; it gives us this Eucharistic banquet at which we can be joined to the Source of all prayer and love for penance. As we say in the Prayer over the Gifts, ". . . fill us, most merciful Jesus, with the same fire of love that St. Francis had so that we may worthily assist at Your holy banquet table."

At Mass today show Christ that you are determined to follow Him by prayer and mortification. At least make a beginning and depend on Him to help you follow through to the conclusion.

June 5—St. Boniface (c. 679–755), Bishop and Martyr

THEME

Each Christian is a missionary. What he has received, he must strive to pass on to others.

Boniface, the apostle of Germany, was an Englishman, a Benedictine and a great missionary. He lead a small band of English missionaries to what we know as Germany.

It is interesting to note that only a few days ago we celebrated the feast of St. Augustine of Canterbury, a Roman, who left his homeland to preach Christ to the English. Within a century the British not only had the faith but they were seeking to spread it. Boniface was one of the leaders in this missionary effort.

APPLICATION

I hope that the point we are making is crystal clear to all. We do not possess the teachings of Christ except through others who have preached it to us. It is not given to us to hoard or to keep under a bushel basket. It is given to us so that we may love and cherish it and then bring it to others. Boniface did that.

Ask him at this Mass, through his example and his prayers, to help you catch the true spirit of Christianity—a spirit which is missionary in theme, missionary in content and missionary in action.

June 6—St. Norbert (c. 1080–1134), Bishop and Confessor

THEME

Each of us is called to be a preacher of the Gospel.

EXPOSITION

Today's saint was a Bishop and a Confessor. He was well educated and possessed exceptionally good connections with the rich and powerful people of his day. Like so many before him, he turned to God and became a priest in order to give his life to Christ. In the Entrance Prayer, the Church points out how he was a great preacher of the Gospel, and through him God founded a new religious congregation in the Church, the Premonstratensians.

APPLICATION

We ask in the Entrance Prayer that the merits and prayers of St. Norbert win the help of God for us so that we may follow his teaching and example. In essence his example was one of devotion to the word of God—the word of God in the Gospel and in the sacraments, the word of God in the Church and dwelling in the hearts of men.

How can we follow St. Norbert's example if we never read God's word, seldom have it on our lips, and could not care less if it is in the hearts of our fellow men? That's admittedly a ridiculous question, but its implications for our lives are far from ridiculous.

June 10—St. Margaret (1050–1093), Queen of the Scots, Widow

THEME

Charity means more than giving money to the poor. It means giving oneself in service to them.

St. Margaret, Queen of Scotland, can be considered under two aspects—her private life and her public life. In private, she was a model wife and mother. She raised eight children in the fear and the love of the Lord. In her public life she was a true queen, a constant support to her husband in his reign and the loving mother of her people.

Her "wonderful love of the poor" is the virtue which the Church highlights for us in the Entrance Prayer as worthy of our imitation.

APPLICATION

St. Margaret teaches us two lessons today. First of all, that a lay person, a mother and a wife, can find holiness in and through her position in life. All of us should be encouraged by her example to seek holiness in our state of life.

The second lesson strikes home more forcefully. St. Margaret loved the poor not just by giving them money but by her personal interest in them. She gave herself to them in their needs. She served them at table; she treated their wounds; she clothed them. There was nothing impersonal about her charity.

During this Mass, as we unite with Christ our Savior, why not ask Him to etch in our minds these two lessons?

June 11—St. Barnabas, Apostle

THEME

God has set each one of us aside to do some special work for Him.

EXPOSITION

The first Lesson of today's Mass gives us a good insight into
the character of Barnabas. He was "a good man, filled with
the Holy Spirit and faith." When there was an urgent missionary job to be done at Antioch, Barnabas was sent. When
he saw how much good could be done for Christ, he did not
hesitate to call upon Paul for assistance. He was Paul's
teacher and leader, destined to be outshone by his disciple in
later years. Barnabas is an example of the early Christian's
almost compulsive need to spread the teaching and love of
Christ among the pagans.

APPLICATION

Barnabas was a Christian of whom we can be proud. It is too
bad that he has become the forgotten Apostle, not forgotten
by the Lord or the Church, but forgotten by ordinary Christians. It is also unfortunate that so many Christians are
forgotten apostles. They are forgotten because they themselves chose to ignore the fact that by their baptism and the
reception of the other sacraments they are meant to be missionaries of the Word of God.

Ask Christ through this sacrifice to help you to be an active
apostle. Don't forget that, like Barnabas and Paul, the Holy
Spirit has set you apart to do the work for which He has
called you. Pray very forcefully after Communion that "nourished by the Lord's sacrament and through the help of the
Apostle Barnabas, all of us may live a life of worthy service
pleasing to Jesus Christ." Pray it forcefully, mean it sincerely,
and live it fully.

June 12—St. John of San Facundo (died 1479), Confessor

THEME

In every way possible try to establish peace among your family, friends and acquaintances.

EXPOSITION

Today's saint is known for his "wonderous gift of reconciling enemies." This Spanish saint won a great reputation at the University of Salamanca as a preacher and director of souls. However, his most outstanding work was in reconciling the young noblemen of his time who were engaging in senseless feuds with their consequent violence and brutality.

APPLICATION

"If at the moment you are bringing your gift to the altar, you recall that your brother has a grievance against you, leave your gift there at the altar. Go first and seek a reconciliation with your brother. Then come and offer your gift" (Mt. 5:24).

Don't these words of Christ apply to us today as forcefully as when He first spoke them? So often Christians are not very Christian to some of their family, friends and acquaintances. We humans are so torn by jealousy and insecurity that we find it easy to dislike and even hate other members of Christ's Body.

The feuds and wars of nations will never be settled until we Christians learn what it means to love one another. Ask St. John today through his merits and prayers to help you to be rooted in God's love so that you will never be separated from Jesus Christ.

134

June 13—St. Anthony of Padua (1195–1231), Confessor and Doctor of the Church

THEME

Seek to regain the full force of Christian love you may have lost or misplaced since the year began.

EXPOSITION

Anthony of Padua, born in Portugal but acclaimed by all the world as an Italian saint, was a Franciscan friar sent to Africa as a missionary. Because of illness he returned to Italy and there developed into an outstanding preacher who was able to convert many people.

Because of his ability as a preacher and his knowledge of Scripture, Pope Gregory IX called him the Ark of the Testament. He did much by the way he expounded the word of God to reform men's lives and to bring them to a deeper devotion and love of Christ.

APPLICATION

Everything that I have said so far is true, but for most of us St. Anthony is famous for something else. He is the saint who helps us find items which are lost. No one seems to know for certain how he got such a reputation, but he has it. Why can't we take advantage of his power to find lost items?

Seek to find through today's saint the full force of Christian love you may have lost or misplaced since this year began. Find it here in this Eucharistic encounter with the Lord. Find it here in this loving assembly united with your brothers and sisters in the Eucharist. Find it through St. Anthony and hold on to it a little more securely in the future because of his help. Just remember that you don't have to lose something before asking for his help. He will help us keep what we have.

June 14—St. Basil the Great (329–379), Confessor, Bishop and Doctor of the Church

THEME

What does it take to be a "Great" Christian?

EXPOSITION

Basil had everything, or at least so it seems. He had a magnificent intellect and great spiritual strength. He had a gift for administration, the power to write wonderful spiritual books, and he was an exceptional theologian. Basil is an author of monastic rule. He was a bishop par excellence, a fighter of heresy, a man who saved the faith of the whole of his region.

He was inspired by a wonderful love of the poor, and his book about the Holy Spirit is still counted a masterpiece of Catholic theology. What a talented man he was! However, he was not called "the Great" because of his talents alone—but mainly because of what he did for the Church and for others with them.

APPLICATION

Not everyone can have or deserves the title "Great" after his name, but it isn't a bad ambition. Perhaps we should forget about "the Great" after our names and just ask St. Basil through this sacrificial banquet to get "the Great" into our minds, our hearts and our souls.

Seek here at Mass for the strength to use your talents, whatever they are, for Christ and His people. Who knows? Perhaps you may find something after your name! It could be "the Great," or even "the Greatest," but you will be most fortunate of all if it is "the Christlike one."

June 17—St. Gregory Barbarigo (1625–1697), Bishop and Confessor

THEME

Pray and work today for the reunion of the great Eastern and Western branches of Christ's Church.

EXPOSITION

Born and educated in Venice, Gregory spent the greatest part of his life in Northern Italy as Bishop and Cardinal. He was so faithful to his duties as shepherd of the flock committed to his care, so zealous in carrying out pastoral reforms, that he was called the second Charles Borromeo. He founded a seminary and college for young priests. His great prayer was that the dissident Greeks might reunite with the Holy See once again. He was renowned, as the Entrance Prayer says, for his solicitude for souls and his love for the poor.

APPLICATION

We concluded the Entrance Prayer by asking God to let us imitate Gregory's example as we honor his good deeds. I am sure all of you realize that within the last few years, the Pope and the Patriarch of Constantinople have met and in other ways have shown an intense longing to achieve the union which Christ wants so ardently.

Gregory would have been pleased at these occurrences. He would have been more than pleased; for he would have prayed with might and main to bring about this reunion.

Today offer your Mass and Communion and all your prayers for this purpose. Devote at least this one day to praying and working toward that goal—the reunion of the great Roman and Eastern branches of Christianity around the Pope.

June 18—St. Ephrem (c. 300–373), Deacon, Confessor and Doctor of the Church

THEME

Ask today's saint to make the deacons of the modern Church true ministers of Christ to all in need.

EXPOSITION

Ephrem lived in the 4th century. He was ordained a deacon and very probably was the head of the Catechetical School of his city. He became a monk and spent most of his life writing commentaries on the Scriptures and composing hymns. He is renowned for his writing and hymns which are said to have kept his people free from heresy.

APPLICATION

Ephrem was not a priest. He was a deacon—one of the most famous deacons the Church has ever had. Vatican II in its *Dogmatic Constitution on the Church* (art. 29), speaks about deacons. It states that they are strengthened by sacramental grace, and in union with the Bishops and his group of priests serve the people of God in the ministry of the Liturgy, of the Word and of Charity. Provision is also made for married men to become deacons and for the reorganization of the diaconate as a permanent rank in the hierarchy.

A deacon preaches the Word of God, administers Communion, performs weddings and baptisms. His is a ministry of service to the poor and needy throughout the world. The United States has a great need for dedicated men who will assume the duties and responsibilities of the diaconate.

Ask St. Ephrem the deacon to help the Church choose the right men to fill the ranks of the diaconate. May such men be worthy of their title and their heritage. May they stir up the sacramental grace which will be given to them and be worthy sons of the Church, Christ's ministers to the poor, the sick and the underprivileged.

June 19—St. Juliana Falconieri (1270–1341), Virgin

THEME

The Eucharist is going to be a great consolation to us when we are dying. Why not appreciate it even more now?

EXPOSITION

Juliana came from a wealthy Florentine family. Her uncle was one of the founders of the Servite Friars, so she was attracted to embrace its rule of life. At the age of 15 she renounced her inheritance, and was the first to receive the habit of the Mantellete Nuns from St. Philip Benizi. So severe were her mortifications that she developed acute stomach trouble and was unable to eat or even receive the Host.

In the Prayer of the Mass, the Church mentions how God miraculously nourished blessed Juliana by the precious body of his Son when she was at the point of death. When the Eucharist was brought to the dying Juliana, its very presence gave her great comfort. A miracle is said to have occurred. As the Host was laid against her heart, it disappeared and she died with a radiant smile on her face.

You may think that this is a pious fairy tale. Who knows? The incident does remind us how important it will be for us when we are dying to receive the Eucharist. What a comfort it will be at that time! Such considerations suggest a most important question: If the Eucharist is going to be so important for us when we are dying, why not make it important for us now?

If you live close to the Eucharistic Christ each day of your life, have no fear about dying. Christ will never let you die alone or without His aid.

June 21—St. Aloysius Gonzaga (1568–1591), Confessor

THEME

It is too bad that this patron of youth is so often misrepresented to young people.

EXPOSITION

Aloysius Gonzaga was born in 1568. At an early age he decided to become a Jesuit even though his father vigorously opposed the decision. He became a Jesuit at 17 and died six years later a victim of the plague. So Christlike had he become that he was almost immediately acclaimed a saint by those who knew him.

APPLICATION

Aloysius Gonzaga has been named the patron of youth by two popes. It is unfortunate that so many people, in discussing this patron of youth, stress his angelic purity and his complete dedication to God from an early age. Young people on the whole cannot relate to such virtues, and adopt a "why bother even trying" attitude. They realize that they themselves do not think or act like angels. Many of them will admit that they have not yet made a commitment to Christ.

The aspect of Aloysius' life that we should stress is his ministry of service to the poor and uneducated. As a student in Rome, he gave every spare moment to instructing poor children in the Faith. He visited the hospital to care for the sick. In fact, he died of the plague he contracted while caring for its victims in the hospitals.

Young people today are interested in service. They want to help the world and to make it better. Aloysius felt the same urge and he did something about it. No one denies that he teaches us a great deal about purity, but he also teaches us a much-needed lesson of concrete, down-to-earth, "get-your-hands-dirty" service to our neighbor. Don't admire St. Aloysius! Imitate him! Serve the poor and the sick as he did, and do it for the same reason—they are Christ asking to be loved and helped.

Young people are attracted by the real Aloysius. If they first imitate his dedication to the poor and unfortunate, they will not ignore his ideals of purity for long. Young people find it hard to live like angels but they will do their best to work like angels of mercy. Don't sell them or Aloysius Gonzaga short!

June 22—St. Paulinus (c. 354–431), Bishop and Confessor

THEME

A man "on the go" for God's poor.

St. Paulinus was a young man "on the go." At an early age he became a Roman senator, then counsel, and finally Governor of Campania. It was here that he was converted to the faith. He resigned his offices and returned to Gaul where he was born. He was ordained a priest in Spain, became a hermit and finally was made Bishop of Tours.

Paulinus was in contact with the great churchmen of his day—Ambrose, Augustine, Martin of Tours, Jerome. He is noted for his poverty and his love toward the poor. It is said that when he had given everything he had away and a woman asked him for money to ransom her son, he gave himself into slavery. So much did he love the poor!

APPLICATION

What a wonderful thing it is to have two saints back to back like Aloysius and Paulinus. Aloysius was a youth of the 16th century with a love for God's poor which knew no bounds. In the Prayer after Communion we ask the Lord through this Holy Sacrifice to give us the same devotion and humility that the holy Bishop Paulinus drew from this divine source.

The divine source that he drew upon was the same as ours— the Eucharistic meeting with Christ. Aloysius knew the value and the strength of the Eucharist. Paulinus in his century knew it. Do we in our century know it? Will we be able to carry on the work of men like Aloysius and Paulinus?

June 23—The Vigil of the Birth of John the Baptist

THEME

We Christians of the 20th century must prepare the people of our generation for Christ's coming.

No one should question the fittingness of this vigil; for next to Christ, John the Baptist is the most striking figure in the Gospels. He is a bridge between the Old and New Testaments.

His work was to announce the coming of Christ. The Gospel account mentions that John the Baptist "will bring back many of the sons of Israel to the Lord their God. And he will himself go before Him (Christ) with the spirit and the power of Elijah. . . . to prepare a well-disposed people for the Lord." John was a fitting precursor of Christ. In his own being he felt the stirrings of greatness. He was a strong man and a striking figure whose mere presence was a most effective sermon for reparation and penance.

APPLICATION

In one of his missionary journeys, St. Paul came upon some disciples of John the Baptist. They did not know Who the Holy Spirit was or Who Christ was. They had been baptized by John. Paul's way was made easy because he just showed them how John had prepared the way for Christ and for the coming of the Holy Spirit. The Baptist's disciples readily believed and were instructed by Paul. So well had John done his work of preparation!

Every Christian alive today must serve Christ as John the Baptist did. It is amazing that after almost two thousand years of Christianity so much needs to be done, so much *must* be done. We, like John the Baptist, must prepare the people of our generation to receive Christ. We must begin with our families and neighbors and move on from there.

Ask the precursor as you prepare to celebrate his feast to help you fulfill this vital part of your Christian vocation. Since your task is so similar to his life's work, chances are he will help you.

June 24—The Birth of St. John the Baptist

THEME

There was a man, one sent by God, whose name was John.

EXPOSITION

After a day of preparation, we come to the birthday of John the Baptist. Jesus said of John that among those born of women, there had not risen a greater than John the Baptist. He was the greatest prophet of them all because he prepared the way for Christ.

St. John the Evangelist declares in the prologue to his Gospel: "There was a man, one sent by God, whose name was John." These words were often applied to Pope John XXIII. It is easy to see why. In that lovable, portly old man, God's goodness and love were so very apparent.

John the Baptist shows forth other attributes of God. He practiced in a heroic degree the virtues of purity, prayer, penance and especially humility. He had one all-consuming purpose—to announce the coming of Christ. He was to shine like a meteor in proclaiming his message and then die.

APPLICATION

Yesterday we spoke of John the Baptist and how his mission was much like our mission today. Think today especially of John the Baptist's words: "He (Christ) must increase, I must decrease." As you follow Mass, participating as best you can, offer yourself to God as John the Baptist did.

At Communion unite yourself to Christ as John did. When you leave, have the same purpose as John. He did everything in his power to see Christ increase. He was not interested in

himself, not concerned with improving his image. He was
interested in Christ. That's how we should feel about Christ.
Do we?

June 25—St. William (1085–1142), Abbot

THEME

What are some 20th century mortifications?

EXPOSITION

St. William discovered his vocation while on pilgrimage to
the grave of St. James the Apostle at Compostella, Spain. He
returned home, became a hermit and built a monastery where
he gave those who gathered around him a rule similar to that
of St. Benedict. He believed according to the spirituality of
his day that he had to perform austere penances and mortifications if he was ever to get to heaven.

APPLICATION

The spirituality of our day has lightened the emphasis on
austere mortifications. Nonetheless, we must mortify ourselves
today, but in a different way. We realize that the body and
the soul are not enemies; they are co-workers for the better-
ment of the person, of mankind and the universe.

What mortification do you practice every day? St. William
had no trouble with smoking, T. V., overeating, alcohol, or
reckless driving. Do any of us? If we do, and some of us do,
then these are the areas for 20th century acts of mortification.
St. William did a good job in his day. Can we do as well? It's
worth a try!

himself, not concerned with improving his image. He was

June 26—Sts. John and Paul (died 362), Martyrs

THEME

Our faith makes us brothers and sisters in the Lord Jesus
Christ.

EXPOSITION

In the Gospel (Lk. 12:4-8) Christ challenges us to a fearless
confession of His name, and pledges that if we accept the
challenge He will acknowledge us before the angels of God.
The saints whose feast we celebrate today took Our Lord at
His word. The little that we know of them tells us that they
were imperial officials who were martyred and buried in their
own home. They chose Christ rather than the emperor. These
brothers in the flesh were also brothers in the spirit because
they shared the same faith and the same martyrdom.

APPLICATION

We, too, are brothers and sisters in the family of God. We
should ask Almighty God today through this Mass to give us
a true Christian family spirit. Achieving such an outlook on
life is and always will be difficult. Our beginnings are enthusiastic, but somewhere along the line we lose steam. Don't
be discouraged. Begin again, and work harder at it this time.

May Christ help us to realize the great bond of charity that
should exist among all of us because we share the same faith,
follow the same Lord Jesus Christ and enjoy the blessings of
His sacrifice and sacraments. Don't ever underestimate the
forces which will try to tear you from Christ's family. On the
other hand, don't ever underestimate the grace of Christ, Who
first called you into His family and isn't going to desert you
now.

June 28—The Vigil of the Feast of St. Peter and St. Paul

THEME

"Lord you know that I love You; today I will prove it."

EXPOSITION

We come together today to celebrate a vigil in preparation for tomorrow's feast. It is a great feast of the Church on which we honor the two Apostles Peter and Paul. In spirit we go with Peter to the temple and see how he acts towards the paralyzed man. Silver and gold he had not, but what he had he gave him. In the name of Jesus Christ Peter told the man to stand up and walk. The man did just that.

In the Gospel Christ three times asked Peter if he loved Him. Three times Peter replied, "Yes Lord, I do love You." Finally the third time Peter in exasperation said, "Lord, you know all things, You *know* that I love You."

APPLICATION

Today we should take to heart the words of Peter to the paralyzed man. We must arise and walk in the spirit of the apostles Peter and Paul. The words of Our Lord to Peter could be addressed to us also. "Do you love Me?" Make Peter's reply yours: "Lord You know all things, You know that I love You." Then add: "I will show my love for You, I will prove it. I will prove my love throughout this vigil as we prepare for the feast. I will make the sentiments I express at Mass carry over into my daily life."

How can I do all these things? By patience with a nagging wife or an alcoholic husband. By enduring a busybody neighbor or fellow worker. By kindness and sympathy toward those

in need. "How" is not the question. "Will you do it?" That's
the question.

June 29—Saints Peter and Paul, Apostles

THEME

Our faith rests upon the firm foundation of the Apostles.

EXPOSITION

"We have just heard Peter's profession of faith in Christ.
"You are the Messiah, the Son of the Living God." In response to this great act of faith, Christ conferred upon Peter
the primacy of the Church and gave to him the power of the
keys. The Epistle story recounts how Peter was saved from
the hands of Herod and the hatred of the Jews. Christ continues to protect Peter's successor just as effectively today.

APPLICATION

In the ancient Church today was a day of great joy. It was
similar to a second Easter: for it commemorated the birthday
of Christian Rome. In 1967 Pope Paul proclaimed a Year of
Faith which would begin on today's feast. It is good to have
the oportunity of today's Mass to realize how firm a foundation the Apostles gave to the Church. Their faith is our faith.
Their strength is ours.

Today at Mass when we say the Creed together, make it a
real acknowledgment of your faith in Christ and in His
Church. During the day and during your life often renew
your act of faith also. Imitate Saint Peter and Saint Paul
whose faith was strong enough to follow Christ to death and
beyond.

148

June 30—The Commemoration of St. Paul, Apostle

THEME

Paul, help us to give ourselves to Christ as completely as you did.

EXPOSITION

Today we commemorate the great Apostle, St. Paul. Paul, persecutor of the Church as he mentions in the Epistle, was called by God to be an Apostle even in the very act of persecuting the Church. He was destined to be a chosen vessel of God's election. Paul, the great missionary, traveled far and wide to spread the good news of Christ. He wrote most of the Epistles, suffered hardships beyond description for the sake of Christ, and was finally martyred in Rome.

APPLICATION

Yesterday we honored the two Apostles, Peter and Paul, but Peter received most of our attention. Today, we celebrate a special feast in honor of St. Paul. Why not join the two feasts together? Realize that you are not asked to follow just one of these Apostles but both of them.

If you have fallen and denied Christ, follow Peter and come back as magnificently as Peter came back. If you have persecuted Christ or turned your back on Him, *now* recognize Him.

Don't be lukewarm in you allegiance. Give everything you have. Paul was not a lukewarm persecutor of Christ, and he certainly was not a lukewarm lover of Christ. Don't you be either. Ask Paul to help you today to be the type of lover that he was.

149

July 1—The Feast of the Precious Blood

THEME

In heart and mind we unite with Christ as He offers His Precious Blood to the Father for our salvation.

EXPOSITION

We do not intend to fragmentize Christ when we honor on one occasion His Holy Name, then His Sacred Heart, and now His Precious Blood. What we are trying to do in our very limited way is to realize the immensity of Christ's love and what He means to us.

We honor His name because it is holy, and it makes us holy. We honor His Sacred Heart because it is the symbol of the love which prompted Him to do so much for us. We honor His Precious Blood because by this Blood of the new and everlasting covenant we are saved. "This Blood has been shed for you and for all men so that sins may be forgiven."

APPLICATION

At holy Mass today Our Lord continues to offer His blood to the Father for the forgiveness of our sins. Let us unite our hearts and minds with Our Lord as He offers this sacrifice. "Whenever you do this, you will do it in memory of Me." Remember often during the day that the shedding of Christ's Blood was the price of redemption, the price He gave willingly, the price He would give again if it were necessary.

Do we realize with what intensity Christ loves us? Do we realize how we must love Him in return to make at least a small repayment for His love? The answer to both questions

150

is "No." We can never realize completely (make completely real) these things; but with a little effort, we can do a mighty fine job. Let us begin now by uniting with Christ as He offers His Precious Blood to the Father for our salvation.

July 2—The Visitation of the Blessed Virgin Mary

THEME

Mary came to Elizabeth prompted by the purest motives of humility to help her cousin.

EXPOSITION

After Mary had been informed by the Angel Gabriel that she was to be the Mother of God, she was not filled up with her own self importance. She was filled with a desire to be with her cousin Elizabeth. The Angel had mentioned almost in passing that Elizabeth was in her sixth month of pregnancy. When Mary arrived, she was greeted by Elizabeth with the words, "Blessed are you among women and blessed is the fruit of your womb. And who am I that the Mother of my Lord should come to me?"

Mary did not seek praise or preference. She hurried to Elizabeth because she wanted to be of help to someone who needed her. She brought with her Christ the Lord. With Mary there came peace and joy, the quiet joy and contentment of having God dwelling in one's home.

APPLICATION

We Christians are like Mary, or at least we should be. We should bring Christ to those with whom we live and work. We should seek to fulfill the mandate of loving service to our

151

neighbor which was the central theme of the life of Jesus and Mary. Our motives for doing so may not be as pure as theirs; our humility may fall far short of theirs, but at least we will be trying in our own feeble way to follow them. That in itself is a giant step forward.

Think about these things during this Eucharistic sacrifice which brings Christ the Lord to you. Leave here determined to bring Christ to all you meet today.

July 3—St. Irenaeus (c. 125–c. 202), Bishop and Martyr

THEME

Irenaeus, by name and nature a peaceful man, help us to live in peace.

EXPOSITION

Today's saint was named Irenaeus, which means peaceful. He was a disciple of Polycarp, who in turn had been instructed by St. John the Apostle. Irenaeus was thus in close contact with the teachings of the Apostolic Church. He became Bishop of Lyons in Gaul and was the first great ecclesiastical writer of the West. As Bishop he was able to counteract heresy by his teachings, and to restore peace to the area. He was by name and by nature a man of peace.

APPLICATION

The Church is very anxious to stress the peaceful nature of Irenaeus and what he accomplished. He teaches us to find in peace and its consequences the means to overcome all dangers, "for there is a future for the man of peace" (Gradual). He was one of the first and most outstanding witnesses to the special place which the Church of Rome has in teaching and guiding the followers of Christ.

Ask him through this Mass for the grace to be men and women of peace, devoted to the ideals of Christ your leader, and loyal to His Vicar, the Bishop of Rome.

God Almighty "grant us peace in our day and keep your people steadfast in their holy religion" (Entrance Prayer).

"O God, author and lover of peace, to know You is to live and to serve You is to reign" (Prayer after Communion). Help us to know and serve you in peace.

July 4—Ferial Day, Independence Day in the United States

(It is suggested that the Mass of the Sunday be offered with the prayers from the Mass of Thanksgiving.)

THEME

For all Americans, the 4th of July should be a day of thanks, of prayer and of dedication.

EXPOSITION

Today is a national holiday, but it also has religious overtones. Christ has exerted a strong influence on our country's history and its people, so it is fitting that we offer a Mass of thanksgiving to Almighty God. Today is a day of thanks for past growth and freedom. It is a day of prayer that we may enjoy and fulfill the promise of freedom in our country's history. It is a day of dedication to the future greatness of our country and to a more responsible use of our freedoms.

APPLICATION

We citizens of the United States should be proud of our country and its history. However, let's not rest on our laurels.

153

Our past greatness and liberty were won at a high price, and any future greatness will be even more costly.

As we face the prospect of another long hot summer of racial unrest and discontent, we know what our country demands from us. Tolerance, love for all our fellow citizens, respect for their rights and, especially, a helping hand for the needy. These are the necessary ingredients for future greatness. Are we willing to supply them?

Offer your Masses and Communions today so that the United States will achieve the greatness of its promise. If we are true Christians and citizens, our country will be great. If we are not, we can forget about our dreams for a United States where justice and liberty are not just empty words.

July 5—St. Anthony Mary Zaccaria (1502–1539), Confessor

THEME

Toward internal renewal of the Church in the spirit of St. Paul.

EXPOSITION

At a time when Martin Luther was rejecting the Church, Anthony tried to reform it from within. He founded the Clerks Regular of St. Paul, commonly known as the Barnabites. These men dedicated themselves to a thoroughgoing reform of the Church. They were interested in the physical as well as the spiritual well-being of the laity.

All was done in the spirit of St. Paul, the great patron of Anthony. That is the reason the Entrance Prayer tells us we should ask God to teach us according to the spirit of the apostle Paul that knowledge of Jesus Christ which surpasses all understanding. It was through this learning that Blessed

Anthony was instructed and founded new religious families of men and women for the reform of the Church.

APPLICATION

Once again we return to our favorite theme. We live in an age in which the Church is reforming herself. There are men and women who desert the Church today because she has not given them a fair deal or because she is not moving fast enough toward the desired renewal. Will you follow their lead? I hope not!

Strive to imitate men such as St. Anthony. Walk in the spirit of St. Paul asking God to help you achieve that knowledge of Jesus Christ which surpasses all understanding. Be loyal members of Christ's Church; a Church ever reforming, ever in need of reform. Offer this sacrifice to God through Jesus Christ for the grace to be loyal members of the Church. Pray also for those who have deserted her that they may return to their true home.

July 7—Sts. Cyril and Methodius (9th Century), Confessors

THEME

A willingness to change from old ways and adopt new methods has characterized great men in every age.

EXPOSITION

Cyril and Methodius were brothers in the flesh and became brothers in religion. They were living a monastic life when the Emperor called them to evangelize the people in Moravia. They went and did such a wonderful job of bringing Christ to those people that they were called to Rome and consecrated bishops. Cyril died there. Methodius resumed his missionary activities and became the apostle to the Bohemians and to the other Slavic nations. Cyril and Methodius are the patrons of the Slavic nations.

APPLICATION

These two men could have stayed in their monastery and lived a life very pleasing to God. They could have clung to their former ways, but they did not. They launched out into the deep with the faith of the apostles, with the firm conviction that Christ was calling them to do His work. They were outstanding missionaries of Christ. They are patrons of the liturgy and were confirmed vernacularists convinced that people should worship God in their own language.

We have need of their inspiring example today. We must accept the liturgical reforms of Vatican II with the same enthusiasm and love that Cyril and Methodius showed toward their missionary activities. In the Prayer of the Mass we ask to be companions of Cyril and Methodius in heaven. Let us ask for another favor through this Mass. May we follow in their footsteps here on earth by our enthusiastic support of all liturgical reforms.

July 8—St. Elizabeth (1271–1336), Queen of Portugal and Widow

THEME

Are you available as a peacemaker?

EXPOSITION

Elizabeth, the daughter of the King of Aragon, was married at a young age to the King of Portugal. In her life as Queen and

Mother she was an example of every virtue. Above everything else, Elizabeth was a woman of peace and a maker of peace. Her birth was the means of restoring peace between her father and grandfather. This was only the beginning of her life's great work.

All her life she worked at promoting peace in her family and in her country. She worked at being a Queen, and she was a good one. Her most outstanding achievement, as mentioned in the Entrance Prayer, was to end the devastating wars which plagued her country and its neighbors.

APPLICATION

We need such women today, especially in our families. So often a family is torn apart by minor feuds and frictions. Someone is needed whom the combatants love and respect. This person will be able to draw the family together again. Even if the hurt prevents immediate reconciliation, the peacemaker will show that she loves both parties, and will be a bridge between both parties. When time has dulled the wound, she will show them the way to reconciliation and peace.

It's not a pleasant job but it's a wonderful work. A peacemaker has so delicate a task that she must possess the wisdom of Solomon and the patience of Job. What I am trying to say is that she must be another Elizabeth. Are there any volunteers for the position?

July 10—The Seven Holy Brothers (died c. 162), Martyrs— Sts. Rufina and Secunda (3rd Century), Virgins and Martyrs

THEME

Uncompromising loyalty to Christ and what it costs.

The Roman widow, Felicity, had to endure more than one martyrdom for Christ. She had to watch her seven sons sacrificed, struck down in horrible ways because they would not desert Christ and sacrifice to the pagan idols. She, herself, four months later followed in their footsteps. The other two saints of today, Rufina and Secunda were called upon to do the same thing a century later.

APPLICATION

We concentrate today upon the seven brothers. These young men were promised anything they wanted if they would sacrifice to the pagan idols. Not one of them agreed. True to their mother and to Christ they worshiped together, stayed together through fire, torture and martyrdom.

We are great believers in compromise and negotiation these days. We give a little here and take a little there, stretch the truth at times, and modify our position occasionally (which is double talk for reneging on a promise). There is nothing wrong with an honorable compromise, but there are limits to its application.

Our faith in Christ, our personal and Christian dignity and that of other human beings should never be compromised. Ask today's saints for the help you need to be uncompromisingly loyal to Christ, to yourself and to others.

July 12—St. John Gualbert (died 1073), Abbot

THEME

For the sake of Christ can you forgive anyone anything?

EXPOSITION

Today's saint was a soldier in Florence, Italy, during the 11th century. He was a man of great courage and of deep loyalty to his family. When his brother was murdered, John set out to avenge the crime. He soon found the murderer and was prepared to strike a death blow when the killer threw himself on his knees, made the Sign of the Cross, and begged for his life because of the Passion of Jesus Christ.

Who of us can imagine the tremendous conflict of emotions that must have occurred in John's heart? Would the desire to avenge his brother's death or love for Christ carry the day? Christ and His grace were victorious. John embraced the murderer and forgave him because of Christ's Passion. Later John became a Benedictine and founded his own religious order to promote the reformation of faith and morals throughout his country.

APPLICATION

What a scene that must have been when St. John Gualbert met his brother's murderer! It is difficult to comprehend how the love of Christ overcame his desire for revenge. St. John could say, "For the love of Christ I can forgive anyone anything." Could we say it? Could we say: "For the love of Christ I will forgive the person who slights me and talks behind my back; the person who is unfair to me, corrects me or ignores me"? For the love of Christ, can I forgive those who passed me over for a promotion; can I work with them and the one promoted over me?

Some of these things are important; others are trivial; but each of them has an emotional impact on us. Once our feelings of revenge and annoyance get aroused, we find it difficult to maintain our Christian perspective. St. John found it almost impossible, but he adhered to God's will despite his emotions. He has a lesson to teach us, doesn't he? Let's learn it well!

July 14—St. Bonaventure (1221–1274), Bishop and Doctor of the Church

THEME

Bonaventure sought to achieve two things in his lifetime—Christlike gentleness and Christian unity.

EXPOSITION

Bonaventure has been called the second founder of the Franciscan Order because he did so much to carry out the ideals of St. Francis of Assisi. He became a Franciscan at 20 and at a very early age became Superior General of the Franciscans.

Because of his writings, which are filled with his penetrating genius and burning love for God, he has been declared a Doctor of the Church, the Seraphic Doctor. He was chosen by the Pope to direct the Council of Lyons where a temporary union was established between some of the Oriental Churches and the Church of Rome. He died in the midst of his work for Christian unity.

APPLICATION

To his own age Bonaventure was the model Christian gentleman. He was learned, he was pious, he was affable. He had the gentle and beautiful qualities of Christ Himself. Bonaventure was also dedicated to Christian unity.

We have need of the ideals that sparked the life of Bonaventure—Christlike gentleness and a willingness to work for unity among all Christians. We need these things *today*. In our highly efficient, automated and impersonal world, we need the gentle and beautiful qualities of Christ and Bonaventure *today*. We need people who are dedicated to the ideals of Christian unity and who are willing to pray, to work and to sacrifice for it *today*. Ask Bonaventure to help you live a life dedicated to these ideals, not tomorrow but *today*.

July 15—St. Henry (died 1024), Emperor and Confessor

THEME

Henry realized the Christian implications of his state in life and lived them to the fullest.

EXPOSITION

Henry was chosen Emperor of the Holy Roman Empire in 1002. He was one of the strongest rulers of the Empire, and yet, one of the kindest and most saintly men of his time. He was the Emperor, but first and foremost he was a Christian. Devoted to promoting Christian living throughout his whole Empire, he and his wife gave an example of holiness upon the throne of Germany which has rarely been matched.

APPLICATION

St. Henry realized the Christian implications of his state in life and lived them to the fullest. That was no small accomplishment even for an Emperor. How about us? Do we realize that no matter who we are or how we earn our living, we are Christ? St. Henry knew his dignity and responsibility as Christ's chosen follower.

This meal we share together should inspire us to follow his example. With its nourishment can we not dedicate ourselves once again to realizing the implications of our Christ-life? Don't just realize what they are! Live them to the fullest!

161

July 18—St. Camillus of Lellis (1550–1616), Confessor

THEME

It is good to pray for a happy death but don't forget to live a happy life.

EXPOSITION

The Church sets before us in the next few days three examples of heroic charity. These three saints teach us how to love our neighbor. Today's saint had a special gift of love to help the dying in their last agony. He has been declared the patron of the sick, of nurses, and all those in the nursing professions.

St. Camillus founded a religious order whose members devoted their lives to nursing the sick, caring for plague victims, troops at war, and prisoners. His work was not a pleasant occupation, but St. Camillus was a happy man despite the dirt, the filth and the sickness. He laid down his life for his friends not by one magnificent act, but by a lifetime of loving concern for the poor and the sick. Truly greater love than this no man has than to be able to live day in and day out a love like that.

APPLICATION

The Church today reminds us of the love which St. Camillus had for the sick, and of his ability to console the dying. Then she urges us to ask Almighty God for the grace of a happy death. In the Prayer after Communion, we say: "May your sacraments strengthen us at the hour of our death, cleanse us from sin, and bring us happily into your merciful arms."

The Church is right in asking us to pray for a happy death; for dying is a very important part of our lives. The Church also wants us to realize that living is important. She wants us

162

to have a balanced picture of today's saint. He died a happy death because he lived day in and day out a life of heroic love for the sick.

Pray for a happy death, but also pray for a happy life which is a life of dedication to God's people and work.

July 19—St. Vincent de Paul (died 1660), Confessor

THEME

God's organization man for the poor.

EXPOSITION

Vincent de Paul is a name that means charity in action. He was a peasant priest who rose to such great heights that he could even influence the royal family of France. He rose high but never forgot the poor and unfortunate. He is outstanding for the many charitable organizations which he established. Just to list what he did is breathtaking.

He founded an order of priests to give missions to the poor and help train seminarians. He organized a group of wealthy ladies to perform works of charity and a group of younger girls to assist the ladies in this work. From the second group came the Sisters of Charity of St. Vincent de Paul.

He was God's organization man for the poor. He started many things on a small scale and when the demand multiplied, he skillfully organized the work and the workers. During his life he received immense sums of money which he spent wisely because he considered it God's money for the poor. He aimed at rehabilitation, not just temporary relief.

The Society of St. Vincent established in many parishes was a forerunner of the role of the laity in modern times. The society is an organization of laymen quietly and effectively caring for the poor and the needy.

163

Vincent teaches us the need of great love and compassion when dealing with the poor. We should never lose the personal aspect of charity. We as individuals help other individuals who are in need.

He also tells us that we need organization for this great work. There must be competent professional people plus many volunteers who are willing to work under their supervision. If such harmony is achieved, then everyone will profit from it. Ask Vincent to help you work with the organizations that are caring for the poor today. Always be on the lookout for ways to do this work better.

In the liturgy St. Vincent comes before us with all the souls that have followed his example and all the poor who have been helped by what he did. These people urge us to follow in his footsteps. They urge us to love and serve Christ in the poor and needy. Don't let Christ in the poor go unloved or uncared for any longer!

July 20—St. Jerome Emilian (1481–1537), Confessor

THEME

Give your love to some neglected child soon, and grow as you love.

EXPOSITION

Today we close the triduum of charity which the Church gives us during July. Two days ago we honored the saint of the sick and dying while yesterday we rejoiced with the saint of the poor. Now we honor the patron of orphans and abandoned children. He was a soldier from noble family. As happened so often in the Church's history, he learned in captivity that he was not following the right leader. When he escaped, he gave himself completely to God's work.

He took as his special apostolate orphans and the victims of war and plague. He kept the orphans in his home, clothed and fed them and educated them. As his fame spread, he was able to establish many orphanages in different parts of Italy. He died as so many saints of charity have died—from a disease he caught while visiting the sick.

APPLICATION

We Christians are not orphans. We are loved with a never-ending love. There is no reason why we should feel deserted or alone. If at times we do, we must forget ourselves and try harder to love others. So often in giving love to a neglected or underprivileged child, we receive more ourselves.

Think about orphans today! They need love so very much. They are cared for; they are fed and clothed, but they need love. They crave for someone to love them and to take their love in return. Resolve now to visit an orphanage and get to know the children. Get to love some neglected child and grow as you love.

From this Mass in honor of St. Jerome, we learn that serving God in a Christian way does not stop at the liturgy. It extends to the way we love and the way we live after we have left the liturgy. In a sense, we do not leave the liturgy. We take it with us and make it spark the activities of our day.

July 21—St. Lawrence of Brindisi (born 1559), Confessor and Doctor of the Church

THEME

Wisdom and fortitude—necessary virtues for your apostolic efforts.

EXPOSITION

St. Lawrence was born in Italy in 1559. He was educated by the Franciscans and imitated his teachers by becoming a Capuchin Franciscan. He had a natural bent for languages and is considered the greatest linguist among the Doctors of the Church. His many-sided apostolate included such positions as army chaplain, teacher of Scripture, diplomat, and leader of the Counter-Reformation. God favored Lawrence with the combined spirit of wisdom and fortitude to measure up to any hardship he might face in fulfilling his apostolate.

APPLICATION

"Grant that in the same spirit we may recognize our obligations and fulfill them with his help" (Entrance Prayer). Our apostolate may not be as many-sided as Lawrence's was. Our abilities certainly could never match his.

Nonetheless, we should ask God through St. Lawrence to give us that combined spirit of wisdom and fortitude which the Entrance Prayer mentions. The wisdom we need will help us to know what God wants us to do, and will show us how to do it. The gift of fortitude will help us to measure up to the hardships of the apostolate. Wisdom and fortitude—these virtues form the ending of our homily. Make them the beginning of your efforts to be an apostle.

166

July 22—St. Mary Magdalene, Penitent

THEME

Mary Magdalene owed a great debt to Christ. She tried to pay this debt by a life of loving service to Him and His disciples.

EXPOSITION

Mary Magdalene was one of the women who followed Our Lord. She had been cured by Him of evil spirits. St. Luke says that she had been freed from seven devils (diabolical possession does not imply a state of sin). There is no need to spend time discussing who she was or why she was with Christ. She was there. She was in the company of the women who took care of Him. She stood at the foot of the Cross with the Blessed Virgin Mary. She was in the garden for the first appearance of the resurrected Lord. As a witness to Christ's Death and Resurrection, she has few equals.

APPLICATION

Mary owed Christ a great debt of gratitude. After she had been freed of the evil spirits, she joined with the other women who cared for Christ and His needs. Mary Magdalene shows us how we can repay the debt that we owe to Christ by loving service to Him and to His disciples, be they men or women.

Let us rededicate ourselves today to the ideals of serving Christ and those who preach His name and do His work. Support your Church and its missions. Support most of all, by your prayers and your Communions, the priests, sisters and lay people who have dedicated themselves full time to spreading the message of Christ.

167

Ask the Lord through the merits of Mary Magdalene to accept the gifts we offer this morning as He once accepted her humble homage and service. Mary Magdalene realized that gratitude to Almighty God does not end with "Thank You, Lord." It begins there and must continue in loving service to Him and His followers.

July 23—St. Appollinaris (died c. 200), Bishop and Martyr

THEME

The Mass gives us the Eucharist as the dynamically relevant means to carry out the instructions of Christ.

EXPOSITION

Apollinaris, Bishop and Martyr, was sent to Ravenna, Italy, to preach Christ. He evangelized the city and its environs, became its first bishop, and its only known martyr. He was killed at Ravenna after withstanding many trials and exile.

He knew well the teachings of St. Peter; he must have read his epistles often. Apollinaris realized that the Apostles had not merely given him an instruction, but a message for life, a spirit of service to God and His people. Apollinaris lived and died for this message of Christ.

APPLICATION

At Mass today we honor Apollinaris. The Church instructs us by the readings and indicates what we are to seek from God by the prayers of the Mass. In the Eucharist we receive the grace needed to put into practice the instruction and directions which the Church has given us.

Christ wants the Eucharist to be dynamically relevant to

our lives and to be the means of putting His teachings into practice. Why is it that we so often receive the Eucharist almost nonchalantly? It is meant to be relevant, to be the dynamo which electrifies our lives and makes them conform to Christ's teachings.

Why doesn't the Eucharist achieve its full potential in us? I don't know! Can you supply any clues? Whatever your answer is, during the Canon join with the priest in saying: ". . . as we receive from this altar the Sacred Body and Blood of your Son, let us be filled with every grace and blessing." May these words help you "come alive" to the full meaning of the Eucharist.

July 25—St. James, Apostle

THEME

Can you drink the cup which I am going to drink?

EXPOSITION

The first of the apostles to suffer martyrdom was James the Greater, the brother of St. John the beloved Apostle. He was one of the three disciples who were privileged to be with Christ at some of the most important parts of his life. He was the first Apostle to die for the sake of Christ. His martyrdom receives just a few words in the Acts of the Apostles. Herod Agrippa "killed James, the brother of John with the sword" (Acts 12:2).

He is venerated as the patron saint of Spain, and his relics are said to be at Compostella in Spain. We may not believe that St. James' relics are at Compostella. Actually it really doesn't matter. What we know of him tells us that he was a

Son of Thunder, a man of great courage and an intimate friend of Christ.

When the mother of James and John asked Jesus for the favor which is recounted in the Gospel this morning, Christ turned to them and said, "You do not realize what you are asking; can you drink the cup which I am going to drink?" They replied unhesitatingly, "Yes, we can." They did. James drank of the cup at the Last Supper and again when he was killed by Herod Agrippa.

APPLICATION

Our Lord asks us today the same question he asked James and John: "Can you drink of the cup which I am going to drink?" St. James the Apostle will help us, through the merits of this Mass, to answer that question of Christ affirmatively. There may be no Herod Agrippa to behead us with the sword, but there are people waiting to cut us down to size.

They will try to destroy our attachment to Christ. We must love such people, and by our actions convert them to Christ. It will not be easy. They want nothing to do with Christ, His Church, religion or anything else. They will never be convinced by words; only a lifetime of Christlike actions will touch their hearts.

This is the cup that Christ offers us. Will we accept it or will we throw its contents on the ground?

July 26—St. Anne, Mother of the Blessed Virgin Mary

THEME

We know and love this woman because of the influence she had upon her daughter.

EXPOSITION

Anne, the mother of the Blessed Virgin Mary and the wife of Joachim, is not mentioned at all in the Gospels. We know about her only from non-Biblical sources. Some scholars doubt that she was named Anne, but no one doubts that the Blessed Virgin Mary had a mother. By all standards she was a valiant woman, a worthy wife in whom her husband could be well pleased, whose child would rise up to praise her.

APPLICATION

St. Anne devoted herself to educating the child Mary, teaching her the wonderful truths of God's great glory. She showed Mary how to live a saintly life. We need women like St. Anne today, women who will accept and will fulfill their responsibilities as Christian mothers.

The Mayor of New York has said recently that the cities of this country have so many problems that they can no longer ignore the great benefits that women bring to city government. The Church likewise can no longer ignore the great benefits that women confer upon her. Today at Mass ask Our Lord in honor of St. Anne to grant to the Church Christian mothers who will carry out His goals for the whole world.

Years ago there was a saying much in vogue with single women: "Good St. Anne, get me a man as quick as you can." Let's change that saying to read: "Good St. Anne make me a Christlike man as quick as you can." "Good St. Anne make me a Christlike woman as quick as you can."

July 28—Sts. Nazarius and Celsus (dates unknown), Martyrs; Sts. Victor I (died c. 200) and Innocent I (died c. 417), Popes

THEME

Lord, teach us the real meaning of witnessing to you.

EXPOSITION

Today we commemorate four martyrs of the Church. It is unusual to group together people from different times and from different states of life, but that is what we do today. Nazarius was a mature man while Celsus was just a young boy. Victor and Innocent were Popes and martyrs also. We honor them today because they were witnesses to Christ. In fact, we say in the Entrance Prayer: "Defend us, O Lord through the holy witness of your saints and let their merits support us in our weakness."

APPLICATION

Some people have the idea that they can witness to Christ just by good example. What they mean is this: keep to yourself; try to be the best possible Christian and keep the commandment, but don't get involved in what's going on outside your little world. "Don't get involved" is the motto of such people. Such an attitude will never make you a witness to Christ as today's saints were.

We must be witnesses to Christ *by our words.* When we speak, everyone should know that we are men who love and follow Christ. We must be witnesses *by our actions,* by the love that we show to our neighbor, by the love that we give to the poor and to the oppressed. We must be witnesses to Christ *by our daily lives* which tell everyone: "Here is a man who believes in something besides money and pleasure."

That's what it means to be a true witness to Christ, and it isn't easy. Ask today's saints to show you how to do it because they did it successfully. All of us can use some good coaching in this task of witnessing to Christ.

July 29—St. Martha, Virgin

THEME

We should not let one sentence said in exasperation color our whole picture of a person.

EXPOSITION

When Jesus came to visit at the home of Lazarus, Martha and Mary, there was much to be done. He was such a close friend and so important a person that they wanted to make Him welcome. Martha hustled around trying to get everything ready. Then she realized that her sister Mary was doing nothing but listening to Jesus. This annoyed her and in exasperation she told the Lord that Mary wasn't doing anything and there was so much to be done. Jesus replied that Martha was worried about many things but only one thing was necessary and Mary had chosen the better part.

Some people delight in criticizing poor Martha. There is little foundation for such criticism. We don't hear of Martha throwing dishes at Jesus because He took Mary's part. She accepted it, calmed down, and listened a little more carefully to what He was saying.

APPLICATION

One sentence said in exasperation should not color our whole picture of this woman. Martha was a good woman. Jesus

173

found in her and her family friends with whom He could always feel at home. She wanted to take care of Him and His disciples. She was devoted to Him. Let us be devoted to Christ in the same way.

There is one lesson we should learn from Martha's mistake. Try to give everyone the benefit of the doubt and to acknowledge that in everyone there is goodness. Try to find that goodness. Don't let a sentence or a whole paragraph or a whole speech spoken in anger color your opinion of a person. Look at all the facts and make your judgment of that person in the light of what you see. Judge him in the light of Christ's love for him and for you.

You have chosen the "better part" by being here at this banquet where the love of Christ is given to us. Don't throw away this "better part" by refusing to give the love of Christ to others.

July 31—St. Ignatius Loyola (1491–1556), Confessor

THEME

Christians by their baptism and confirmation are soldiers of Christ, and that demands complete dedication to Him and His work.

EXPOSITION

As we look around the world today, we see that military men are serving as heads of state in many countries. Ignatius, whose feast we celebrate today, was a military man who would have made a first-rate head of state. However, he was not satisfied by his life. He wanted to be a soldier, but he realized that he had to devote himself to something more than fighting battles for an earthly king. Ignatius, through his enforced

174

convalescence after a battle wound, realized that he was called to the service of God.

He and his early companions took not only the three vows of poverty, chastity and obedience but also a special vow that they would always do what the Pope commanded. Ignatius was a man of great spirituality, and his *Spiritual Exercises* have been used for centuries to guide Christian men and women.

APPLICATION

"O God, in order to promote the greater glory of Your Name, you fortified the Church militant with a new army through the work of Blessed Ignatius. May this help and example bring us through our battle on earth to be crowned with him in heaven." The military aura pervades the prayers of today's Mass and reminds us that we are fighting in a war also. There are battles to be won or lost; there is a war which must be won.

Ask St. Ignatius for the grace to realize that you are a soldier. You must give all that you have for your God as a soldier gives his all for his country. Is it too much to ask? Ignatius didn't think so. Do you?

August 2—St. Alphonse Mary Liguori (1696–1787), Bishop and Doctor of the Church

THEME

The law of Christ is a law of love.

EXPOSITION

Today's saint is the patron of all confessors and moralists. Alphonse Liguori was a lawyer, priest, founder of the Redemptorists, but above all a lover of God's law. He did not fall in love with the law of God but with the God whose law it was. We're not playing with words here but with the deepest reality. Alphonse felt about God's law as the composer of Psalm 118 felt when he sang: "I love your Law . . . I put my hope in your word" (v. 113-4). Alphonse is an example to all of the gentleness and moderation needed in applying the law.

APPLICATION

Ask Christ at Mass today for grace to know that in loving His law, you are truly loving Him. Ask to be gentle and moderate in the way you enforce your rules, especially with your family. To rule by love is much harder than to rule through force and fear but it is much more effective. Let Christ and St. Alphonse show you how to rule by love.

August 4—St. Dominic (c. 1175–1221), Confessor

THEME

Knowledge of our faith should lead to greater union with Christ.

EXPOSITION

Dominic de Guzman, a young Spanish priest of the 13th century, fought against the Albigensian heretics and brought many of them back to the truth. He achieved such great results because of his intellectual powers but primarily because of his gentle "don't-burn-them-at-the-stake" approach. He knew the power of love, kindness, joy, and shared experiences before any hippie ever coined the word "flower power."

Dominic founded the religious family which has assumed his name even though technically they are the Order of

176

Preachers. He endowed his order with a theological basis and the belief that by teaching people the truth, they will turn toward God.

APPLICATION

Who of us could not grasp more fully the truths of our religion and use them to grow closer to God? Each of us needs to learn more about our Faith and especially about this great act of worship. When was the last time you read an article, pamphlet or book about the Mass? Don't try to worship God with a child's faith when you are no longer a child. An adult needs a mature understanding and love of his faith and all its parts. If you don't have it, now is the time to get it.

August 5—Dedication of the Church of Our Lady of the Snow (c. 435)

THEME

On this feast we should ask Mary to help us realize that we are dedicated to Jesus more than any church could ever be.

EXPOSITION

Today we recall the dedication to God's service of the Church of Our Lady of the Snow. Because of its antiquity and dignity, it is the greatest of all the churches in Rome dedicated to Our Lady and is popularly known as St. Mary Major.

APPLICATION

An the anniversary of this church's dedication we should check on our devotion and dedication to Jesus Christ. We should be aware of Mary and the very important role she

177

plays in our lives and in our salvation. She shows us in the flesh what it means to be completely at God's service.

During Mass and at Communion today ask Mary, your mother, to share with you some of the secrets of her complete dedication to Christ, her Son and your Brother. She is just waiting to be asked.

August 6—Transfiguration

THEME

Lord, it is good to be here at Your sacrificial banquet.

EXPOSITION

Peter's almost uncontrollable desire when confronted by the vision of the transfigured Jesus was to see that it never ended. "Lord, it is good that we are here. With Your permission, I will set up three tents here." By providing a fitting dwelling place for Jesus and His two prophet-companions, Peter sought to insure their presence on the mountain-top forever. Who can blame Peter for such feelings? Who would ever want to trade such a vision for the drab emptiness of worldly pleasures?

APPLICATION

It is good to be here at Mass also, but we, like Peter, cannot stay here forever. We have to go down into the valley of everyday life, cherishing the vision that we have of Christ just as Peter did. Only we do not have to keep it to ourselves. We must share it. Ask Jesus and His three apostles through this Mass to help you in your efforts to share your priceless vision of Christ.

178

THEME II

This feast confirms our faith in Christ's Divinity. It also gives us an appreciation of the great dignity which is ours as adopted sons of God.

EXPOSITION

In the Epistle Peter gets right to the point. In a no-nonsense fashion, he lets us know that Christ is no myth and His Divinity no farfetched story. It is the truth which has been vouched for by God Himself and Peter was there as an eye-witness. He warns us to pay close attention to the prophetic message also because it and the facts of the transfiguration prove that Christ will come a second time.

APPLICATION

We follow Christ not just because of our feelings but because of the witness of the Father Whose words Peter quotes. Someday we hope to hear the Father use the same words of us as He did of Christ: "My Son, my beloved, in whom I take delight, this is He" (II Peter 1:17). If we center our lives on Christ and grow more like Him through our Masses and Communions, then we definitely will hear those words.

August 7—St. Cajetan (1480–1547), Confessor

THEME

Each of us must join Christ in His search for souls.

179

When Cajetan heard the message of Christ to seek first the kingdom of God and His will, he believed what he heard. He not only heard and believed, but he acted on the message. Cajetan had such great trust in God that he did not worry about his daily needs. God would provide. Today's saint trusted in God's fatherly love and devoted himself to the salvation of souls. He was so interested and zealous in this apostolate that he won the title, "Hunter of Souls."

APPLICATION

Christ is hunting for souls today just as He did in the time of St. Cajetan. He is doing so through us. How are we doing? Just tall tales, fish stories about the ones which "got away," or are we working right along with Christ? Do we really trust in Him and in our mission to others? Talk it over with Christ today at Mass and offer Him all your talent in His continuing "hunt" for souls.

August 9—St. John Mary Vianney (1786–1859), Confessor

THEME

St. John teaches us that prayer and penance are necessary weapons in our search for souls.

EXPOSITION

John Vianney is the patron of parish priests. The reason for this special honor is not hard to uncover. For 40 years he labored without letup in a poor, uninspiring parish in France.

180

He gave everything he had to the service of God's people. He was and still is an example of priestly zeal and unflagging fervor in prayer and penitential works. St. John became known as the "Saint of the Confessional" because of his long hours in hearing the confessions of people from all over the world.

APPLICATION

We just prayed "May his intercession and example enable us to gain the souls of our brothers for Christ, and with them attain to everlasting glory." Use the strength and grace which you gain here at Mass and Communion to go out and be true to yourself, but make it your best self—your most Christ-like self. If you can even come close to that goal, you will help to gain the souls of your brothers and sisters for Christ. In so doing, you will be saving your own soul. Who could ask for better pay?

August 10—St. Lawrence (3rd Century), Martyr, Deacon of Rome

THEME

We must love Christ in and through the poor whom we are privileged to help.

EXPOSITION

St. Lawrence was tortured by a Roman prefect who wanted him to reveal the whereabouts of the Church's treasure. Lawrence brought a great number of the poor before the prefect and pointed to them saying: "Here is the Church's treasure." It was a nice gesture but it cost dearly. Lawrence had spent his life loving and waiting upon Christ in His poor and hun-

181

gry people. He is a wonderful example to us of how to love Christ. Lawrence loved Christ to the very limits, to torture, pain, death and beyond. Lawrence loved Christ not as some unreachable ideal, but in and through the poor to whom he ministered.

APPLICATION

Try to love Christ as Lawrence did. After all, it is easier to find a poor person to love and help than to be tortured on a gridiron; at least under the present conditions.

Cf. Parsh Vol. IV, p. 314, where he draws a beautiful comparison between Christ, Lawrence, and the Christian community, basing it on the seed which dies and then brings forth an abundant harvest.

August 12—St. Clare (c. 1193–1253), Virgin

THEME

Never underestimate the power of a woman to follow Christ.

EXPOSITION

St. Clare is renowned as a perfect example of the Franciscan ideal. Her life is a very beautiful adaptation to female circumstances of a way of perfection which seemed almost impossible even for men because of its rigors and its almost complete dependence on charity for the necessities of life.

St. Clare, a girl of beauty and wealth, gave up a most comfortable life and future to follow that "impractical" plan of life devised by St. Francis of Assisi. It was impractical to the worldly-wise, but to her it was, as we will pray in the Communion hymn: "going forth to meet Christ, the Lord."

Follow her example and with the strength you gain from this Mass and Communion, do as she did: "go forth to meet Christ" your Lord today in everything that you do.

August 14—Vigil of Assumption

THEME

How does Mary want you to prepare for her great feast?

EXPOSITION

Recently we explained the purpose of a vigil. Today's is a very important one. We are preparing for what is perhaps the greatest of all Marian feasts. The feast of St. Lawrence had a vigil also (August 9) but his feast did not mean as much to us. Mary is special. She is Our Lady and our Mother; she is a big part of our daily life.

APPLICATION

Tomorrow will be a great day for her and for us. Let us prepare well today. Why not ask her at Mass today what she wants you to do in preparation for her feast.

August 15—Assumption of Mary

From her throne in heaven, Mary, God's lowly handmaid, encourages us to persevere.

Today we rejoice with Our Lady at the great privilege which she had of being taken up body and soul into heavenly glory. However, the Gospel says nothing at all about her Assumption, but tells us of Mary's visit to her cousin, Elizabeth. Why does the Church use this Gospel and not one which mentions something about Mary's Assumption? The reason is simple. The Gospel is the story of Christ, and Mary plays only a secondary part in it. Her name is mentioned just a few times and her words are recorded even less frequently. The section which we have just read contains the longest talk of Mary.

In a sense today we see Mary's life as a ladder. The Assumption shows us the top of the ladder with Our Lady sitting close to God in heavenly glory, while the Gospel shows us the lowest rung of the ladder with Mary calling herself God's lowly handmaid.

Most of us are not world-famous personalities, but just lowly people who are trying to do their best. We need Mary's example of humility and lowliness to show us that there is meaning to our existence. We also need the vision of our Blessed Mother in heavenly glory to encourage us and to lead us to

184

our Father's house. At Mass and Communion today ask your Mother Mary to help you to live your life in union with her Son so that you, too, will one day reach the top rung of the ladder of life.

August 16—St. Joachim, Father of the Blessed Virgin Mary

THEME

This feast sets before us once again the human ancestry of Jesus Christ.

EXPOSITION

St. Joachim is presented to us today as one of the just men of the Old Testament, loyal to his God, generous to the poor, one tested by adversity and yet always faithful to his ideals. Today's feast reminds us of Christ's ancestry and reaffirms once again that He was truly one of us.

APPLICATION

As we think about Christ's humanity, it is well to think of Mary and her parents. They along with Joseph are part of our Christ-family. The Alleluia verse brings home quite forcefully what St. Joachim can do for us. "O Joachim, husband of St. Anne—father of the kind Virgin—help your servants to save their souls."

In the Prayer over the Gifts we beg God to accept the sacrifice we offer. Once again St. Joachim is joined with his wife and most blessed child. His is a family with enormous influence with God and one which is ever ready to help us. Call upon this blessed family often. Start now at Mass.

185

August 17—St. Hyacinth (1185–1257), Confessor

THEME

Don't just keep the Faith, spread it as an Apostle should.

EXPOSITION

St. Hyacinth, a Dominican friar, earned the title "Apostle of the North" (Poland, Russia, Scandinavia, etc.). He had a great devotion to Mary, Queen of the Apostles. It may be hard to grasp but each of us is an Apostle also. We are called to spread the love and trust of Christ to all we meet. There is an expression which is often used when religious people part which goes, "Be good and keep the faith." The usual reply is: "Don't keep it, spread it." There's a lot of good theology in that remark.

APPLICATION

Ask Mary, the Queen of Apostles, and today's saint to help you realize that you are an Apostle. You must not clutch the Faith to your heart but spread it. Get a running start here at Mass and then go out to change your world, my fellow Apostles.

August 19—St. John Eudes (1601–1680), Confessor

THEME

Our rule of life must be: "Can I do what God wants me to do?"

St. John was a zealous preacher of missions and an outstanding confessor. He also founded religious institutes for men and women. He was the first to urge public devotion to the Sacred Hearts of Jesus and Mary.

The Entrance Hymn speaks of "the law of God being in his heart." By that we mean that he was fully and completely united to the Father's will. He lived his life, acted, thought and desired according to one rule: "What does God my Father and Christ my Brother want me to do at this moment?"

APPLICATION

Why not follow St. John's example and live always with "the law of God in your heart?" Our rule of life has to be: "What does God expect of me at this moment and under these circumstances?" It's not always possible to answer that question infallibly. Thank God we don't have to answer it that way. We do our best to find out what God wants. Then we do our best to do it. It won't be easy but we have Christ as a dynamo of strength. His strength is our strength through each Mass and Communion.

August 20—St. Bernard (1091–1153), Abbot and Doctor of the Church

THEME

The members of our families should be influenced by our love of Christ.

St. Bernard brought new vigor to the Cistercian Order which he entered at 22. He was the adviser of Popes and rulers, promoting peace among nations and opposing the forces of evil and untruth inside and outside the Church.

St. Bernard had great influence in the world but even a greater impact on his own family. Four of his five brothers and an uncle entered the Cistercians with him as well as 26 other friends. Later in life, his father and younger brother also entered the monastery of which Bernard was the Abbot. He must have been quite a Christian to impress his family so much because, as we all know, it's almost impossible to deceive one's family.

APPLICATION

Ask Bernard through this Mass for the grace you need to impress your family as he did to make them love Christ more. It isn't easy to play the part of a good Christian to a family audience. In fact it's impossible. You have to *be* a true Christian to win their sincerest praise—their imitation. As the saying goes, God and Bernard are "ready, willing, and able" to help you in this task. How about you?

August 21—St. Jane Frances de Chantal (1572–1641), Widow

THEME

We need "gentle strength" to live the Christ-life.

EXPOSITION

St. Jane de Chantal was of a noble family, married to a wealthy Baron, the mother of his children, generous to the poor, widowed by a hunting accident, and finally the founder of a new religious order for women. These bare facts do not really convey the strength and love of this woman. Perhaps one story will. The man who accidentally shot her husband on a hunting trip asked her to be the godmother of his son. She did so to console the father and to show her forgiveness openly.

St. Jane vowed always to do what she understood to be most perfect. Her great strength of character urged her to do this. St. Frances de Sales, her spiritual director, strove to teach her the need for moderation and gentleness. She learned so well that her motto could have been "gentle strength."

APPLICATION

All of us could use a greater dose of one or the other of the virtues of gentleness and strength of character. Most of us could certainly use a better balance of the two. At Mass ask God for such gentle strength. Imitate today's saint. Isn't there a woman in your life whose example you might profitably follow?

August 22—The Immaculate Heart of Mary (Several suggestions are offered for this feast as its Mass formulary is used on the First Saturdays)

THEME

Mary's role in achieving peace is dear to her Immaculate Heart.

EXPOSITION

First proposed as a feast of the Church in the 17th century, devotion to Mary's Immaculate Heart was promoted by Popes

Pius VII and XI. However, it took the horrors of a World War to give this feast to the universal Church. In 1942 Pope Pius XII solemnly commended the whole human race to her most gentle Heart and established this feast on a universal basis. He hoped "that with the help of the holy Mother of God all nations would receive the gift of peace and the Church of Christ the blessing of freedom." Today's observance, therefore, is a kind of "votive feast" in memory of Mary's motherly protection during World War II.

APPLICATION

Does any one dare to say that Mary's protection is not needed at this moment to promote peace? Once again rededicate yourself to God through His Mother's Immaculate Heart. Here at Mass ask for the "peace which the world cannot give," the peace which Christ has promised, and which only He can give. Ask for it at Mass; build it by your dedication to being a peace-loving person yourself and bring it to your environment.

THEME II

The love of Mary's Heart must be our love.

EXPOSITION

Today's feast is similar to the feast of the Sacred Heart of Jesus not only because it was inspired by the already existing feast of our Lord, but also because of its purpose. As with the Feast of the Sacred Heart, today's feast does not seek to honor just a physical part of Mary, but everything that the heart stands for physically, socially and culturally.

To use the words of St. Bernardine of Siena: "Today we honor the one who merited to be made God's Mother, who for nine months gave the hospitality of her heart and of her womb to God Himself. What treasure could be better

than that Divine Love with which the heart of the Virgin
burned . . . ?"

APPLICATION

The love of Mary's heart must inflame our love. Ask Mary
today at Mass for the grace to have your heart burn with
divine love; love for God the Father, Son and Holy Spirit.

THEME III

Ask Mary to help you live in accordance with the wishes of
God's Heart.

EXPOSITION

The Entrance Prayer speaks of God preparing a worthy
dwelling place for the Holy Spirit in the Heart of Mary.
Then we who devoutly celebrate this feast of her Immaculate
Heart ask to live according to the wishes of God's own Heart.
As always we direct our prayer to God even though we honor
Mary. Because even the slightest acquaintance with Our Lady
makes us realize that she was completely occupied with doing
God's will, we ask for the same grace.

APPLICATION

This prayer of the Mass asks for the best possible gift—to live
in complete accord with the wishes of God. Repeat this request often during this Mass, especially when the celebrant
invites you to do so with his words, "Let us pray."

THEME IV

Mary's Heart is sensitive to every emotion of our hearts.

EXPOSITION

In Mary's Immaculate and divinely privileged Heart, the
noblest sentiments and emotions found expression and yet

191

her sorrow-filled soul experienced all the sufferings that can weigh upon mankind. Her compassionate and motherly heart is able to comfort and strengthen the many children given to her by her Divine Son because she experienced great sorrow in her own life.

APPLICATION

In every difficulty, trial or sorrow we can find solace and encouragement in the heart of Mary, our Mother. Christ has given her to us and visa versa. It's a two-way street and we have to travel it often, going to her as Mother and recognizing the duties we have as her children.

August 23—St. Philip Benizi (1233–1285), Confessor

THEME

Things look different when viewed in the light of our final goal.

EXPOSITION

In the Entrance Prayer we acknowledged that God has given us an outstanding example of humility in the person of St. Philip Benizi. Then we asked for the grace to follow today's saint and . . . to strive after the treasures of heaven. The petition in this prayer ties in quite nicely with Christ's words in the Gospel: ". . . your heart will be wherever your treasure is" (Lk. 12:34).

APPLICATION

It's a nice prayer and flows off our lips with little effort and even less impact on our approach to the absorbing process of earning a living. Our treasure is in heaven and we have to make every effort to remind ourselves of that fact.

Ask God through St. Philip to help you see things in the light of your final goal. Don't be surprised if you work harder at earning a living when you see things in this light. You'll know where you're going and you'll want to develop all your talents, to provide for yourself and family and to help to build God's kingdom on earth. It's a big job, but you can do it with Christ and for Christ.

August 24—St. Bartholomew, Apostle

THEME

Give your best in the service of Christ.

EXPOSITION

When Christ saw Philip bringing today's saint to Him, He said, "Here is an Israelite worthy of the name; there is nothing false in him" (Jn. 1:47). St. Bartholomew is an example of someone who gave sincere service to Christ. As soon as he met Christ, he was His man, His follower. There was no holding back, no deception or fraud in his allegiance to Jesus.

APPLICATION

What about you? Are you a Christian worthy of the name? Are you being yourself with God? Or are you trying to pull the wool over the eyes of the One Who made you? Be yourself with Christ because that's the way He made you. But always try to be your best self . . . to give the best that you have in His service. St. Bartholomew can show you the way. Ask him through this Mass to do just that.

Theme II

What have you done recently that could be called the work of an Apostle?

Exposition

St. Philip led Bartholomew to Christ. You can do likewise by showing forth to all you meet, but especially your families, what it means to follow Christ. You are an Apostle by your baptism, but mainly by your confirmation.

Application

What have you done lately that could be called the work of an Apostle? Are you the type of Catholic whose motto is: "Pray, pay and obey," or do you go beyond this bare minimum? Do you try to explain, spread and publicize the faith of Christ? Are you an Apostle at home, at work, on the golf course, the dance floor, or in the neighborhood tavern? If not, ask St. Bartholomew at Mass today to make you what you should be—an Apostle of Jesus Christ.

Theme III

Christ seeks to mold and form us as His Apostles.

Exposition

Jesus was particular about whom He chose as His Apostles. Notice how He took His time, looked them over very carefully, and then spent the night in prayer before making the final decision. They were not spectacular people, but they were individuals with whom He could work.

194

Christ was also particular when He made you one of His followers. He seeks to form and mold you to be an Apostle. Open yourself to His grace here at this Eucharistic sacrifice and banquet. When you receive Him today, ask for an ever-deepening union with Him, a greater share in the zeal and misison of St. Bartholomew and all the other Apostles. You wouldn't be here unless you were a little Apostle—start to grow! Don't be an Apostle Bartholomew—be an Apostle "you." Bartholomew lived 2,000 years ago and did fine work then. You live now and the verdict on your work is yet to come.

August 25—St. Louis (1215–1270), King-Confessor

THEME

As followers of Christ the King, we share in His royal heritage.

EXPOSITION

St. Louis is needed in our day of rampant materialism. He shows us how to live in the world and yet not forget God. He used the great wealth, power and influence of his kingdom to spread the Church, to help the poor, and to fight against those who attacked the shrines of the Holy Land. He was a worthy ruler filled with fatherly concern for his people and country. When King Louis came before the King of Kings to make an accounting of his years on earth, he surely heard the words, "Well done, good servant" (Lk. 19:17).

The Entrance Prayer of the Mass moves from the earthly kingdom which St. Louis inherited to the kingdom of heaven which he gained by his holy life. Then we ask St. Louis to help us become sharers in the heritage of the King of Kings.

Ours is a royal heritage, more priceless than any earthly kingdom imaginable. We do not appreciate how deeply honored we are to be called to share such a close relationship with the King of Kings. May St. Louis, who knows both sides of the coin, enlighten our minds at Mass today to the dignity which is ours as Christians.

August 27—St. Joseph Calasanctius (1556–1648), Confessor

THEME

Making God and His love relevant for today's youth demands all the assistance we can get.

EXPOSITION

Joseph Calasanctius, a Spaniard working as a priest in Rome, saw that the children of the poor needed his help. They were trapped in the vicious quicksand of ignorance and vice. To bring Christ to these youngsters, Joseph founded a new order. He was outstanding in this apostolate because of his power to form young people in the spirit of understanding and of piety. We can use his help today in promoting juvenile decency.

APPLICATION

Ask Christ at Mass through St. Joseph to give young people the grace to know and to love God. They must be challenged to give of themselves for Christ's Church and poor. Such a challenge to their idealism will not go unanswered. It has a

"Pied Piper" quality about it which they find almost irresistible.

Young people are in danger of losing their souls because they can see no relevance in religion. Perhaps you, by your words and example, with St. Joseph's help, will be able to convince them that God and His love are relevant. There is just one "hitch." You can only do so if God and His love are relevant to you. Are they?

August 28—St. Augustine (354–430), Bishop and Doctor of the Church

THEME

Each of us must come to Christ in his own way and at his own time. Most often love lights the way and hastens the time.

EXPOSITION

Here is a man who was the salt of the earth and the light of the world, but he was not always such. He had a good mother who taught him well, but he had to reach Christ by his own way and at his own time. He finally did with the help of her prayers and sacrifices, and through the influence of the great churchman, St. Ambrose.

"Our hearts are restless until they rest in Thee." Christian art pictures Augustine with a burning heart to symbolize the love of God which permeated his whole life after his conversion. This love is especially evident in his writings. Augustine tried to fill his heart with earthly satisfactions but soon found that such things could never do the job. Then it was that he realized that: "Our hearts are restless until they rest in You."

Maybe you, even though you have the faith of Christ, have not been the salt of the earth or the light of the world. Ask Our Lord at this Mass to help you to realize your capabilities and talents. Go out from this Mass and try to work as earnestly for Christ's Church today as Augustine did once he turned from his sinful ways.

Rest your heart in God's love and ask Him during the sacrifice to bind you more and more to His love.

August 29—Beheading of St. John the Baptist

THEME

To die for one's ideals is not to die in vain.

EXPOSITION

A little more than two months ago we celebrated the feast of the Nativity of St. John (June 24th). Today we commemorate his martyrdom. He died the victim of a man's lust, an ambitious woman's fearful revenge, and a young girl's hateful request. He died in prison, brutally, and under shabby circumstances. And yet his death was a glorious one because he died for noble ideals. He was fearless in life and we can be sure that he met the executioner with the same calm, manly courage. Perhaps John was defeated by Herodias' plots, but it was only an apparent defeat. His death was not an end or conclusion to his work but just an interruption.

APPLICATION

John the Baptist still waits to lead us to Christ today at Mass, to prepare us for the coming of our Messiah, Christ the Lord. He still repeats for our benefit those wonderful words: "I must decrease, He (Christ) must increase" (Jn. 3:30).

Truly he can teach us many things by his words but mainly by his heroic example. Ask this man, so close to Christ by blood and purpose, to teach you by love and holiness to love Christ in everyone you meet. He is anxious to start right here at this Mass.

THEME II

We could use strength and determination like St. John's.

EXPOSITION

Herod was weak and lustful, Herodias was strong and determined to destroy her enemy. John the Baptist was certainly not a weak-willed individual. Did you ever think that there are two people to imitate in this triumvirate? Both of them knew what they wanted and were willing to fight to achieve their goal. Herodias did not rest; she planned well and by her cunning played upon Herod's weaknesses to get what she wanted.

APPLICATION

If only we were as anxious to save our souls as she was to gain her objective, we would have little to fear. However, we have a less unsavory example of strength and determination in St. John. He knew what was right and he was not afraid to preach it no matter what the consequences. He should be our model as we seek ways to serve God more fully each day. Let us ask God our Father to give us through this sacrifice a share in St. John's great strength and determination.

August 30—St. Rose of Lima (1586–1617), Virgin

THEME

Seek a share in Christ's attractive and enchanting holiness.

EXPOSITION

The feast of the first canonized saint of the Western Hemisphere must not pass unnoticed for she can be the catalyst to spur all of us on to great holiness.

In the Entrance Prayer we call her a "flower of purity and patience." By these and other virtues she accomplished many things. She drew people to Christ by just being herself.

APPLICATION

Spurred on by her example let us urgently repeat the application which the prayer made to our lives. "May we also become pleasing enough to draw others to Christ." The only glimpse of Christ some people get is that provided by the lives of the Christians with whom they associate. We need to become so attractive by our virtue and holiness that others will want to serve the Christ we follow. Ask Christ to give you, through this Mass and Communion, a share in His own very attractive and enchanting holiness.

August 31—St. Raymond Nonnatus (1204–1240), Confessor

THEME

Raymond shows us how to see Christ in every human being, especially the lowliest.

EXPOSITION

Raymond spent himself completely in the Christlike work of freeing Christians who had been enslaved by the Mohammedans. Raymond acknowledged Christ in every Christian. He served such persons in every possible way because he saw Christ in them. He did not just give money or a comforting word; he gave himself in this work even to the point of becoming a hostage so that others might go free. When he met his Master, he was ready and God truly set him over all his goods. God valued today's saint above many others because Raymond freely gave of himself for Christ.

APPLICATION

Maybe Raymond can help us through this Eucharistic celebration to see Christ in every Christian. Sometimes it is not easy because many Christians do not act very Christlike, but with our saint's help we will try to uncover the Christ Who dwells in every baptized person. Our chances of success in this endeavor are fairly good. With a little effort we can make them better.

September 2—St. Stephen (975–1038), King and Confessor

THEME

The Church needs many "Stephens" to complete what Vatican II began.

EXPOSITION

Today's saint certainly used God's gifts to their best possible advantage. Stephen was King of Hungary, the Apostle of Christ to his people whom he led into the Church, and a loving father to all. He is noted for his love of the poor, his generosity to the Church, and his devotion to Mary whom he chose to be the Patroness of Hungary. With all of this he was a soldier of great courage.

The Entrance Prayer highlights Stephen's role in spreading the Church by the conversion of Hungary—his work as "Apostle-King" of his country. The Prayer after Communion points out how his zeal for spreading the faith made him worthy "to pass from an earthly kingdom to a glorious throne in heaven." We ask the grace to follow his example of faith.

APPLICATION

Seek through this Mass and Communion to follow his example of faith because we need many Stephens if the Church is to continue its growth. You must be one of them because the Second Vatican Council has said that the laity "are called upon, as living members (of Christ's Body) to expend all their energy for the growth of the Church" (*Dogmatic Constitution on the Church,* Art. 33).

September 3—St. Pius X (1835–1914), Pope and Confessor

THEME

St. Pius X teaches us to restore to Christ all that we are.

EXPOSITION

Today's saint was a "chosen one" raised up by God "from the people." He was a peasant boy with a fine mind and a determination to serve God before all other persons or things. As he said in his last will: "I was born poor, I have lived poor, and I die poor."

He became a priest, a bishop, and then the Cardinal of Venice. Finally in 1903 he was elected Pope. Simple and humble as he was, once he realized that he could not refuse the election because it was the will of God, he accepted the papacy and its burdens.

He was every inch a Pope, the only Pope in the last 400 years to be canonized. To know him was to love him; to meet him was to be convinced that one was face to face wth a saint. As Pope he sought "to restore all things to Christ," and stressed daily Mass and Communion as a way of doing just that.

APPLICATION

The People of God have come a long way since Pius' time. Many of our advances, especially the liturgical renewal, can be traced back to Pius X. He can help us appreciate the great value of the liturgy and particularly this Mass we offer together.

You cannot imagine how anxious St. Pius is that we profit from this Eucharistic sacrifice-banquet. He had such a deep appreciation of the power and value of the Eucharist. Surely we can call upon him with confidence to help us by this Mass to continue his life-long efforts to promote a better understanding of what Christ in the Eucharist means to us.

Ask him also to strengthen you to follow his teaching and example and thus "restore to Christ" all that you are and have.

September 5—St. Lawrence Justinian (1381–1455), Bishop and Confessor

THEME

The glory of a true bishop is to be a loving father and guide for his people.

EXPOSITION

Today's saint was noted for his humility but also for another virtue. Pope Eugene IV called him the "Ornament and Glory of Bishops." St. Lawrence was Bishop of Venice and its first Patriarch. Because he was such a good, saintly, humble bishop, he should remind us of our own bishops. They have a heavy burden to carry; they are responsible for all the souls in their dioceses.

Just a casual reading of Vatican II's *Decree on the Pastoral Office of Bishops* reveals the awesome responsibilities such men have to teach, to preach, to sanctify and to rule. Above all else, they must show forth to their people the loving kindness, concern and firmness of God the Father.

APPLICATION

Today here at Mass and in Communion, ask St. Lawrence to guide and protect our bishops as they seek to fulfill the truly frightening duties of their office. Pray with special fervor for our bishop. He appreciates your help in his sublime task of being a loving father and guide for all his people.

September 8—The Nativity of the Blessed Virgin Mary

THEME

The best observance of Our Lady's Birthday is our full and active sharing in this Eucharistic celebration.

EXPOSITION

Today we rejoice because it is the birthday of Mary. With this event, the story of our salvation begins because "from this spotless Virgin came the Sun of Justice, Christ, our God" (Magn. Ant.). Once again we have an opportunity to honor Christ's Blessed Mother. We do so by recalling to mind quite vividly what we owe to Mary and by rededicating ourselves once again to her Son, Christ, our God.

The best observance of Our Lady's birthday is our full and active sharing in this Eucharistic celebration. Certainly if we do so at this Eucharistic celebration, we will have observed our Lady's birthday in a most fitting manner. There is really very little said in today's Mass about Mary's nativity except for the proper prayers, but great emphasis is placed upon her divine motherhood.

APPLICATION

Although we are celebrating a feast in her honor, there is no undue concentration on this fact; rather there is a wholesome referring of everything to Christ. Our Lady in the liturgy never stands alone but always close to Christ and subordinate to Him. Let us become more aware of this relationship and as we honor her here today, let us turn in worship to her Son. She would be pleased if we did so at this Mass, which we should offer as a people united in our love for Jesus and His Mother.

September 9—St. Peter Claver (1579–1654), Confessor

THEME

Everyone we meet is Christ no mater what his race, color, creed or education.

EXPOSITION

St. Peter Claver is the special patron of all Catholic missionaries working among the Negroes. This young Spanish Jesuit devoted his whole priestly life to caring for the slaves that were brought to the central slave market of Spanish America, Cartagena in Colombia. He is an example of the active and true love of neighbor which we seek through this Mass. It is a gift that all of us need in ever greater abundance.

APPLICATION

We need peace between the races. St. Peter Claver can show us the way to achieve this peace. He is telling each person offering this Mass today the secret of success in this endeavor. Everyone we meet is Christ no matter what his race, color, creed or education. Once we have this truth firmly in mind and put it into practice, we'll get the peace that we want between races because we will treat every person as an individual, a human being like ourselves, someone made in the image of Christ.

St. Peter is telling us today to forget about going down to the slave ships. They don't exist any more. Now we have the slums, the ghettos, the areas of blight and discrimination. This is the arena in which we must fight to achieve peace among races. Wouldn't it be wonderful if we treated everyone we met, no matter what his color, as we would treat Christ? If we are to do that we certainly need much help from God. We can get it at this Mass today. At least we'll get a running start.

September 10—St. Nicholas of Tolentino (1245–1305), Confessor

THEME

Mass—the most effective and valuable gift we have to give.

EXPOSITION

This man truly had his heart and his treasure in the same place and in the right place—in God. St. Nicholas was a daring preacher of the Faith who used sidewalk preaching or street corner preaching as a way of reaching the people. Often after he had offered Mass for some soul in purgatory, he would have a vision of that soul being released to go to heaven. Obviously there was no need to convince our saint of the value of the Mass.

APPLICATION

We who offer this Mass together may never have such an effective proof of the value of what we are doing. However, we can be sure that our Masses are worthwhile and more helpful to those for whom they are offered than we imagine. Try to appreciate the value of this sacrifice. Also, be sure to offer this Mass and every Mass for a specific intention. Do not neglect this wonderfully effective gift of God.

September 12—The Holy Name of Mary

THEME

We honor not just a name but a person today.

EXPOSITION

How familiar to all of us is this scene from St. Luke's Gospel. We have heard it so often that perhaps we do not realize how frequently Our Lady's most holy name occurs in it. What is there in a name anyway? For us moderns, there isn't that significance. However, a person's name means much more in the Bible and the Liturgy because it stands for the whole individual, his nature or being. It is the expression of his personality.

Today's feast was instituted by the Church not to honor just a name, but to honor a person. Not just any person, but that very special woman who is Mother of the Church and all its members.

APPLICATION

Ask Our Lord at this Eucharistic banquet to help you "rejoice in the protection of the most holy Virgin Mary and delight in her name" (Entrance Prayer).

Today try to think of Mary often and to realize how frequently you use her name. Try to use it with love and respect as befits the name of her who is your mother and constant helper in fulfilling God's will.

208

September 14—The Exaltation of the Holy Cross

THEME

Christ on His glorious Cross of victory draws us to Himself.

EXPOSITION

"It behooves us to glory in the Cross of our Lord Jesus Christ" (Entrance Hymn). There is to be no sorrow today. Good Friday is the feast of the Holy Cross when our hearts are deeply touched by Christ's suffering and death. Today we experience only joy because of this symbol of victory over *sin*. It was because of the Cross that God exalted Christ above all else, and bestowed upon Him that Name which is above every other name.

From His position on the Cross, Christ does "draw all men to Himself." He is drawing us to Himself now as we gather around this altar. In the Prayer over the Gifts we say: "We are privileged to venerate this holy Cross; grant that we may also enjoy for all eternity the salvation it has purchased for us."

APPLICATION

Through this and every Mass we are privileged to venerate the holy Cross, our sacred symbol of victory. From His sacrificial Cross Christ draws us to Himself right now in this community of love. Be aware of the action of Christ within your hearts. Give yourself fully to Him so that He may "draw" you even closer to Himself.

September 15—The Seven Sorrows of the Blessed Virgin Mary

THEME

Close to Jesus to the last.

EXPOSITION

Today we once again turn to Our Lady as we have done so often this month, but this time it is to recall her seven sorrows. This feast of Our Lady follows logically from yesterday's feast of the Exaltation of the Holy Cross. Mary's greatest sorrow was to stand beneath the Cross. The Sequence Hymn puts it very nicely: "At the Cross her station keeping, Stood the mournful Mother weeping, Close to Jesus to the last." By this rather long yet beautifully moving poem, we prepared ourselves for the reading of the Gospel.

APPLICATION

Think of Mary's sorrows. Compare them with your own. Surely yours are no greater than hers, and probably almost insignificant in comparison to hers. As you stand here at the foot of Calvary at this reenactment of her Son's sacrifice, ask her for the grace to bear your cross of sorrow as she bore hers. She will not refuse you this favor. Ask her also through this Mass to win for you the grace to be "close to Jesus to the last."

September 16—Sts. Cornelius and Cyprian (c. 250), Martyrs

THEME

To stand with Christ no matter what.

EXPOSITION

Bishops, martyrs, and friends in Christ, Cornelius the Pope and Cyprian the Bishop of Carthage had a vision of life with Christ which made them place the right value on the things of this world.

Both men gave their lives for this vision. Today we are not often called upon to pay such a price, although that possibility is not to be ruled out. However, we may be called to be martyrs in a different sense. Each follower of Christ may have to face subtle persecutions, undramatic little slights which accumulate to such a point that they almost overwhelm us. These things were the lot of Christ and His followers whom we honor today. Should we expect to escape?

APPLICATION

Ask Sts. Cornelius and Cyprian for the help you need to stand with Christ no matter what the opposition. If union with Christ, achieved through your Masses and Communions, is the source of strength and encouragement as it should be, there is nothing to fear.

September 18—St. Joseph of Cupertino (1603–63), Confessor

THEME

We are in a race for heaven.

EXPOSITION

Joseph of Cupertino was certainly not a very promising candidate for sainthood—at least not on the surface. His holiness was far from apparent. One had to live with him to discover his obedience and patience under severe criticism, his spirit of poverty and his angelic purity.

APPLICATION

None of us is a sure "winner" in the race for sainthood but we are in the race to stay. Mass and our other contacts with God must be the training ground where we develop the stamina to win the victory and the crown. We win the crown in the school of "hard knocks," in that mixture of "ups and downs," joys and sorrows, "one step forward, two steps backwards" which is our life.

Ask St. Joseph of Cupertino most urgently during this Eucharistic Liturgy to help you rise to Jesus by learning to accept and to live your daily life to the fullest. If you do, you will still not be a "sure winner," but you will be an "odds-on favorite."

September 19—St. Januarius and His Companions (c. 304), Martyrs

THEME

A love that never grows cold.

EXPOSITION

Today we are reminded of the sufferings and persecutions which God's people have faced and overcome. Glorious testimony to their belief in Christ was given by the Martyrs Januarius and his companions whom we honor at this Mass.

We should pause and reflect upon the words of Christ about persecutions. He told us that there would be many trials and sufferings; that many would fall away from Him. . . . He concluded his warning by revealing that ". . . most men's love will grow cold. Still it is the man who bears up patiently to the end who will be saved" (Mt. 24:12-13).

APPLICATION

Januarius and his companions had the option: "Their earthly life or their love for Christ." They made the right choice— because their love had never grown cold. Beg Our Lord at this Mass for a love like that. Keep your love busy embracing your daily share of trials and difficulties. Then you won't have to worry about growing cold.

September 21—St. Matthew, Apostle and Evangelist

THEME

Christ's magnificent appeal.

EXPOSITION

What a magnificent appeal Christ must have had. He said only two words, "Follow Me," and Matthew left his post at the customs house to become a disciple. Matthew probably knew about Christ and may even have heard Him preach. Certainly he would have been stirred by Our Lord's message of love and forgiveness. But to have Christ call him to be one of His disciples was an unthought of joy. Matthew did not delay for a moment, he did not weigh the consequences of his act. Christ wanted him and that was good enough.

APPLICATION

I hope that you can see the similarity between the scene in this morning's Gospel and your own relationship with Christ. You have been called by the Savior. What was your answer? No matter what it was, use the opportunity you have now at this sacrifice to answer Christ's "Follow Me" as St. Matthew did. Don't resist the urge you have to surrender to Our Lord's appeal. Give in!

September 22—St. Thomas of Villanova (1488–1555), Bishop and Confessor

THEME

As poor as the poor he helped.

EXPOSITION

"Well done! Come, share your Lord's joy." It is not hard to imagine Our Divine Lord greeting today's saint with these words. St. Thomas of Villanova, as we have just mentioned in the Prayer of the Mass, was known for his extraordinary compassion for the poor.

As the *Maryknoll Missal* recounts in its introduction to his feast, he was "a man of infinite charity in word and deed, (who) lived as frugally as the poor who benefited by his unstinted almsgiving." How could the poor Christ not reward so faithful an imitation of His own poverty?

APPLICATION

Today ask Jesus through the intercession of St. Thomas for the grace to love the poor, and to do everything in your power to ease their lot. In so doing you will be proving yourself to be "a faithful and prudent" follower of Christ. You will be one of those who uses God's gifts to help the members of God's family, and God is too good a Father to forget such goodness. He will not be outdone in generosity.

September 23—St. Linus (1st Century), Pope and Martyr

THEME

A pledge of allegiance to the Pope.

EXPOSITION

Today we offer Mass in memory of Pope Linus, the first successor of St. Peter as Bishop of Rome. Not a great deal is known about this man's life, but he must certainly have been quite close to both Saints Peter and Paul. The Liturgy lists St. Linus in the Eucharistic Prayer right after the Apostles, which is an indication of his importance and rank.

APPLICATION

Perhaps as we recall his life and martyrdom for Christ, we could renew our allegiance to Pope Paul who is successor to Peter, Linus and many others. In these days when all authority is questioned or ignored completely, we can use a reminder every once in a while about the predecessors and importance of the man who guides the Church. At each Mass we pray for the Pope. Today let's pray very hard. Why not offer your Mass and Communion for the Pope? I have a feeling he'd appreciate your thoughtfulness.

September 26—The North American Martyrs (martyred between 1642–1649)

THEME

Perseverance no matter what the opposition is.

EXPOSITION

St. Paul in his Second Epistle to the Corinthians proclaimed: "And I will gladly spend and be spent for your sakes." The same spirit of self-sacrificing concern for others drove the North American Martyrs to their destiny. These men are called the "first fruits of the Faith in the northern regions of America." We who live in the land they loved and who share their Faith should be extremely proud of them and their work.

Their martyrdom started long before their heads were crushed by hatchets or their bodies pierced with arrows. They had to leave the luxuries and comforts of the old world to go to the unexplored reaches of the new world. There they found stark naked hatred for themselves and everything they represented. They had to live in conditions which were so inhumane as to be lower than primitive. And yet they were willing to make such sacrifices, to spend and be spent so that the news of Christ might reach the Indians.

APPLICATION

The Prayer after Communion tells us how important the Eucharistic "food of the valiant" was to our American martyrs. "When . . . (they) were strengthened by this same bread, they did not hesitate to lay down their own lives for their

217

brothers." This prayer concludes by putting the following words on our lips: "May we also bear one another's burdens and love our neighbors with an effective and sincere charity."

Try to get those words from your lips into your heart. Then act on them.

September 27—Sts. Cosmas and Damian (3rd Century), Martyrs

THEME

What is the state of your soul's health?

EXPOSITION

Today's saints were brothers who practiced medicine in Syria toward the close of the third century. Although the ties between them and ourselves may be less apparent than with yesterday's martyrs who suffered on this continent, Cosmas and Damian can teach us a worthwhile lesson. They were interested in the "whole" patient, if you will. By their approach to medicine, they converted many sinners and saved others from spiritual ills.

APPLICATION

Bodily illness is so real to us for it has an immediacy and impact which we cannot ignore. Spiritual troubles are not so apparent, but they are nonetheless real. Let these saintly brother-doctors help you through this Mass to realize the state of your soul's health.

If you love every man as Christ, or if you see in your colored or poor brother a person with bodily and spiritual

September 9—St. Peter Claver (1579–1654), Confessor

THEME

Everyone we meet is Christ no mater what his race, color, creed or education.

EXPOSITION

St. Peter Claver is the special patron of all Catholic missionaries working among the Negroes. This young Spanish Jesuit devoted his whole priestly life to caring for the slaves that were brought to the central slave market of Spanish America, Cartagena in Colombia. He is an example of the active and true love of neighbor which we seek through this Mass. It is a gift that all of us need in ever greater abundance.

APPLICATION

We need peace between the races. St. Peter Claver can show us the way to achieve this peace. He is telling each person offering this Mass today the secret of success in this endeavor. Everyone we meet is Christ no matter what his race, color, creed or education. Once we have this truth firmly in mind and put it into practice, we'll get the peace that we want between races because we will treat every person as an individual, a human being like ourselves, someone made in the image of Christ.

St. Peter is telling us today to forget about going down to the slave ships. They don't exist any more. Now we have the slums, the ghettos, the areas of blight and discrimination. This is the arena in which we must fight to achieve peace among races. Wouldn't it be wonderful if we treated everyone we met, no matter what his color, as we would treat Christ? If we are to do that we certainly need much help from God. We can get it at this Mass today. At least we'll get a running start.

needs and if you try to supply these needs, you are healthy. Just ask Cosmas and Damian to teach you some preventive medicine so that you will stay healthy and keep growing in Christ. If you are spiritually ill then seek the necessary remedies in union with the Divine Physician, Christ, the Lord.

September 28—St. Wenceslaus (917–939), Duke and Martyr

THEME

The good never finish last. The world only thinks they do.

EXPOSITION

St. Wenceslaus was a man beset by family troubles and opposition. His grandmother was a saintly woman who encouraged him to be a good Christian and a good ruler. His mother and brother were far different in their outlook and actively sought to destroy all the good that he did. Finally they succeeded in having the saintly Duke assassinated while he was on his way to Mass. Today's saint was worthy of Christ; he shouldered his cross and followed his Lord and Master.

APPLICATION

Although Wenceslaus lived long ago and seems so foreign to us, he can help us to shoulder our own cross and follow Christ. Use the opportunity which you now have at Mass to ask for this gift from the martyred Duke. If your family is divided by petty jealousy and "backbiting," ask today's saint for the grace to love enough to forgive and mend and forget.

September 29—Dedication of St. Michael the Archangel

THEME

Michael—our secret weapon in the battle.

EXPOSITION

Today we commemorate the dedication to St. Michael the Archangel of a very ancient church in Rome. The angels praise and honor God by the faithfulness of their whole being. Michael is revered as the supreme guardian spirit of the universal Church and as the great opponent of the devil.

The Alleluia Hymn which we just said as a preparation for the reading of the Gospel fits in quite well with the picture we have of Michael: "St. Michael the Archangel defend us in the battle, that we may not perish in the dreadful judgment." Also pertinent is the Prayer after Communion which declares: "We rely on the prayers of St. Michael so that the Sacrament which we have received with our lips may always bear fruit in our hearts."

APPLICATION

The two petitions are related. If we receive the Eucharist fruitfully, we will be strengthened for the battle. Make these prayers from the Mass your prayers so that through this Eucharistic sacrifice and banquet you may be strengthened for the battle of life. The forces of evil in the world and within us are often stronger than we realize. Accept and appreciate all the help you can get from today's celebration.

September 30—St. Jerome (c. 342–420), Confessor and Doctor of the Church

THEME

Jerome should inspire us with a love for the Word of God.

EXPOSITION

The guiding passion of St. Jerome's life was the Sacred Scriptures. He spent most of his life reading or translating them, learning more about the languages, customs and areas from which the Scriptures came. It is no wonder that the Entrance Prayer of the Mass terms St. Jerome as "the greatest scholar in the interpretation of the Holy Scripture" that the Church has ever had.

APPLICATION

In our day the Bible is being restored to its rightful place of prominence in the life of the Church and its members. Jerome teaches us many things about the Bible, two of which are of paramount importance for our generation. We must have a profound love and respect for God's Word in the Scriptures. We must realize that the books of the Bible were composed at times and in a culture far different from ours.

It is no simple task to understand the message of Sacred Scripture. To do so we must listen to the experts and study their findings with great care. Above all, we must read the Bible constantly, if possible, daily. Ask St. Jerome for a love of the treasure found in the Scriptures. Learn to love the Word of God set forth in this Mass and every Mass.

October 2—The Holy Guardian Angels

THEME

Ask your guardian angel to show you how to be a truly Christlike human being.

EXPOSITION

Jesus mentions the angels toward the end of the Gospel reading as being the guardian of children and as living always in the presence of God. Today we remember in a special way these heavenly creatures whom God has given us as guardians on our way to Him. These angels protect us from the power of the devil, guide us among the difficulties of life, and inspire us to live our Christ-like ideals.

APPLICATION

We should be more aware of their influence and guidance. In the Prayer of the Mass we ask God that "we may always be safe under their protection and happy for all eternity in their company." Make that your prayer today at this Mass and every day as you pursue your efforts to follow Christ Who is the King of Angels and Men.

Just remember that your goal in life is not to be angelic but truly human and Christian. Many persons have spent their lives pursuing the angelic virtues. Such efforts are doomed to fail. What is worse, such efforts detract from what should be our all-consuming task—developing and Christianizing our human lives to the fullest. Ask your guardian angel to teach you the difference and help you to fulfill your destiny as a Christian man or woman.

222

October 3—St. Teresa of the Child Jesus (1873–97), Virgin

THEME

The little way—a sure way to sanctify.

EXPOSITION

"I assure you, unless you change and become like little children, you will not enter the kingdom of heaven" (Mt. 18:3). These words of Christ and similar expressions from the Scriptures were the means by which St. Teresa solved a vexing problem. She knew that she was no spiritual giant. When she compared herself with the saints, she felt like a grain of sand standing near a towering mountain.

Yet there was in her an almost unbearable desire to be a saint, and she knew that God would not let that desire go unfulfilled. Finally, in the little way of spiritual childhood, she found the answer. She would become as a little child and put her complete trust in God her Father, seeking to please Him in everything as a loving child does for an adored parent.

APPLICATION

Few if any of us are spectacular persons. Have not most of us experienced the same feelings of inadequacy when we compared our performance with that of the Saints? We'll never "make it big" as they did. Our path toward saintliness must be similar to that of St. Teresa.

Ask her through this Mass and Communion to help you respond wholeheartedly to Christ's call to spiritual childhood. "Lord, give us the grace to follow the little way of St. Teresa in humility and simplicity of heart so that we may win an eternal reward" (Entrance Prayer).

October 4—St. Francis of Assisi (1181–1226), Confessor

THEME

Lord, make us instruments of your peace.

EXPOSITION

"Lord, make me an instrument of peace." These words are from a prayer by St. Francis of Assisi, a man who, like Christ his Master, was truly gentle and humble of heart. Don't you think that these words must have been uppermost in the mind of Pope Paul when he decided to go before the United Nations on the feast of St. Francis in 1965 to make a stirring appeal for world peace? Today more than ever, there is need of people who are willing to be instruments of peace, who are willing to follow the peace plan of Christ and the popes.

APPLICATION

There will be no peace in the world until there is peace in the individuals who make up that world. In your prayers and Communion at this Mass, seek for the strength and the grace necessary to bring peace to yourself. Try your hardest to be an instrument of God's peace within your family and neighborhood. Seek for peace within yourself. Then and only then will there be a chance for peace in the world. May the example of St. Francis, so human and good, so gentle and humble, inspire you to be an instrument of the Lord's peace.

THEME II

The Christ-like Francis encourages us to take up the mild yoke of the Lord.

If ever there was a man who took the Gospels literally, it was today's saint, Francis of Assisi. Francis read Christ's words about giving up the things of the world to follow Him. He knew that Jesus had lived a life of poverty and hardship. Francis never hesitated but dedicated himself to following this ideal of Christlike poverty.

He took the yoke of Christ upon his shoulders and found it refreshing indeed. He found that Christ was gentle and humble of heart, that the Lord would provide for him and those who followed him. Today's saint loved poverty and the Cross. He did not despise the world for he loved all creation, but above all created things he loved their Creator.

APPLICATION

As you offer this Mass and receive Our Lord in Communion, ask for the grace to follow Christ as St. Francis did. At the very least, admire Francis and try to bring your life closer to his Christlike ideals.

October 6—St. Bruno (1030–1101), Confessor

THEME

Solitude and prayerful union with God are necessary virtues in our "jet" age.

EXPOSITION

Although Our Lord loved being with people, He often sought in solitude the opportunity for prayerful union with the Father. These intervals seemed to refresh Him and to give

Him the strength needed to do the work of the Father. Today's saint felt a similar longing for solitude and prayerful union with God.

St. Bruno was well-born and educated, and he rose quickly in the Church. However, he turned from all these honors to seek God in solitude. He founded the Carthusians, the most penitential Order in the Church. He left the world for peace and solitude but then was called back by the Pope to assist him in the many duties of his office. Even among all the hectic activity of the Papal Court St. Bruno always strove to keep his sense of solitude and prayerful union with God.

APPLICATION

We in the 1960's, surrounded by all our technological miracles, cannot live like Carthusians, but we can follow the example of St. Bruno in our own lives. Ask him through this Mass to gain for you the grace of preserving your prayerful union with God even among the many distractions of your daily life. Especially in this Communion bind yourself more firmly to Christ so that you will maintain and intensify your closeness with God through your Eucharistic Lord.

October 7—Our Lady of the Rosary

THEME

Our interest in and enthusiasm for the Rosary will grow as we become more aware of its intimate connection with the Mass.

EXPOSITION

"Let us celebrate the solemnity of the Rosary of the Virgin Mary; let us adore her Son, Christ the Lord." These words from the Divine Office might be the motto for our celebration of the Mass. As we renew the sacrifice of Calvary in an unbloody manner, we intend to adore Mary's Son, Christ, the Lord, by our presence here, and to offer this sacrifice in honor of Our Lady of the Rosary.

There is a close connection between the Mass and the Rosary. The Mass sets before us the life, death, Resurrection and Ascension of Christ. In the Rosary we meditate upon these events in Christ's life while saying the prayers.

Each time we recite the Rosary, we should remind ourselves of the Masses we have offered or will offer in the future. While meditating upon the mysteries, we should seek to become aware of the connection which they have with the Mass. In this way we will find renewed interest and enthusiasm for this practice because of its relationship to the Mass.

APPLICATION

Let's not throw away our Rosaries. Let's make every effort to understand and appreciate this great prayer which is so closely related to the Sacrifice we offer here. During this Sacrifice and at the Banquet when we unite body and soul with Christ, may the Lord God "give us the grace to follow the examples they (the mysteries of the Rosary) set before us, and to obtain the rewards they promise." May Mary help us "to draw strength from the mysteries we reverence and obtain the effects of the sacrament" we will receive at this Mass (Cf. Prayer after Communion).

THEME II

Cf. *Maryknoll Missal* p. 1106 for the introduction to Mass where the communal and ecumenical aspects of the Rosary are stressed.

227

October 8—St. Bridget (1302–1373), Widow

THEME

Holiness can be ours if we live up to the responsibilities of our state in life.

EXPOSITION

St. Bridget fulfilled St. Paul's description of a worthy widow. She was "a woman to whom noble deeds bear testimony—the testimony, namely, that she has cared for her children, shown hospitality, washed the feet of the saints, helped those in distress, and been intent on every kind of good work" (1 Tim. 5:10).

Bridget, the patron saint of Sweden, was the foundress of a religious order and a mystic famous for her Revelations concerning the sufferings of Christ. She was also a loving wife and the mother of eight children, one of whom became St. Catherine of Sweden. She was married for 28 years to a prince who died shortly after entering the Cistercians.

Did she become a saint through her marriage and children or only despite these things? She became a saint because she lovingly accepted her state in life and lived it to its fullest. She was a saint when she was a married woman with a husband and children; she was a saint when she was a widow, "left quite alone and with her hopes set on God."

APPLICATION

St. Bridget teaches us that we should strive for holiness no matter what our position in life is. As we offer this Mass with our brothers and sisters in Christ, let us offer ourselves to the Lord so that He may lead us along the road of holiness just as He once did with St. Bridget. He will definitely lead. Will we have the courage to follow?

October 9—St. John Leonardi (1543–1609), Confessor

THEME

Today's saint should make us more conscious of our obligations to the missions.

EXPOSITION

"I have become a minister of Christ—in virtue of the office that God has given me—for I am to fulfill the word of God" (Offertory Prayer). Today's saint certainly fulfilled the word of God as a minister of Christ. He was, as St. Philip Neri said, a "true reformer" establishing a community of priests to undertake the reform of pastoral work. He longed to go to the missions, but could not.

Instead St. John founded in Rome a seminary to train for the priesthood young men from all the mission territories. Because of this he is called the originator of the College of the Propagation of the Faith. Since its beginning, the College has educated thousands of priests of all nationalities and sent them to carry the Gospel of Christ to their people.

APPLICATION

The needs of the misisons in our day are even greater than in the time of St. John Leonardi. He discovered that his mission apostolate was to his own country. The men who are trained at the Propagation of the Faith College know that they will work in their native lands. Do you see the implication this has for our lives? First see what you can do at home for the

229

missions and do it. Then help the mission effort in other lands.

At our Masses and by our Communions we can win from God the graces that are needed; and while entering into the spirit of the sacrifice, we will be inspired to give of our material possessions as well. If we do these things, then we will be imitating the blessed confessor John, professing what he believed and practicing what he taught.

October 10—St. Francis Borgia (1510–1572), Confessor

THEME
The humble Christ is our model and our reward.

EXPOSITION

Have you wondered if following Christ is worth all the sacrifices it entails? If so, you should pause to consider today's saint. St. Francis Borgia surrendered family, fame, wealth and position to follow the humble Christ. We are called upon to make no such sacrifices in our lives. We are not royalty as he was, nor are we wealthy or charged with matters of national import as he was.

Although we may have less to surrender for the sake of Christ, there are sacrifices which must be made. We must be honest at all times and treat our neighbors as brothers and sisters in the Lord. These are not easy sacrifices. It is so simple to cheat on an expense account or in the supermarket. It seems so natural to love our own and look "down our noses" at those of a different color, race or belief. We need quite a dose of humility to realize that such practices are frustrating us in following Christ.

230

Ask St. Francis to help you to offer this Mass in union with Christ Who is the all-satisfying reward of the humble. With such help and such motivation you will surely find in this sacrifice what you need to follow Christ, "the model of true humility and the reward of the humble."

However, the Mass is not a magical formula or incantation which makes you completely holy without any effort on your part. You must offer the Mass humbly and sincerely with the priest and the people of God. Then you must live the Mass in your daily life. That will be the greatest challenge you will face as you seek to walk in Christ's footsteps.

October 11—The Motherhood of the Blessed Mother

THEME

Mary worries about our welfare even as she once was anxious over Christ's welfare.

EXPOSITION

As the Gospel was being read, were you a trifle surprised that it was not the account of our Lord's birth at Bethlehem? Certainly there is no scene which portrays Mary as the Mother of God better than the one which describes how she wrapped the baby in swaddling clothes and laid Him in a manger. Or is there? Today's Gospel story may even be more apt for the occasion than first meets the eye. We have just heard how our Lady and St. Joseph found Jesus in the Temple after a heartrending search of three days.

In this scene Mary is truly a mother, a mother torn by conflicting emotions. She is overjoyed at finding her Son, disappointed at His apparent lack of concern for Joseph and herself, and mystified at His explanation about attending to "my Father's affairs." As she thought about this scene later on and pondered it in her heart, it became a powerful reminder to her that she was the Mother of Him who was both God and Man.

APPLICATION

It should be a powerful reminder to us also of Our Lady's lofty dignity. But above all, it should draw us even closer to her since she is also our mother. She as Christ's mother was anxious about His welfare. She experiences great anxiety right now over us.

Would that our reason for causing her such worry and anxiety were the same as Christ's—that we had to attend to our heavenly Father's affairs. Unfortunately that is often far from the truth in our lives. Why not pay more attention to our Father's affairs, and more honor to Mary, the Mother of Christ and of all those who are His friends?

THEME II

Today's feast sets before our eyes God's Mother and my mother also.

EXPOSITION

This feast was instituted by Pope Pius XI to commemorate the 1,500th anniversary of the Council of Ephesus which defined, as the teaching of the Church, that Mary is the Mother of God. In our own century another great Council of the Church has spoken about Our Lady's preeminence.

Vatican II, in its *Dogmatic Constitution on the Church*, Chapter VIII, acknowledged and honored Mary: "as being truly the Mother of God and Mother of the Redeemer" (art. 53). This document also calls her the "Mother of the members of Christ, having cooperated by charity that the faithful might be born in the Church . . . the Catholic Church

232

honors her with filial affection and piety as a most loved mother" (art. 53).

These two Councils, separated by more than 1500 years, indicate the sentiments which should be ours as we offer this Mass in honor of Our Lady. We should offer this sacrifice fully aware that the Mother of God is also our mother. All who have assembled here are brothers and sisters in Christ and are gathered together to honor Mary with filial affection. Make good use of the opportunity provided for you at this Mass and Communion to grow closer to Christ through His Mother and ours.

October 13—St. Edward (1004–1066), King and Confessor

THEME

Blessed are the pure of heart for they shall see God.

EXPOSITION

St. Edward preserved his innocence even in the midst of a sinful court to which he had been exiled. In 1042, he returned to England as King. He restored peace and prosperity to his country, its Church, and its people.

He so endeared himself to his people that for years after his death, they always referred to him as "good King Edward." He had great devotion to St. John, the beloved disciple of Christ. There was never any question of his manliness or of his kingly bearing, but neither was there any question that here was a man who was pure of heart as well as of body.

In our day when neither purity of body nor of mind is very much respected, we need a saint such as Edward to remind us of some basics in Christian living. We need to reaffirm our allegiance to Christ-like purity of mind and heart, of body and soul.

Use this Mass and Communion to beg God through the prayers of St. Edward for the gift of a great love of purity so that you may be blessed, as he and all the pure of heart are, with the vision of God.

October 14—St. Callistus I (3rd Century), Pope and Martyr

THEME

The dead in Christ—our attitude.

EXPOSITION

Pope St. Callistus I was one of the greatest Pontiffs of the third century. While he was deacon to Pope Zephyrinus, he was in charge of the Christian cemetery on the Appian Way, which is now known by his name. As Pope, even when he was beset with both internal frictions and external persecutions, he still maintained his interest in the ancient Christian burial grounds.

APPLICATION

One of the characteristics of Christianity is its belief in the resurrection of the dead and its consequent care and respect of the bodies of the deceased. What is our attitude toward those who have died in Christ? How do we act at a funeral?

Do we grieve as "those who have no hope," or are we composed and resigned because of our belief in the Resurrection?

Today funerals have taken on all the trappings of high society affairs. Most people seem to be more interested in how the neighbors will view the proceedings than in caring for the deceased. We should remember the phrase "those who have died in Christ" and treat the dead with the respect and honor due to those who are dear "to God and all the saints."

Offer this sacrifice today so that you will believe with all your heart in the resurrection of the dead. May your faith in the resurrection of the dead show you how to surround the bodies of the dead with Christian love and respect.

October 15—St. Teresa of Avila (1515–1582), Virgin

THEME

In our life there must be balance between prayer and activity.

EXPOSITION

If we wanted to do so, we could consider St. Teresa of Avila as two people. She was a woman of tremendous energy and drive who reformed the Carmelite Order to which she belonged, founded many new convents of her Order, and fought for her ideals and reforms against great opposition.

On the other hand, she was so proficient in prayer and gifted with the highest degree of mystical union with God that her writings on the subject are consulted even now. She is the only woman proposed by the Church as a teacher. (Cf. Entrance Prayer.)

However, Teresa was not two persons but just one very extraordinary woman. She achieved in her life a balance be-

235

tween prayerful union with God and an abundance of activities. In fact, all her actions found their source and driving force in her contemplation of the Trinity.

APPLICATION

Most of us feel more at ease in the active life than at prayer time when we are often plagued with distractions and spiritual dryness. Often we fail to see that our prayerful union with God should be the inspiration and companion of our activities for God.

We need a sense of balance in our own lives similar to that of St. Teresa. Such a sense of balance can be acquired at Mass and Communion through our union with God. Strive to do so at this Mass. Persevere in this effort after Mass, striving by your daily activities and prayers to maintain a constant union with Christ.

THEME II

Teresa's vocation as teacher and administrator could be compared to the vocation of a married woman to be a teacher and homemaker. Stress how a mother leads her children to know Christ and the joys of living for Him, provides them with a sense of values, and in short, helps to form a Christian family.

October 16—St. Hedwig (c. 1174–1243), Widow

THEME

Carry the Cross which Christs puts in our way no matter what obstacles the world puts in our way.

St. Hedwig was of royal birth. As a young girl she married the Duke of Silesia. She knew by personal experience many of the roles a woman plays in life—wife, mother, widow and finally member of a religious order. In each of these states of life she embraced the Cross of Christ no matter how hard it was to do it.

She put herself at the service of all, performed the lowliest tasks even to the point of serving the poor and lepers with her own hands. When her husband and later her son died, she accepted their deaths with such wonderful resignation to God's will that we are forced to admire her courage and trust in God even today.

APPLICATION

The Cross casts its shadow over our lives also. We must be ready and willing to accept the Cross no matter when or how it appears. It can come to us in sickness or in sorrow, in poverty or in the death of loved ones.

Our own strength is insufficient for the task. How well we know that fact! We must seek outside ourselves for the strength which we need. Union with Christ the Lord at Mass and Communion can help us to embrace the Cross of Christ.

October 17—St. Margaret Mary Alacoque (1647–1690), Virgin

THEME

Love is all you really need.

Christ revealed many things to St. Margaret Mary when He appeared to her and showed her the treasures of His Heart. He gave her love to be "the root and foundation" of her life. She learned through all the hardships and the opposition which she met in spreading devotion to His Sacred Heart, that the love of Christ surpasses all knowledge. In all her 43 years, she found that His yoke did lie easy and His burden was light; for He was always gentle and humble of heart to her.

APPLICATION

In the Entrance Prayer, we asked St. Margaret Mary to win for us the grace to love our Lord *above all things* and *in all things*. St. Paul in the Epistle prays: "May love be the root and foundation of your life." Modern rock and roll singers blast out the news. "All you need is love; Love is all you really need!"

It doesn't matter what words are used, as long as you get the message. Once you get the message, give it to others fast. Here at Mass give yourself completely to this act of love and seek from it the strength to love Christ above all things and in all people.

October 18—St. Luke, Evangelist

THEME

Luke's insights can help us to understand the hearts of Jesus and Mary.

EXPOSITION

St. Luke is known as the author of the Third Gospel and the Acts of the Apostles. His Gospel is called "the Gospel of the Merciful Heart of Jesus" and also contains some of the most cherished descriptions of our Blessed Mother. The Acts of the Apostles centers upon the work of the two most important Apostles, devoting the first part to St. Peter and the second to St. Paul. Luke was a constant companion of St. Paul in his missionary activities and during his first imprisonments.

Luke is also called the "Beloved Physician" and is said to have been an artist. Luke, like a good physician, knew what a sick man needs, and so he gave us an account of the loving, merciful heart of Jesus. In so doing, he also painted the most beautiful word-picture which we have of the Blessed Virgin Mary.

APPLICATION

Have you ever felt that it's impossible for you to get close to Jesus? He seems so distant and irrelevant to the people of the late 1960's—to you. I would not be ashamed to admit that this has been a problem. Everyone seems to face it sometime and to some degree. Luke faced this problem in his day but he did something about it. From his contacts with Mary and the Apostles he learned the facts his Gospel recounts.

Why not use his "life" of Christ to learn more about the Savior? Luke's insights can help us understand the Christ we follow. If Luke cannot do the job by himself, don't give up! There are three other authors waiting for their turn at bat.

October 19—St. Peter of Alcantara (1499–1562), Confessor

THEME

Evaluate all things in the light of Christ.

EXPOSITION

One of the greatest mystics of his century, St. Peter became a Franciscan at the age of 16. He was famous for his remarkable spirit of penance and the highest gift of contemplation. He not only reformed his own order by evaluating its work and spirit in the light of Christ, but he also assisted St. Teresa of Avila in her reform of the Carmelites by using the same criterion.

APPLICATION

It is necessary for us to evaluate our life and its purpose in the light of Christ to see if we have strayed from the right path. Is the success we seek, the comfort we desire, and our approach to work, prayer and sacrifice worthy of Christ? Ask St. Peter of Alcantara through this Mass to win for you the grace to start immediately upon a re-evaluation of your life in the light of Christ.

Be completely honest with yourself and God as you seek to "restore to Christ" everything in your life. That's a tall order for any person to carry out, but do your best. Use the love and strength which you receive at this banquet table to help you be honest with yourself.

October 20—St. John Cantius (1397–1473), Confessor

Lord, give us the grace to act kindly toward our neighbor.

"I was eyes to the blind—and feet to the lame was I—I was a father to the needy." These words of Job, which form the Offertory verse, are quite properly referred to today's saint. He was the best possible father to the needy of his day. Except for a few years as a parish priest, most of his life was spent as a professor at the University of Cracow in Poland.

During this time, his pockets were always empty because he gave everything to the poor. Often he gave away his own clothing and shoes. When he realized that he was dying, he distributed what little he had to the poor. He knew that Christ would care for his "good and faithful servant."

Do we always see our neighbor's needs and do what we can to help? Or are we like the people St. James talks about in his Epistle (Ch. 2) who give words of comfort but nothing more? As the result of this Mass and Communion we will ask to imitate the charity of St. John. Will we mean what we say or is it going to be another example of noble inspiring words falling on deaf ears? Make the request of God and mean it. Then go out and show your neighbor that you meant it.

Holiness in a professor is not so extraordinary that we must comment on it. Nonetheless, St. John does exemplify that what we believe and know can and should influence our lives as followers of Christ.

October 23—St. Anthony Mary Claret (1807–1870), Bishop and Confessor

THEME

Lord, give us zeal for the souls of those with whom we live, work and recreate.

EXPOSITION

St. Anthony Mary Claret is a relatively recent saint and one who has special interest for us because he was Archbishop of Santiago, Cuba for six years. He wanted to go to the foreign missions but poor health did not allow this. Instead he worked in Spain and its territories, founding new religious communities for men and women. Through his efforts there was a remarkable spread of devotion to the Blessed Sacrament and to the Immaculate Heart of Mary.

APPLICATION

Today's saint wanted to serve God and save souls by going to the foreign missions, but this was not to be. God took Anthony with all his apostolic zeal for souls and showed him how much could be done right at home. This is not the first time that God showed one of his saints that there was work to be done on the homefront as well as on the battleground of the missions.

The same message is given to us today. There is much to be done right where we live, work and recreate. As we unite with Christ and one another through this Mass and Communion, let us ask Him to give us zeal for the souls of those with whom we live and work. Brothers and sisters in Christ—that's our mission territory. Let's not forget it.

October 24—St. Raphael, Archangel

THEME

Raphael, heal us of our ailments and be our companion in this life and in eternity.

EXPOSITION

Raphael's name means "God has healed." The Gospel story was chosen as a reminder of Raphael's healing powers. The Epistle mentions two incidents which exemplify this power, namely, the healing of the elder Tobias who was blind, and the freeing of Sara from the influence of the devil. Raphael accompanied the younger Tobias on his journey and thus won the reputation of being the angelic protector of travelers.

APPLICATION

In the Entrance Prayer the Church asked God to send us Raphael so that we might ". . . be guarded by him always and strengthened by his assistance." We members of Christ's Mystical Body who are still on earth are said to be *"in via"*—on the way. It's an apt expression for many reasons. Our life on earth has its dangers and pitfalls. We barely reach the end of one growth stage before we have to move on to the next with its own peculiar difficulties.

243

A good companion can make or break us in this undertaking. Raphael was certainly a good companion to young Tobias. Why not ask St. Raphael to be your companion in this life and the next?

October 25—St. Isidore, the Farmer (12th Century), Confessor

THEME

Faithful performance of the uneventful duties of one's life is the surest road to holiness.

EXPOSITION

St. Isidore may be called the patron saint of the humdrum life. He was a married peasant who spent his life as a farm laborer working for other people. He knew the dull routine of farming; the repetition of the growing cycle year after year—plow, plant, tend and harvest. Into this monotony he introduced a sense of purpose—love for Christ and for all his fellow Christians.

Christ had said: "If you remain united to Me and My word remains a part of you, ask for whatever you want and you shall have it" (Jn. 15:7). Isidore did not seek to run away from his humdrum life. He tried to unite even the smallest and most menial tasks to his love for Christ.

APPLICATION

What lesson can we learn from St. Isidore? Are we to follow him into farm work? No, indeed, that is not what we need to learn. We have to realize that there is much of value in the ordinary tasks that face us each day. Dishes, diapers, meals and money problems, farms and factories, employers and employees, etc., etc. Our lives can become so much a routine that every spark of interest and attractiveness seems to have evaporated. St. Isidore shows us that there is great value in even the most monotonous lives. Learn to see this value. Have a sense of purpose as St. Isidore had.

Use your encounter with Almighty God through this Mass and Communion to develop a new outlook on your daily life. Then use the graces gained at this sacramental encounter to guide your life according to your new outlook which will really be Christ's outlook.

October 28—Sts. Simon and Jude, Apostles

THEME

To follow in the footsteps of the Apostles is definitely asking for trouble, but it is also asking for heaven.

EXPOSITION

As we read the words of the Gospel taken from Christ's "farewell address" to his Apostles at the Last Supper, we should be amazed at how literally they have been fulfilled in the last 2000 years. No follower of Christ has been more important than his Master. None who was worthy of the name "Christian" has escaped the predicted persecutions.

Simon and Jude suffered martyrdom because they were convinced that Christ was God. They wanted everyone to know this wonderful news about Christ. These men, who were joined so closely to Christ by love and friendship, sought and gained the honor of being united to Him by their sufferings and death.

245

If we are going to follow the example of Simon, Jude and all the other Apostles, let us get one thing perfectly clear in our minds. There will be opposition to our course of action; for none of us can follow Christ faithfully without sufferings and persecution.

At this Mass we should be united in love with Saints Simon and Jude and all here present. If we can achieve such a union of love, we will be able to unite our lives with Christ, His apostles and one another. Ask God for the grace to follow in the footsteps of the Apostles, even though it means asking for trouble. When the trouble comes, do not back away. Fight on with courage because you have the best possible comrades-in-arms, the Apostles of every land and generation.

November 1—All Saints Day

THEME

Today, the Family of God rejoices that so many of its members are eternally united to the Trinity in love.

EXPOSITION

Today is a family celebration. We are honoring all our brothers and sisters who have "taken up their cross daily and followed the Lord" to their own Calvary and beyond that to heaven. We honor the famous canonized saints. We honor the unnamed and unnumbered holy people of all the ages who are united eternally with the Trinity in heaven.

We are united here around the altar as a family—a family

246

praying together so that it can stay together on the road to God and remain together forever in heaven.

Finally, this is a family affair because of the close bond of love which unites God's family whether in heaven or on earth. We honor the saints and they win God's grace for us. We rejoice in their happy state, and they encourage us to follow their example. Their successes revive our weary spirits and help us try once again to love God as we should.

APPLICATION

We are a family here although not always a very united or loving family. We are so separated by our weaknesses and by our reluctance to love Christ in each other. We are torn apart by our selfish excesses. This Mass can be the beginning of a new family spirit among all Christians.

Ask Our Lord through this Eucharistic sacrifice-banquet to nourish and protect this beginning—to be the source and foundation of our family life and love. With the strength that we gain at Mass we can live in union with Christ and with all the saints. It is only a possibility now. We alone can make it a fact. Work hard to make it a fact and look forward with confidence to the All Saints Day which will honor you along with all the other saints.

THEME II

The Epistle may be sheer torture to lectors, but it does highlight the absolute universality of the Church's membership.

November 2—All Souls Day

THEME

Today is a family feast during which we reach out a helping hand to our brothers and sisters suffering in purgatory.

EXPOSITION

Yesterday we rejoiced because so many of our Christ-family have followed the Lord to heaven. Today we turn our thoughts to the souls in purgatory. They suffer now for a while but are assured of reaching heaven. As the saying goes: "They have it made." We who are still on the way—whose destiny is still in doubt—we should rejoice with them. We should also realize that our prayers and good works, our kindnesses and charity help the souls in Purgatory.

This Mass is the greatest gift that we can give them. Who in the world could possibly fathom the power of this sacrifice? Christ, our Brother, is the Priest; Christ, our Brother, is the victim. We join with Him in this action which gives immense glory and worship to our Father. By our Communion we become a most intimate part of this sacrifice-banquet. This is where we can help our suffering brothers and sisters most of all.

APPLICATION

Offer your Mass today and often during the year for the souls in purgatory. Pray frequently for them. Pray especially for the soul in purgatory who on earth was most like you in talent, personality, troubles, temptation, and vocation. Love your Christ-family in this most concrete and worthwhile way.

November 3—St. Martin de Porres, Confessor

THEME

In those dioceses where this feast is celebrated, it is certainly worthwhile to discuss social justice. St. Martin has been officially designated as the Patron of Social Justice. It would be good to underline the fact that he treated all as Christ. That is the essence of social justice—to see and love Christ in everyone.

November 4—St. Charles Borromeo (died 1584), Bishop and Confessor

THEME

St. Charles' example encourages us to work to implement the Decrees of Vatican II just as loyally and as energetically as he did those of Trent.

EXPOSITION

Charles, the nephew of Pius IV, a Cardinal at the age of 23 and Archbishop of Milan, was the great hero of the Catholic Reformation. Milan was the center of his wonderful pastoral zeal. He was the product of the nepotism that had so weakened the Church throughout the ages, but he was an exception to the rule. His loyalty and love for the Church are unquestioned. Because of his influence with the Popes, he helped to complete the Council of Trent. Then he went to the great Archdiocese of Milan and put the Council's decrees into effect.

If we are to find the strength to be faithful to the hopes and aspirations of Vatican II, we will find it in the Mass at our family worship of God. From this source of strength we must go forth and implement the hopes of Pope John, Pope Paul, and all the Council Fathers. "St. Charles, help us by this Mass to be full and active members of our reformed and ever-reforming Church. You traveled the rough road to reform and renewal. Help us to follow your lead."

November 9—Dedication of the Archbasilica of Our Savior

THEME

Each Christian is the living, and should be loving temple of God.

EXPOSITION

We commemorate at Mass today the dedication of a famous church to Our Savior. The more common name for the Arch-basilica of Our Savior is St. John Lateran, the Cathedral of the Pope and the site of five ecumenical councils.

In the prayers and readings of the Mass there are several references made to the dedication of a building to God, but another emphasis is apparent. God does not dwell primarily in buildings but in His people. Christ enters Zacchaeus' house to seek and to save that which was lost—the soul of the master of the house.

APPLICATION

As we commemorate the dedication of a church to Almighty God, let us remember that our own dedication to God is greater than that of any building. I do not mean to disparage your profound respect for a church in any way. A church, basilica or archbasilica is more than a mere building. It is a symbol of the heavenly Jerusalem where God is present. It is a manifestation of Christ to the world. It is a witness to His self-sacrificing love and wholehearted generosity.

A church is all of these things, but we are much more. We are not brick, mortar, marble, limestone. We are flesh and blood made to the image and likeness of God. We have been dedicated to God as His living, loving temples.

At Mass today realize that you and I are more holy than the building whose dedication we commemorate; than any church building. May God help us to realize how real and personal our dedication to Him is. May we become what we are called to be—living and loving temples of God.

THEME II

On this date in 1965 much of the Eastern Coast of the United States and some parts of Canada experienced a total blackout. We never realized how much electricity meant to us until we didn't have it for a while. Let's not wait until it is too late to realize how much God and His grace mean to us.

November 10—St. Andrew of Avellino (1521–1608), Confessor

THEME

Our Mass should be a preparation for life as well as death.

EXPOSITION

Andrew was a lawyer in the ecclesiastical courts of Naples. He was a *lover of truth*, a reformer of clerical and religious life. He lived a strong and active Christian life, but his death was really his crowning glory. He died as he was starting Mass. It was a fiitting crown to his life of service to Christ living in the poor, in his fellow religious and clerics.

To die as St. Andrew did just as he began Mass is a beautiful way to meet death. We can become very lyrical about how Andrew finished in heaven the Mass that he started on earth. You and I have started a Mass now and more than likely we will finish it here on earth.

Mass gives us the great joy of union with God, with our Brother Christ, with the other members of the family of God who have gathered here. It does all these things and more because it is a family feast. After this family feast we will go into the world to live out in the happenings of our daily lives this union of love with Christ and each other that we have experienced at Mass. That would be a happy ending for the story and it is the way this story should end. What are you going to do to make it end that way?

November 11—St. Martin of Tours (died 397), Bishop and Confessor

THEME

We must see Christ in those we meet, especially the most un-Christlike people.

EXPOSITION

Today we honor St. Martin of Tours. Martin, a soldier who became a saint, is the inspiration of all belated vocations.

The first of a long line of soldiers who gave up fighting for the world to fight for Christ, Martin should inspire all of us. The story of how he met a beggar and shared his cloak with the beggar who was Christ, is well known. He did many other wonderful things. He was a bishop of whom the Church can be proud. He was a Christian with whom we can relate.

APPLICATION

The story of St. Martin and the beggar teaches us one lesson. Look for Christ in everyone we meet. If we can learn to do that, our hearts should burst forth in joyful "Alleluias." We will be perfect.

Even in the most unlikely people, Christ is present. Think of the most obnoxious, boorish, and insulting person you know. Christ lives in that person. Think of the person who was the butt of the last nationality or racial joke you told. Christ lives in that person and his nationality or race. Think of the Protestants and Jews whom you distrust and shun. Christ lives in them.

Ask St. Martin to help you see, love and serve Christ in everyone. By now we all know that it isn't easy. So ask him most humbly for the grace to look for and love Christ in everyone you meet.

November 12—St. Martin I (died in 655), Pope and Martyr

THEME

Suffering comes to those who strive to preserve and to spread Christ's teachings.

253

Martin I was elected Pope in 649, and died in exile in 655. During those years, the Church was being torn apart by internal disorders and disagreements. The Emperor during St. Martin's reign was constantly interfering with the government of the Church. He considered matters of faith as his special concern and was willing to compromise its teachings for the sake of political expediency. Pope Martin opposed him in such matters.

This led to such bitterness that the Emperor, claiming to be the friend of Christ and the Church, banished the Pope to exile and death. What a sad spectacle it was to see Christians fighting among themselves! What a mockery it was to wound the Church of Christ so deeply and then to claim that it was done for the honor and glory of God.

APPLICATION

Within the Church today there are internal difficulties and disagreements. There is the fear that this garment of Christ will be torn asunder. Please God, Christlike patience and understanding will win the upper hand. Pray for the Church, for its unity and the purity of its teachings. These are things loved by Saint Martin more than life and its comforts. Do we dare to love the Church less today?

This Church of Christ is a wounded Church, not because of Christ, but because of us. It suffers because we, its members, are not Christlike. The Emperor of St. Martin's day was not the only Christian who has sacrificed the faith for political, business or social gain. He has many followers even now.

You know whose follower you are. Make sure you have not begun to compromise your faith in any way or for any thing. Be a loyal, a loving member of the Church. Do not wound it more than it has been wounded. Seek by your loyal action and by your love to heal its wounds.

November 13—St. Frances Xavier Cabrini (1850–1917), Virgin

Theme

St. Frances Cabrini challenges us to repeat in our own lives her "American success story."

Exposition

Frances Cabrini fell in love with the Christ who said: "Take My yoke upon your shoulders and receive My instructions; because I am gentle and humble of heart" (Mt. 11-29). Even though she was never a very healthy woman and did not like the sea, she traveled constantly across the Atlantic and worked tirelessly on both sides of the ocean to care for souls.

She founded a new religious order dedicated to the Sacred Heart of Jesus, and was the principal cause of its rapid spread. She became a naturalized citizen of the United States, and died in Chicago in 1917. In 1946 she became the first U. S. citizen to be canonized.

Application

Her life is an American success story we can all admire and follow. She went from "rags to riches," to the riches of many souls brought back to the practice of their religion, of countless women who joined her in her missionary work. She established orphanages, schools, and hospitals all over the Americas. Her holiness and missionary activity challenge us to follow in her footsteps. We who are soon to be fed sacramentally with the Body and Blood of the Lord, will be given the means to follow her example. Will we accept the challenge or will we reject it?

November 14—St. Josephat (1579–1623), Bishop and Martyr

THEME

The unity of Christ's Church must be defended today just as strongly as in the time of St. Josephat.

EXPOSITION

Today's saint is one of the patrons of Poland. As Bishop, he tried to be a good shepherd of his flock and always sought to stay within the one flock of Christ. In his youth his Church was reunited under the Pope. Later, as Archbishop, he fought tirelessly against the forces which were trying to destroy that unity. His fight was to the death; for he was beaten to death in a riot caused by his opponents.

APPLICATION

St. Josephat's devotion to Church unity should inspire us to treasure this unity. However, we cannot merely treasure it; we must work hard each day to make it a living, meaningful reality. The unity we seek today is the union of all Christian Churches into the one Church of Christ. Such a dream will not be fulfilled without effort. It cannot be fulfilled if we Catholics present at this Mass are not united in determination to promote Christian unity.

As we share in this Eucharistic meal, we should be filled with the spiritual strength of the martyr-bishop Josephat. It was this strength which made him victorious in defending the Church (cf. Prayer after Communion). It can and will do the same for us if we receive this food worthily.

November 15—St. Albert the Great (1193–1280), Bishop and Doctor of the Church

THEME

Albert, saint and scientist, proves that there need be no conflict between science and religion.

EXPOSITION

St. Albert the Great was one of the most brilliant and learned men of the medieval period. He deserved the title "Great" because of his intellectual powers and learning, especially in the field of the natural sciences. He was so impressive in this regard that the Church has chosen him as one of her universal Doctors, and has named him as Patron of the Sciences.

APPLICATION

We can and should admire Albert's learning and intellectual ability, although we cannot hope to imitate him in these things. We can and should admire his faith and deep humility, and these are qualities we can imitate. Ask St. Albert the Great to help you to be "great" even in a small way in the virtues of faith and humility.

There is no conflict between true religion and true science. That is an impossibility since God is the source of both. St. Albert showed us how science and religion could be forged into a harmonious whole. He was a competent scientist and a complete Christian and he was not embarrassed or retarded in his scientific work by his Christianity, nor was his belief in God undermined by his studies.

Teilhard de Chardin in our own century has demonstrated

the validity of this position once again. Ask St. Albert for the necessary balance between the search for worldly wisdom and divine wisdom. Since God our Father is the source of both, there can be no conflict if our religion is true and our science accurate.

November 16—St. Gertrude (13th Century), Virgin

THEME

Life centered on the Mass.

EXPOSITION

Gertrude was a Cistercian nun of the 13th century. She was an exceptionally gifted woman and used her natural talents well. When she was twenty-five, Christ began to appear to her. At His command she wrote several works about her mystical experiences. She herself was a mystic whose whole life was centered on the Mass and the Passion of Christ.

A vocation leaflet once had the saying on it: "My Day, A Mass." If only we could put that motto into practice, and make our whole life the echo of our daily encounter with Christ at Mass. Our union with Christ and His members here should be one of such intimacy and love that it will help us overcome our daily difficulties. The Mass should be the high point of each day acting as the dynamo from which we get the strength to live Christlike lives. The Mass meant all that and even more to St. Gertrude.

APPLICATION

Ask her to help you understand and value your daily Mass. Seek in many ways to participate more actively and maturely in this sacramental encounter with Christ. The more you put into it, the more you will get out of it. That expression is as true of the Mass as of other things. That expression, however, does not go far enough; for Christ will see that you get much more from the Mass than you put into it.

November 17—St. Gregory the Wonderworker (died 270), Bishop and Confessor

THEME

The greatest wonder that we can work is to lead others to Christ by our example.

EXPOSITION

Faith that can move mountains is rare. St. Gregory had it according to one legend which relates that when he wanted to build a church where a mountain stood, he ordered the mountain to move and it moved.

He was a man of great learning and holiness. Outstanding miracles and prophecies graced his life and work. When he started his work, there were only 17 Christians in his city, a large urban center. When he died, there were only 17 non-Christians. That one statistic tells us more about his apostolic zeal than a hundred pages.

APPLICATION

If only our lives produced such conversions to Christ in our families, co-workers and neighbors! Unfortunately this is not often the case. Pray for this grace at Mass today as you communicate with Christ in the most intimate way possible.

Ask to be made wonderworkers. Do not ask to move mountains. Moving a mountain is a small thing compared to moving a soul into Christ's arms. Ask God for the grace to do the greatest of all wonders: to lead other souls to Christ. Ask for such grace sincerely and fervently. Then go out and work at being a wonderworker.

November 18—Dedication of the Basilicas of the Holy Apostles Peter and Paul

THEME

We Christians possess a proud heritage, rooted in Christ and his Apostles, Peter and Paul.

EXPOSITION

Today, as on November 9th, we commemorate the dedication of a church to God. In fact, today we celebrate the dedication of two churches, one built over the tomb of Peter and the other over the tomb of Paul. We go in spiritual pilgrimage to these churches today. They remind us that we are a people who possess a proud heritage.

Our faith is founded upon Christ. The twin pillars which support our faith are Peter and Paul. They are our spiritual ancestors; we are the heirs of their apostolic glory and zeal. They teach us that we must sink our roots deeply into Christ Who is the one and only foundation.

APPLICATION

Today we celebrate the dedication of two churches of mighty dimensions. Do you realize that one Christian who follows in the footsteps of Peter and Paul completely dwarfs any church no matter how imposing it is? Why? Because God made our hearts to be his home, and a dwelling of brick and mortar can never be anything but second best.

At Mass today be proud of your heritage, be proud of Sts. Peter and Paul. Seek to follow their lead. Rededicate yourself as a temple of God and sink your roots deeply into the foundation of Christ and His Apostles.

November 19—St. Elizabeth of Hungary (1206–1231), Queen and Widow

THEME

When compared with the kingdom of heaven, all other things fade into insignificance.

EXPOSITION

When Christ told the parable about the hidden treasure (Mt. 13:44), He was pleading with us to have a sense of values. He wanted to teach us the true worth of the kingdom of heaven. Queen Elizabeth of Hungary understood Christ's message. She knew what was valuable in life. Her life was the usual mixture of good and bad. She was of royal background and had a fine husband, a loving family, great wealth, dignity and honor.

She was a wonderful Christian during the good times and an even better one when misfortunes galore befell her. She lost her husband, was dispossessed of her great wealth and deprived of her royal prerogatives. No matter what happened, she never doubted Christ's loving concern for herself and her family. Elizabeth shows us how to accept from God the good and the bad. In fact, she shows us how to love God in everything that happens to us no matter what it is!

261

Each of us will find that our lives are a mixture of good and bad, of "ups" and "downs." Our "ups" may not be so high as hers; our "downs" may not be so low, but we will have both. Let us hope that our commitment to Christ, reinforced through Mass and the sacraments, will help us to accept whatever happens as St. Elizabeth's did. Pray that we will be able to preserve our sense of values, and to seek always and before all else the kingdom of heaven.

November 20—St. Felix (died 1212), Confessor

THEME

Each Christian has been called by God to do the work of Christ in his life.

EXPOSITION

Little is known of today's saint except that he received a call from heaven to make his life's work the ransoming of Christians captured by pirates in the Mediterranean.

APPLICATION

We also have a call from God to do His will in our lives. We Christians of Vatican II must, with God's help, make ourselves the most efficient instruments of the Church in the modern world. We cannot shun this world; we cannot turn our backs on its sufferings, its desires and hopes. We have to bring Christ to our world. Better yet, we have to be Christ in the modern world.

Ask for this grace in all that you do. The most opportune

time and place to ask for this grace is right here when you are united with your family at the sacrifice of Christ which is offered through the hands of Christ.

November 21—Presentation of the Blessed Virgin Mary

THEME

Mary was not merely presented to God. She was completely consecrated to God and to His work.

EXPOSITION

Today we celebrate an ancient tradition that Our Lady was taken by her parents to the Temple to be presented to God. God gave a child to the parents, and they acknowledged that fact by presenting the child in the Temple, by consecrating the child to God.

In the Entrance Prayer of the Mass, the Church describes Mary as the dwelling place of the Holy Spirit. She is the new temple of the Savior. Then the Church prays: "May we be worthy through her intercession to be presented in the Temple of God's glory." It is a good thing to be concerned with heaven, but let's not forget what must be done here on earth where we must become worthy dwelling places for the Holy Spirit.

APPLICATION

Our baptism brought us into the family of God, into a loving relationship with God and all the other baptized members of Christ. We became dwelling places of the Holy Spirit as Mary was. We have been consecrated to God as she was, and we must live out the implications of that consecration. At

263

Mass when the priest consecrates the gifts we offer, remember that they only represent us. Let's make sure we offer the reality along with the symbol.

November 22—St. Cecilia, Virgin and Martyr

Theme

The power of Christlike love to lead others to the Savior.

Exposition

Cecilia, child of a wealthy patrician family of pagan Rome, dedicated herself completely to God. Forced by her father to marry a young pagan, she lived a life of virginity, converting both her husband and his brother. When both of them were martyred because they buried Christian martyrs, Cecilia buried them and was herself arrested. She showed the strength of what we so euphemistically call the weaker sex. She did not deny Christ. She was loyal to Christ, to her husband, and to the things that she had taught him.

Application

If we love with a Christlike love, it is so easy to attract others to follow the Lord. It isn't a self-conscious, phony sort of make-believe. People are not fooled by such pretense for any length of time. It is a matter of seeing and loving Christ in others and letting Him do the rest. Cecilia did it, and many others have done it.

If we have not been able to do the same, the fault lies with us and no one else. We have not loved as Christ wants us to love. His love is set before us in this sacrificial banquet. It is ours for the asking. Will we ask for it? I hope so, and let it be today!

November 23—St. Clement I (died c. 100), Pope and Martyr

THEME

Ask Clement for some of his steely strength and iron-willed determination to follow Christ.

EXPOSITION

Today we celebrate the feast of a man of distinction. Clement is a link with the apostles. He was the co-worker of Peter and Paul, the third successor of Peter as Bishop of Rome. Paul mentions him in today's Epistle. "Clement and my other co-workers, all of whose names are in the Book of Life." Clement was heir to the words of Christ: "You are Peter and on this rock I will build My Church." He was heir to the promise and to the fulfillment of that promise. Even when exiled he worked to convert pagans to Christ. He died because he refused to stop leading souls out of the darkness into the light of Christ's love.

APPLICATION

A man like Clement can fire our imagination, can give us the enthusiasm we need to follow Christ. He was a man of great strength and determination. In the face of persecution, in the face of death, he still preached Christ. If only all Christians, especially all of us (here at Mass) could follow his example.

At Mass today ask Clement for some of his steely strength and iron-will determination in following Christ. The Church needs strong men today to carry forward the great work of

renewal begun by Vatican II. Don't let George or Clement
do it. St. Clement did his part. Now you do yours!

November 24—St. John of the Cross (1542–1591), Confessor and Doctor of the Church

THEME

An unwavering love of the Cross is the mark of a true Christian.

EXPOSITION

John of the Cross was born in Spain and became a member of
the Carmelite Order. He was a great friend of St. Teresa of
Avila and her faithful ally in her restoration of the Carmelites
to their original rule and fervor. Because of his efforts at reform, he was imprisoned and he had to suffer many spiritual
and physical torments. He had asked God for such trials and
God gave them to him. By his life of intimate union with
God he earned the title, "Doctor of Mysticism."

APPLICATION

In the Prayer of the Mass, we ask that John, who was gifted
with the spirit of complete self-denial and a deep love of the
Cross, may help us to follow his example. We need his spirit
of self-denial and his love of the Cross in our own age. We
need to reform our lives according to the standards of Christ.
As you offer Mass today, make it your intention to offer it so
that you will continue to reform your life and grow in your
devotion to the Cross of Christ.

November 25—St. Catherine of Alexandria (early 4th Century), Virgin and Martyr

THEME

We need a faith that no argument or violence can shake.

EXPOSITION

Catherine of Alexandria is the patron of philosophers. It is said that the emperor assigned a number of philosophers to shake her faith in Christ. They failed and, in the end, Catherine converted them to Christianity. In desperation the emperor attempted to win his point by torture, but this did not work either. There is a legend that angels carried her body to Mt. Sinai in Arabia after she was beheaded.

APPLICATION

The Prayer of the Mass recalls this legend and then asks that God would grant, through the merits and prayers of this saint, that we may reach the mountain which is Christ. We need to strive through persistent faith to seek Christ. He really is not a mountain which is completely unapproachable except by expert climbers or by the wings of angels. He is our Lord and our Savior. He is our ladder. He is present here at Mass.

Seek at this Mass to know Him more fully, to love Him more truly. Sink the roots of your faith deeply into Christ so that no intellectual arguments nor physical torture will ever shake your alliance with Him. Almighty and most merciful Father, may Your will be done in us who follow Your Son. Give us a faith in Christ which no argument or violence can shake.

267

November 26—St. Sylvester (1177–1267), Abbot

THEME

Death can be a cruel but remarkably effective teacher.

EXPOSITION

The Entrance Prayer of today's Mass states the reasons why we honor Sylvester. "God gave him his vocation to be a hermit as he stood before an open grave contemplating the vanity of this world." Sylvester was an outstanding student and clergyman in his native city. He gave up his position to become a hermit when he saw the dead body of a once handsome relative. Many men followed Sylvester and he organized them into a religious order.

APPLICATION

Death can be a remarkably effective teacher. It taught Sylvester to flee the pleasures of the world and to become a hermit. Death has a different message today. It isn't telling us to turn our back on the world and become hermits, but to stay in the world and bring it to Christ. We share in Christ's mission to our world. In fact, He wants us to be front-line troops in His campaign.

Part of the blame for the present situation must fall on us Christians who preach one thing and practice the opposite. Some of us have portrayed God not as a loving Father, but as the almighty "bully in the sky" who delights in trapping poor humans in the act of sinning. The world refuses to accept such a caricature and so should we. Our mission to the world must begin with a change in our ideas about God, and in a greater harmony between our words and deeds.

It might be easy to turn away from the world and become hermits. It is harder to stay and fight for Christ. Why can't we? It will not be an easy task. To do it properly will require much help from God. That help is available here at Mass. Get as much as you can, and then go out and use it to convince the world that Christ is important.

Six Longer Homilies
By Way of Example

Ember Wednesday in September

Ember Day of Joy

The striking thing about Ember Wednesday in September is the joyful mood which characterizes its Liturgy.

The Introit sets the tone of our celebration when it proclaims: "Sing joyfully to God, our Strength—Take up a pleasant psalm with the harp." The Communion proclaims: "Be not sad for the joy of the Lord is our strength."

Some may say that it is much easier to be cheerful on Ember Days now when we are not required to fast any more. Perhaps for some this may be true, but such people do not experience the Christlike joys to which we refer. Our joy today is of such intensity and depth that it eagerly embraces voluntary penances, not limiting itself to what authority commands.

God Is Good and Generous

Amos, the shepherd prophet, speaks in the First Lesson of the future prosperity of the restored kingdom of Israel. This kingdom is a figure of the Messianic kingdom of Christ. We are living in a realization of that kingdom now—the Church.

In and through the Church we have received a superabundance of material and spiritual gifts from God. We are prosperous because of Christ Who is the cause of all our blessings. "Truly who is like the Lord, our God, Who is enthroned on high and looks upon the heavens and the earth below?"

God has blessed us with His law. The joy of the people who listened to Esdras read the Book of the Law of God must be our joy as we strive to hear and obey God's will as it is contained in the law. We should love the law for one reason only—because it is the expression of the Will of God Who has first loved us.

God blesses us with the Word of Christ in the Gospel. Jesus asks us, as He asked the man in the story: "Do you have faith?" What is our answer? It could be a resounding, roof-lifting "Yes, Lord." Is it?

Christ recalls all of us to the primacy of faith in Him, to the need for penance in our lives if we are to conquer the evil spirit. With the father of the boy possessed by the unclean spirit we must cry out to Christ: "I do have faith, help my lack of faith."

With the Apostles we must learn that penance, prayer and fasting are needed for victory over the devil. Have the words: "Why could not I overcome the evil spirit" never slipped from our lips? If they have, then we definitely need to learn this lesson.

The Joy of Eucharistic Union

With minds and hearts rejoicing in the Word of God spoken to us by Amos, Esdras and Christ, we move into the sacred action of the Mass. We offer our gifts in the joy of a family united in love giving something to our Father. Our joy swells as we see our gifts accepted and transformed by God. With limitless graciousness God returns our gifts at the banquet table. In the union which we find with Christ in Communion, all God's gifts are contained and surpassed.

The joy of our Eucharistic sacrifice and sacrament makes

all other joys pale before it. That is why Ember Wednesday is an ember day of joy and has us sing out: "Today is holy to Our Lord. Do not be saddened this day, for rejoicing in the Lord, that is your strength."

Ember Friday in September

Joyful Penance Leading to Renewal

Ember Friday in September is a day which stresses penance and expiation for past failures. The Mass has this penitential tone, but there is also evident a quiet spirit of joyful thanksgiving.

The Entrance Hymn urges us: "Rejoice all hearts that seek the Lord. Give thanks to the Lord, invoke His Name." The Offertory Hymn continues this theme: "Bless the Lord, O my soul—and forget not all His benefits. . . ."

At Mass today we are given the opportunity to look back over the past three months and to assess our successes and failures in God's service.

We Start with Sorrow

The prophet Osee greets us with words of warning and yet of comfort also. "We must return to the Lord, our God, and say to Him: 'Forgive all iniquity.' " If we turn to God in sorrow and say "Yes" to His invitation of love, there need be no fear of His wrath.

"Let him who is wise, understand these things; let him who is prudent, know them" (First Lesson).

271

After reviewing our failures and expressing our sorrow, we must move on to other things. Sorrow is not an end in itself. It should lead us to plan better for the future.

Perhaps the woman in the Gospel might suggest a resolution for the next three months. Do you remember how she treated Christ? She seemed so fond of Christ, so eager to serve Him, to express her affection, admiration and love. She positioned herself close to Christ and was not going to let the scorn of the Pharisees drive her away.

Why not try to imitate her? Try to bridge the distance which separates you from Christ. We moderns are very anxious about how we relate to people. We should be even more anxious about relating to Christ. Quite obviously we relate to Christ here at Mass. However, we should relate to Him in others as well. Do we?

Let's Get Down to Earth

What about our families? Are we kind, considerate and agreeable with them? We might ask ourselves further questions about our dealings with our fellow-workers, with the poor, Negroes, foreigners, people of other religions. Are we honest and reasonably human in our treatment of them? Are they trash in our eyes or does the fact that Christ lives in them really mean something to us? The key to success in this endeavor is to respect each man as Christ.

If you consider the Mass as a sacrificial encounter with Christ, you will relate to Him in a most beneficial way. In the intimacy of this union with Christ, talk over the events of the past few months. Tell Him that you are sorry for the failures; rejoice with Him over the successes. Plan well for the future.

Resolve to take the treasures of Christ's love which are yours at Mass and to return them to Christ living in your neighbor.

272

Ember Saturday in September

Day of Atonement and Thanksgiving

Ember Saturday in September often coincides with one of the more famous Jewish feasts, Yom Kippur. This is a day of atonement and penance in preparation for the Fall festival.

The Church recognizes the need for atonement at this time of the year also. In fact, she has always stressed the necessity of penance. We Christians should realize that we must atone for our sinful ways, and now is the acceptable time to do so.

Today Mass has another important theme—that of thanksgiving. Once again the Church blends together what might seem like conflicting emotions—atonement and thanksgiving. However, these emotions or sentiments are not so much conflicting ones as they are complementary. We atone for the good things which we wasted in the past three months. We give thanks for the blessings of life which God has showered upon us. "Praise the Lord. . . . all you peoples! For steadfast is His kindness toward us—and the fidelity of the Lord endures forever" (Tract).

A Link with the Past

The three readings of this Mass form a link with the past, highlighting how deeply into Judaism our Christian roots are sunk. In the first reading we hear the Lord tell Moses of the Day of Atonement (Yom Kippur). It was, as we said, a feast of preparation and purification for the great harvest festivals. The Church uses the Ember Days in general and especially this Ember Saturday in September as such a feast of purification.

The second reading compares the sacrifices of the Old and New Testaments. St. Paul tells how the former sacrifices just pointed to Christ, Who would replace the blood of goats with His own blood and thus achieve eternal redemption.

In the final reading, Christ forcefully reveals how the Sabbath Law yields to the greater law of love for one's neighbor.

Follow the Crowd

". . . the crowd rejoiced at all the marvels He was accomplishing." Just this once let's follow the crowd. Let us rejoice at all the marvels that Christ did, but especially should we rejoice because He Himself is the greatest marvel of all.

We must become more aware of how deeply we are committed to the cause of Christ; how closely linked our destinies are with Christ and His Church. The Second Vatican Council, in its *Dogmatic Constitution on the Church,* has revealed the true nature of the Church and our dignity as its members.

The Church is not primarily an organization. The Church is a "mystery of love." It is a Church of service to mankind but especially to the poor. We are members of this pilgrim Church. We belong to God's holy people. What wonders would be worked if every Christian realized his true worth and dignity!

Use this Eucharastic sacrifice-banquet for atonement and thanksgiving. Give thanks especially for the greatest of all gifts, Christ, the Lord. Make this Mass the occasion for strengthening your commitment to the work of Christ. Remember that Christ unites our destiny with His own at every Mass.

274

September 3—St. Pius X

A Man of the People

"God exalts the lowly" is not only the sentiment of Mary in the Magnificat but of many other biblical personalities. Today's saint was a "chosen one" raised up by God "from the people." He was a peasant boy with a fine mind and a determination to serve God before all other persons or things.

As he said in his last will: "I was born poor, I have lived poor and I die poor." He became a priest, a pastor, and a bishop. Then he was named Cardinal Patriarch of Venice and in 1903 was elected Pope.

No matter what his position was, his manner of living never changed if he could help it. He did not turn his back on his humble beginnings. He had been a priest of the poor and he was the Pope of the poor, also.

The Pope of the Eucharist

Simple and humble as he was, once he realized that he could not refuse to be Pope because such was the will of God, he accepted the burden. He was every inch a Pope—the only Pope in the last 400 years to be canonized. To know him was to love him; to meet him was to be convinced that one was face to face with a saint. As Pope he sought "to restore all things to Christ," and he stressed daily Mass and Communion as a way of doing just that.

You cannot imagine how anxious Saint Pius X is that all of us profit from this Eucharistic sacrifice-banquet. He had such a deep appreciation of the power and value of the Eucharist that we can call upon him with confidence to help us by this Mass to continue his efforts "to restore all things to Christ."

In the Entrance Prayer of this Mass we mentioned how God gave St. Pius "the wisdom of heaven and the courage of His Apostles so that he could defend the Catholic faith and restore all things to Christ." Then we prayed to be able to follow his teaching and example.

Pius X faced many trials in his eleven years as Pope. They were difficult times in and outside the Church. The final and greatest trial of his life was that he could not prevent World War I. He recognized that there would be a great war. He tried to prevent it. He died worn out and brokenhearted because the big powers would not listen to his pleas for peace.

When he was asked to bless the armies of one of the countries, he replied: "I bless peace, not war."

There hasn't been real peace since Pope Pius died in 1914. Pray a little harder today that the Pope of Peace will win from God the peace we need so desperately. Why not offer this sacrifice for that intention?

September 8—Nativity of Blessed Virgin Mary

Salvation Begins

Today we rejoice because it is the birthday of Mary. With this event the story of our salvation begins because, "From the spotless virgin came the Sun of Justice, Christ, our God" (Magn. Ant.). There was no fanfare when Mary was born; just the quiet joy of holy parents blessed by God with a daughter to love. Even though no angels sang "Glory to God in the highest" at Mary's birth, it was an occasion of great joy for us because her birth was the beginning of our salvation.

Once again we have an opportunity to honor Christ's Blessed Mother. We do so by recalling to mind quite vividly what we owe to Mary and by re-dedicating ourselves once again to her Son, Christ, our God. The best observance of Mary's birthday is our full and active sharing in the Eucharistic celebration. Certainly if we do this, we will please Our Lady more than we could ever do otherwise.

Everything for Christ

Today's first reading shows us Mary as Wisdom speaking to us and telling us how she was in God's mind even before Christ. The Gospel tells us something of her ancestry by detailing that of Joseph, her spouse.

There is really very little said about Mary's nativity in the Mass except for the Proper prayers. However, great emphasis is placed upon her divine motherhood throughout the whole Mass.

Although we are celebrating a feast in honor of Mary, there is no undue concentration on this fact; rather there is a wholesome referral of everything to Christ. That was the way Mary lived on earth—by referring everything to her Son. That is the way she wants it now, and the Church uses this approach.

As Pius Parsch says: "In the Liturgy Mary never appears in solitary grandeur but always in relation to Christ." Let us become more aware of this relationship between Mary and her Son. Mary still teaches us to refer everything to Christ. As we honor her here today, let us turn in worship to her Son.

Only the Best

I like people to remember my birthday. You do also, I imagine. We may not want to tell people our age, but we surely like them to remember the occasion. Does not Mary feel the same way? Of course she does!

We should want to give her only the best on her birthday.

277

In fact, she wants only the best and will not accept less. Our best is easy enough to give. The best observance of Mary's birthday is our full and active sharing in this Mass. The best gift we can give is our effort to follow her example and refer everything to Christ. Do your best for Our Lady on her birthday.

September 14—Exaltation of the Holy Cross

Cross of Glorious Victory

The words of the Entrance Prayer are still ringing in our ears: "It behooves us to glory in the Cross of Our Lord Jesus Christ in Whom is our salvation, life and resurrection, by Whom we are saved and delivered."

Although it may not be easy to do, we are told that we should glory in the Cross of Christ. There is to be no sorrow today. Good Friday is the feast of the Holy Cross when our hearts are deeply touched by Christ's suffering and death.

Today we are to glory in the Cross; it is the symbol of our victory over sin. It was because of the Cross that God exalted Christ "above all else, and bestowed on Him that Name which is above every other name. . . ."

We face many difficulties on our way toward Christlike maturity. There are the world and the devil. Even more fearful and dangerous for our Christ-life, there are our self-love, our pride and our exaggerated sense of independence. We need to be reminded that the victory is ours. The Cross of Christ is our assurance of glorious victory over all these opponents.

Please pay special attention to the Offertory Prayer and try to make its sentiments yours as you offer this sacrifice: "Protect your people, O Lord, through this sign of the holy Cross, from the snares of their enemies, that we may pay You a pleasing service, and our sacrifices may be acceptable to You."

Christ on the Cross!

In the Gospel Christ tells the crowd how He is going to overcome Satan: "and when I am lifted up from the earth, I shall draw all men to Myself." St. John adds that Jesus said this to indicate what sort of death He was to die.

Our Lord took His position on the Cross—His throne of pain and suffering; from this position He overcame Satan. From this position Christ continues to "draw" all men to Himself.

Christ is drawing us to Himself now as we gather around this altar. Soon we will say in the Prayer over the Gifts: "O Lord, our God, we are to be nourished by the Body and Blood of Our Lord Jesus Christ, Who made the Cross a sacred symbol. We are privileged to venerate this holy Cross; grant that we may also enjoy for all eternity the salvation it has purchased for us."

The Cross and the Eucharist

Through this and every Mass we are privileged to venerate the holy Cross, our sacred symbol of victory. In this Eucharistic celebration Christ draws us to Himself as we gather here in a community of love. We are drawn not only to Him but also to all the others who are in Christ through Baptism.

Be aware of the action of Christ within your hearts. Give yourself fully to Him so that He may "draw" you even closer to Himself.

Be aware that every Mass is the gathering of God's family at the foot of Christ's Cross. Find in this and in every Mass you offer the means to give yourself more thoroughly to God and to your neighbor through the crucified Christ.

Homilies for Lent,
Easter and Pentecost

Ash Wednesday

THEME

Make Ash Wednesday the dynamic impetus which will assure that this Lent will be the best one you have ever lived.

EXPOSITION

Christ detested insincerity, pretense or hypocrisy. He wanted the people of His time and us to worship God sincerely. Nothing in all God's dealings with the Israelites, nothing in Christ's dealings with the Jews of His day was more of a disappointment than that false worship which looked so perfect and holy on the outside but was so empty and corrupt on the inside. Jesus commanded us to perform acts of self-denial and of mortification not to win praise from others but to please our Father in heaven.

Today we will receive ashes. The ashes are worth nothing in themselves. They are merely a symbol that during Lent each of us is going to practice true interior self-denial and mortification. These forty days are given us to prepare for Easter, to seek rebirth and resurrection, and to stir up within ourselves the graces of our baptism.

APPLICATION

Whatever self-denial you practice during Lent is your decision. Here are some guidelines you might follow. (1) Do something positive during Lent. Perform at least one act of kindness each day. Show your love for God and neighbor in this practical concrete way. (2) Do not mortify your family, friends or co-workers. That is not your function during Lent. If your Lenten self-denial is making you unbearable, and a torture to your loved ones, give it up. Start all over with a positive approach. (3) Your Lenten mortification is as pagan as your neighbor's pampering of himself if you do not use what you save to feed, clothe, and shelter the poor and unfortunate.

Choose well and practice mortification this Lent because you love Almighty God. Make it a sincere act of worship or don't do it at all. You are not hearing things or listening to heresy. It is better to tell God quite frankly that you are not going to do penance this Lent than to try to fool Him. At least He can respect your honesty.

Offer your Lenten penance to God with the other gifts during this Mass. Ask Jesus to consecrate your effort and to help you through this Mass to reach your Easter goal. What you do here today should explode into a dynamic impetus which will spark all your Lenten activities. Can you find all of that in this sacrificial union with Christ and the whole Christian community? It is there. Do not ignore it!

Thursday after Ash Wednesday

THEME

Lord, how should we pray?

EXPOSITION

The disciples once asked Christ how they should pray and He taught them the Our Father. Today's Mass also answers the disciples' question: "How should we pray?"

281

In the first reading, King Hezekiah prayed with tears, simplicity and trust. The centurion in the Gospel also prayed well. There was a simple statement of what he wanted. He made it humbly: "Lord, I am not worthy that you should come into my house." He had complete confidence: "Just give an order and my boy will get better."

During Lent, pray often and well. Pray as the Church teaches you in today's Mass. At Communion when you say: "Lord, I am not worthy . . ." mean it with all your heart. Mean all your prayers.

The Mass is the greatest prayer you have. Everything that has been said about prayer should be applied to this and to every Mass you offer. Remember you need three ingredients for successful prayer and for your part in the Mass: simplicity, humility and confidence.

If you have them, at least to some extent, develop them during Lent. If you don't have the necessary ingredients, why not spend this Lent acquiring them? It will be the best investment of your time and effort you ever made.

Friday after Ash Wednesday

THEME

"It is not the manifestation of virtue but its motivation that God rewards" (St. Jerome).

EXPOSITION

Christ's words in this morning's Gospel: ". . . what is so extraordinary about your conduct?" should make us think: "How would we answer that question?" Christ has told us that we cannot love only those who love us. We have to love the ones who hate us and the ones who are completely indifferent to us. He has told us: "You must be perfect as your heavenly Father is perfect."

Do not act virtuous. Be virtuous. Recall the theme of these last three days—Christ wants sincerity. Anyone can appear virtuous, but God does not judge by appearances. He has a better standard and a clearer vision of what we really are.

APPLICATION

The prayers of this Mass show us what Lent should be. In the Entrance Prayer we ask Christ to let "this bodily penance also be a truly spiritual exercise to make us strong." What we do during Lent must have an effect upon our whole being, not just on our bodies.

St. Jerome has told us that it is not the manifestation of virtue but its motivation that God rewards. What are the motives for our Lenten mortifications? They can range from mere playacting to the purest, most unselfish love for God and neighbor. Where do our motives fit into such a scale of values? Are they the best? I hope so, but each individual must make that judgment for himself. If love is your motive, you will never have to worry about any other.

In the Prayer after Communion we ask God: "fill our hearts with the spirit of your love." Everything we do during Lent must be sealed with the spirit of Christ's love. His spirit teaches us to love and serve Christ Who dwells in our neighbors and co-workers. At this Eucharistic sacrifice find the strength to follow the promptings of Christ's spirit of love.

Saturday after Ash Wednesday

THEME

May each reception of the Eucharist strengthen us and make us hunger still more for greater intimacy with our Eucharistic Lord.

EXPOSITION

In today's Gospel the apostles are utterly and completely astonished when Our Lord calms the sea. It is not a surprising reaction, and yet they should have known that Christ was truly interested in their welfare. He would not let them be harmed.

The people in the second part of the Gospel story recognize Christ and go scurrying about the whole countryside looking for the sick so that He can heal them. Did these people have to be told about the great love Christ had for the sick and deformed? Not at all! They knew how He loved every human being, especially the unfortunate.

APPLICATION

Christ was the same in both sections of the Gospel account. Isn't it strange that the apostles doubted Christ's love and concern while the ordinary people never even thought to question what seemed to them to be a self-evident truth? The apostles should have known Christ so well that they would never have doubted His love.

However, let us not be too harsh on them. We can be guilty of the same fault, and often are. The apostles grew more certain of Christ's love as the months of His public ministry passed. We, likewise, can and should grow more aware of Christ's loving concern for us. The Eucharist helps us in this effort. Each reception of the Eucharist should strengthen us and make us more certain of Christ's desire and ability to protect us.

Monday after the First Sunday of Lent

THEME

Our eternal fate depends on how we treat one another, but especially the poor.

EXPOSITION

Our Lord's description of the last judgment is a real "eye-opener." When He comes to judge us, He will divide the good from the bad. The norm by which He will make this division is a simple one.

It isn't how pious I look at Mass or during my prayers. It isn't how many times I strike my breast and say: "Lord, Lord!" The norm is: "Whatever you did for one of these brothers of Mine, insignificant though they be, you did it for Me!" On the last day the important thing will be the answer to the questions: "How did I treat others? Did I not only see but serve Christ in my neighbor?"

APPLICATION

Isn't the norm that Christ uses unfair—at least by human standards? It isn't fair of Him to ask us to treat everyone as we would treat Him. He should see some of the people in my neighborhood or at work. They certainly aren't Christ! Don't worry about them for now. What about yourself? Are you Christ in their eyes?

Why don't you try to be more like Christ in your neighborhood and at work. It is just possible that those around you will follow your good example. Even if they don't, you will be better for your efforts. During Mass today ask the Lord of salvation to "change our hearts and enlighten us by Your heavenly teaching" (Entrance Prayer).

Tell Christ that your eyes are on Him for guidance and help just as the eyes of servants are fixed on their master in order to know and fulfill every desire. If this Eucharistic encounter with Christ does not help you to be more like Him, then something is wrong. It certainly isn't His fault, is it?

Tuesday after the First Sunday of Lent

THEME

During Lent we should try to discover exactly what Christ means to us.

EXPOSITION

In the Gospel we are told that the whole city of Jerusalem was demanding to know: "Who is this?" Christ showed them who He was by His justifiable anger toward those who had made His house not a house of prayer but a bandits' den. The children in the temple precincts caught the message. That is why they cried out, "Hosanna, Son of David." In another Gospel passage our Lord tells the priests who want Him to rebuke the children and make them stop: "If they do not cry out, then the very stones of the temple will."

APPLICATION

We know who Christ is. We can rattle off a description of Him and his mission without even thinking. Perhaps that is the difficulty. It's too simple. Christ is not a shallow type individual Who fits into our convenient categories. He is far above us for He is God. His thoughts are not our thoughts and His ways are not our ways. As high as heavens are above the earth, so far are His ways above our ways and His thoughts above our thoughts (Cf. Isaiah 55:8).

During this Lent, aim high. Try to find Christ. Examine what He means in your life. Is He an expendable convenience or a vital part of your existence? What influence does He have on your attitudes, your ideals, your actions? Spend some time during Mass answering those questions. Discover once and for all exactly what Christ means to you!

Wednesday after the First Sunday of Lent (Ember Wednesday)

THEME

In the Mass we have a Man greater than Jonah, wiser than Solomon; for we have Christ doing the will of His Father.

EXPOSITION

Today's Mass is pregnant with meaning. Moses in the intimate union with God on Mt. Sinai, Elijah walking for 40 days strengthened by the angel's food, both are feeble fore-runners of the Christ Whom we meet at Mass. The words of our Lord in the Gospel are true. There is a greater prophet than Jonah here. Someone wiser than Solomon is here to help us appreciate the Mass.

This is the One who says: "Who is My mother? Who are My brothers?" and answers His own question: "Whoever does the will of my heavenly Father, that person is brother and sister and mother to Me."

APPLICATION

In this Mass we do have Someone wiser than Solomon, greater than Jonah. We have Christ the Lord enshrined in the act of doing His Father's will on Calvary. Do we appreciate the

Christ Who comes to us through this Mass? Do we at least *try* to appreciate what Mass means to us? I hope so!

Let us at this Mass become the brother, the mother, the sister of Christ by doing the will of the heavenly Father. In just a few minutes when we pray together the Our Father, let us say the phrase, "Thy will be done . . ." with special meaning. Let us mean: "Thy will be done, O Father Almighty, by us and by all Christ's followers.

Thursday after the First Sunday of Lent

THEME

Persistent faith overcomes all obstacles.

EXPOSITION

Jesus seems to have met His match in the Canaanite woman. She was not going to let Him escape before He granted her request. She had faith in Christ and knew that He could do what she asked. He was not going to grant her wish at first, but she kept asking, and asking, and asking. So persistent was she that the Apostles pleaded with Christ to give in just to get her to stop.

When Christ made those very cutting remarks, she humbly accepted what He said, and then turned the remark to her own advantage. He tested her, and she came through with flying colors. This is the only instance in the Gospel where our Lord was backed into a corner. He had to grant her wish because of her persistent faith or face the possibility of being kept in that corner.

Such faith overcomes all obstacles. We need that type of faith. We do believe in Christ and in His willingness to help us, but something seems to be lacking. Our faith is so weak, almost like a "good weather" flower that dies in a storm. We stop believing when our faith should be growing through adversity. What's wrong with our faith? We become discouraged too easily. Look at what the Canaanite woman had to overcome, and yet she never stopped believing in Christ.

At Mass today ask our Lord in honor of the Canaanite woman to help you have a persistent faith. Join with the priest in saying: "Grant all Your Christians, O Lord, an understanding of the faith they profess, and a deep love of the heavenly sacrament they receive" (Prayer over the People).

Friday after the First Sunday of Lent (Ember Friday)

THEME

I haven't anyone but You, Lord.

EXPOSITION

In the Gospel the sick man is the epitome of helplessness. For 38 years he had been crippled, and for most of them he had been waiting for a cure. But there was no one to get him to the pool on time. Christ was there, but the sick man did not recognize Him. Christ said: "Stand up, pick up your mat and walk." Immediately the man was healed. Christ acted swiftly—so swiftly that the man never even knew Our Lord's name.

The cured man still had to learn the fuller meaning of Christ's act. Our Lord does not do things halfway; He found the man and cured His spiritual sickness. "No more sinning for fear that something worse happen to you."

How often have we said in times of difficulty: "I haven't anyone"? That's not true. We have Christ to show us the way to perfect health of soul and body, to lead us through all our difficulties. He is the way, the truth, and the life. If we follow Him, we will always have someone to help us over the rough spots.

Don't take Christ for granted though, because no one likes that. Listen to His words: "No more sinning," and obey them. Jesus is no "pushover." He means what He says about not sinning any more, so let's not play any games with Him.

Vatican II has said: "The life of the Church grows through persistent participation in the Eucharistic mystery." Our life in Christ must grow in the same way. Lord, make it grow through this and every Eucharistic celebration! Teach us that we do now and always have Someone who cares.

Saturday after the First Sunday of Lent (Ember Saturday)

THEME

The transfigured Christ calls us to come to the joy of the Resurrection through the self-denial of Lent.

EXPOSITION

Today we stand looking forward to the second week of Lent and the rest of this holy season. On this Ember Saturday we must look both forward and backward before we go further into Lent. We must look back to see how we have done in the last three months. We must look forward to see where we are going.

Moses reminds us in the first reading that we, like the Israelites, are God's people. We must obey His commandments. Paul tells us how to live as God's people. In the

Gospel we have the story of the transfiguration. Christ takes His three chosen apostles to the top of the mountain and there is transfigured before them.

Why at this time of the year should we have this Gospel? The Church arranges to have this Gospel passage read today and tomorrow for the same reason that Christ allowed the transfiguration to happen originally. By His transfiguration —this slight glimpse of His divine glory—He wanted to strengthen his apostles for the horrors of His rejection and failure. The Church attempts to reassure us in the same way.

APPLICATION

It is good to have Moses remind us who we are. It is better to have Paul show us how to live as God's chosen people. It is best of all to have Christ transfigured before us. This Lent is a period of renewal of our baptismal dedication to God— renewal of all the wonderful desires that have ever welled up in our hearts to love and serve Christ.

At Mass today the transfigured Christ calls us to come through this period of self-denial to the glory of the Resurrection. Like St. Peter, the words should slip from our lips: "Lord it is good that we are here." As you come down from the mountain of the Mass to your daily tasks, ponder carefully these words: "Tell the vision to everyone so that everything done during Lent will be motivated by the vision of the glorious Christ of Easter."

Monday after the Second Sunday of Lent

THEME

When we present our petitions, we rely not on our own merits but on Christ—God's great mercy in the flesh.

In the Gospel Christ tries to tell the crowds His identity and His mission. He lets them know that He does not do His own will but that of Him Who sent Him. These people do not understand Him because they do not want to understand. They ask Him repeatedly: "Who are You?" When He answers their question, they are deaf to His message.

Only then does Christ describe the chasm which separates Him from His listeners: "You belong to what is below; I belong to what is above. You belong to this world—this world to which I do not belong." There is only one way for the Jews to be saved: "Unless you come to believe that I am what I am, you will surely die in your sins."

APPLICATION

We, too, have listened to the words of Christ. Will we do better than the crowds to whom He spoke? Yes, we will if we realize who He is and what His mission is. "Christ is the bridge over the chasm separating us from the Father" (St. Catherine of Siena). He is the one who has come to save us from our sins. He is the revelation of God's mercy to sinners. Christ Himself is God's great mercy in the flesh.

At Mass today give yourself completely to Christ. Seek to follow His example and to do the will of God. Some persons are afraid of bridges; but no one need fear Christ, our bridge. He is the one completely secure link to the Father. Let's stay close to Christ. If we can do this we will not die in our sins but rather live in His love for all eternity.

THEME II

Lord, help me not to die in my sins but to follow You to the Cross and beyond.

Tuesday after the Second Sunday of Lent

THEME

Christ is a Man who can say: "I do what I say and you must do likewise."

EXPOSITION

Today's Gospel story is the introduction to that part of Matthew's Gospel where Christ curses the Scribes and Pharisees. These men were the successors of Moses and must be obeyed. However, no one should be fooled. It was another case of "Doing what they say . . . not what they do."

Everything they did was for show. Christ told the disciples that they should obey the Scribes and Pharisees because they were the successors of Moses. Yet Christ was greater than Moses. He not only tells us what to do but shows us how to do it by His actions.

APPLICATION

It is easy to fall into the trap that the Scribes and Pharisees fell into—to become so occupied in telling others what to do that we do nothing ourselves. They sought the appearance of holiness and neglected the real thing. The fight against such tendencies is never ending.

Every Christian must ask himself: "Am I a phony Christian or the real thing?" It's a loaded question—loaded with great significance for Lent and afterward. Let's answer it truthfully and fully. We must continually plead with God as we did in the Entrance Prayer: "Teach us our duties and assist us with Your grace to perform them."

God will grant your petition if you offer this sacrifice in

such a way that you can say: "To You my heart speaks, You my glance seeks."

THEME II

The first lesson highlights two basic Lenten virtues—alms-giving and love of neighbor manifested to a stranger.

Wednesday after the Second Sunday of Lent

THEME

We serve a Master Who taught by work and example the glory of suffering and of service to others.

EXPOSITION

Once again Christ predicts His betrayal, passion, death, and Resurrection. The mother of John and James asks a favor of Christ. He wants to know if they are willing to drink of the same cup of suffering as He. They vow their readiness to suffer with Christ.

Christ did not want to lessen the importance of suffering, but He did want to teach these men and the other disciples a vitally necessary lesson. He sought to give them a balanced picture of the value of suffering and of humble service to others: "The Son of Man has come not to be served but to serve and to give His life as ransom for the rest of men."

APPLICATION

Service to others—called by some the ministry of service—is a constant theme of Vatican II and a basic element of Christianity. Christ is our leader. We have promised faithfully at our baptism to follow Him.

Let us say to Him at this Mass: "Lord, teach us as You

294

taught the apostles the value of serving others and suffering
for Your sake." "Turn the hearts of your people toward
Yourself. Set them on fire with Your Spirit that they may be
firm in faith and zealous in good works" (Prayer over the
People).

Thursday after the Second Sunday of Lent

THEME

The fundamental Christian attitude must be to prefer eternal
happiness to the pleasures of the passing moment.

EXPOSITION

In the story of the rich man and Lazarus we have the personi-
fication of all the world's "haves" and "have-nots." The rich
man is not condemned because he was downright cruel to the
beggar at his door; he is damned because he was completely
indifferent to a fellow-human being. Wealth and the creature
comforts it bought blinded him to anything but his own
pleasure. He paid for such indulgence after death.

Lazarus experienced just the opposite fate. He was abjectly
poor on earth but accepted his lot and gained heaven. The
disparity between the main characters in today's Gospel while
they were alive was nothing compared to the great abyss
which separated them after their final judgment.

APPLICATION

"More tortuous than all else is the human heart." We believe
only what we want to believe. Christ has given us a story
with a moral so clear that it should curl the hair on our
heads, if any still remains there. But we are completely im-

295

pervious to its meaning and go blithely on our way mortgaging our future happiness at every turn for some present pleasure.

"If they do not listen to Moses and the Prophets, they will not be convinced even if one rises from the dead." If we do not listen to Christ as He speaks to us through this Mass, we will not be convinced even when He rises from the dead on Easter morning. Learn now during this second week of Lent that the fundamental Christian attitude is to prefer eternal happiness to any pleasure of the passing moment. Do you not think that eternal happiness is worth any sacrifice?

Friday after the Second Sunday of Lent

THEME

How long do we lease God's property without making a suitable return?

EXPOSITION

Jesus told the story in this morning's Gospel about a man who built a vineyard, leased it out and sought some return on his efforts. He sent his servants and finally his own son to collect the rents. We know the ending—not only were his servants killed, but his son was killed also. Finally he had to destroy the killers and take the vineyard away from them. He gave it to other people who would use it and pay him what he wanted for it.

APPLICATION

We are the chosen ones of Almighty God—chosen by Him to use our bodies, our abilities and our talents for His greater glory and honor. He is a patient God, but He is a just God also. He demands a suitable return on His investment. He has invested His love in us. Jesus, His Son, has saved us from our sins.

How long are we to use God's gifts without a suitable return? Begin now at this Mass to thank Him for everything that you are and have. Use this Mass as an opportunity to dedicate yourselves to a better use of your gifts.

In doing this, you may very well expose yourselves to the envy and jealousy of other people. Joseph and Jesus had to suffer such a fate. From their example learn courage; learn that God can make even envy and jealousy work to His own good. If you are the object of such envy and jealousy, do not be overcome by the evil but overcome it by your loving union with Christ.

Saturday after the Second Sunday of Lent

THEME

The sheer magnitude of God's love for us should leave us breathless in adoration.

EXPOSITION

There is little time for a homily today so we will limit ourselves to a few observations. In the first reading the craftiness and lies are neither condoned nor rewarded. Jacob was to suffer severely later on because of his deception. His own children were to be divided among themselves by lies and jealousy.

The chief lesson we learn is that God always achieves His purpose. God brought good out of evil while still being unalterably opposed to that evil. In the Gospel Christ tells us of the sheer magnitude of the Father's love for His children. No matter what our sins have been, if we turn to God our Father in sorrow and humility, He forgives us.

APPLICATION

The love of God the Father is showered on us each day in many ways. And yet no matter how alert we are, we can only catch glimpses of how much we are loved. At Mass we come closest to this divine love at its source. Try harder today to glimpse how much God loves you.

Once you have grasped this reality, even in an imperfect way, you will be amazed at what a treasure of love you have in this Eucharistic celebration. The sheer magnitude of God's love should leave us breathless in adoration. Why are we so slow to accept and to appreciate His love?

Monday after the Third Sunday of Lent

THEME

Some desire God's gift and are willing to accept it where, when, and how He gives it.

EXPOSITION

In the first reading Naaman almost missed his cure because he wanted things done his own way. He was saved from his hard-headed approach by his servants who showed him the way to faith in the prophet's words. They urged him to do exactly what he was told. Naaman finally humbled himself enough to accept God's gift of a cure when, where, and how He gave it.

In the second reading Christ worked none of the miracles that His neighbors wanted because they did not believe in Him or His mission. He did work one miracle for them—He prevented them from destroying their one claim to fame—Himself. These neighbors of Christ had God's gift in their midst but they were too blinded by jealousy to accept it. They lacked the humility necessary for a 20-20 spiritual vision.

APPLICATION

Do we have the necessary humility to believe in Christ? Most of use would quickly respond "yes" to that question. Certainly we believe in Him. Why else would we be here at Mass? That's a good question. There are many reasons why people come to Mass, some better than others.

Let's try to have the best possible reason—a desire to participate as alert and active Christians in Christ's sacrifice and to seek God's gift of Himself in Communion. Let us be humble enough to admit that we have a long way to go before we really appreciate the Mass. Now that most of the Mass, and especially the Canon, is in English, we must try harder to deepen our appreciation of God's gift among us—His Son in this sacrifice. If we really desire God's gift of His Son, we will be ready to accept it where, when, and how He gives it.

THEME II

Our rejection of Christ is a greater wrong than that of His neighbors.

EXPOSITION

Christ's neighbors were blinded by jealousy of "that boy down the street who thinks that He's too good for His own home town." Their rejection of Christ was wrong but understandable. They had known Him too well as just another human being to think that He could be the Messiah.

299

We don't have that excuse. We have known that Christ is God. Our greater distance from these events should have given us a better perspective from which to judge Christ and His claims. We know His miracles, His holiness of life, His teachings and the astonishing fact of His Resurrection from the dead.

If we reject Him, our is a greater, a far greater wrong than that of His neighbors. If we have in any way rejected Him, let us express our sorrow during this sacrifice. As we prepare to feast with Him and upon Him during this banquet, let us ask for the grace to believe as we should. God will surely grant us that grace.

Tuesday after the Third Sunday of Lent

THEME

Each day in Lent we should grow closer to Christ's ideal of inexhaustible forgiveness toward our neighbor.

EXPOSITION

Christ demands almost superhuman effort at loving and forgiving our neighbor. Peter probably thought that he was being exceptionally holy and generous in offering to forgive his brother seven times. Can you imagine his reaction when Christ replied: "No, not seven times; I say seventy times seven?" What Christ meant should be perfectly clear. His followers must be willing to forgive without any limitation whatsoever.

Have you ever asked yourself the question: "Is following Christ worth it all?" It would be easier to follow another religious leader—even one who would command us to recline on a bed of nails or meditate while standing on our heads. Isn't it almost impossible to do what Christ wants—to forgive inexhaustibly? Yes, it is *almost* impossible but it is not *completely* impossible.

With God's help we can make a good attempt at forgiving and with a better than average chance of success. With His help, we can even love the gossip next door or in the next office, the so-called "friend" who carries tales and delights in our misfortunes; the friend or relative that has turned on us because of some petty misunderstanding.

Through this Mass and Communion find the strength to live the ideal which Christ sets before you. Each day during this Lent try to grow closer to Christ's ideal of inexhaustible forgiveness toward your neighbor. Forgiving comes more easily to one who loves like Christ. It will never be as easy as eating apple pie and ice cream, but it will be easier than hanging on a Cross.

Wednesday after the Third Sunday of Lent

THEME

During this time of renewal we should strive for greater sincerity in our Christ-life.

EXPOSITION

In the running battle which Christ waged against the Scribes and Pharisees, today's confrontation ranks as one of high drama. His response to their question is devastating and sets their traditions in their proper perspective. His words: "You hypocrites" and His quotation from the prophet Isaiah not only scandalized them but fairly demolished their pretensions. Their worship was external and lacked sincerity, while Christ preached an internal whole-hearted response to God's love. Between these two positions there could be no middle ground. Between these two camps there could be no peace.

APPLICATION

There are traces of Pharisaism and legalistic thinking in all of us at times. Some of us do more than the law commands, such as attending daily Mass, but do we think that we are better than the others who do not? Do we despise those who are not here at Mass each day? They may have sound family, business, or health reasons which prevent their coming. Let's not despise anyone. Let's pray for those who want to be here but cannot make it.

Some of us believe that the number of our prayers will save us. How Christ's Heart must ache for such persons. Don't they know that He does not consider the poundage of our prayers, but their sincerity?

During this time of renewal—for that is what Lent is—let us examine the sincerity with which we perform our religious duties. Seek in this sacrificial encounter with Christ to learn the sincerity which He demands from His friends and disciples.

Thursday after the Third Sunday of Lent

THEME

Christ's love for the poor and the infirm is not a sterile, verbal emotion but a tender loving concern for them in their need.

EXPOSITION

The words of the Entrance Prayer certainly characterized Christ's actions in this morning's Gospel. "I am the salvation of the people," says the Lord. "From whatever tribulation they shall cry to Me, I will hear them; and I will be their Lord forever." Christ sternly drove the fever from Simon's mother-in-law. He rebuked the devils and drove them from the persons they had possessed.

His harshness was reserved, as we can see, for the demons and for man's ills. For his fellowman he showed a tender loving concern. He did not specialize in great group miracles. He gave each individual case special treatment and attention. He was interested in every human being as a person.

APPLICATION

The station-church for today is that of Sts. Cosmas and Damian, who were physician-martyrs. They caught the message of Christ contained in this morning's Gospel. They loved all their patients and even their persecutors as Christ had loved His.

We must love as Christ did. We must strive for the virtues of tenderness, kindness and concern for our neighbor. These are the great virtues of a community. These are the qualities that build a community and sustain it in time of need. As we gather here around the altar, we should and must be a Christian community at prayer. Let us ask Almighty God to help us to be community-minded members of Christ's Church.

Friday after the Third Sunday of Lent

"We have heard for ourselves and we know that this is really the Savior of the world."

Did you notice in this morning's Gospel Christ's great patience in dealing with the woman at the well? He attempted to lead her to an acknowledgment of her sins and from there to belief in Him and His mission. This is a perfect example of His approach to sinners. With the woman at the well, He succeeded more by His gentleness and kindness than by His intellectual brilliance. No one denies that His logic and argumentation was good. We just maintain that His gentleness and kindness were infinitely better.

This woman convinced many of her neighbors to come and see Christ. She led them to Him and they began to believe in Him because of her. When they had heard Christ for a few days, they believed even more that "this is really the Savior of the world."

There are two lessons we should draw from this incident. The first is the absolutely unshakable conviction that Christ is gentleness and kindness personified to every sinner who repents. Secondly, we can say with the townspeople, "We have heard for ourselves and we know that this is really the

Savior of the world." Our faith comes through hearing about Christ from others. We in turn have to pass on the good news to others.

At this family gathering of Christians, let us learn once again how kind and gentle Christ is to everyone. Let us offer thanks to the Lord for those who instructed us in the faith. Let us ask Christ through this Mass and Communion to help us lead many others to believe in Him.

Saturday after the Third Sunday of Lent

THEME

"Nor will I condemn you. From now on, stop sinning."

EXPOSITION

Needless to say, Christ did not approve of the woman's adultery. He simply rebelled at the hypocrisy of the people who accused her. His reaction was magnificent in its simplicity, and complete in its exposure of their hypocrisy. "Let the first of you to throw a stone at her be the man who has no sin." Needless to say, no stones were thrown.

APPLICATION

None of us may have violated the marriage contract as the woman in the Gospel did. Few of us, however, can say that we have faithfully observed the terms of our covenant relationship with God which was established at baptism. By that sacrament we were joined more completely to Christ and His Church than any man and woman are by their marriage vows.

When we violate our baptismal covenant or agreement with Christ, we are worse than adulterers. Thank God we can put aside all pretense and admit that we have sinned. Isn't it wonderful to realize that Christ's words are applicable to us as they were to the woman? "Nor will I condemn you. From now on, stop sinning."

In the intimacy of the union which we experience with Christ and His members at this sacrifice-banquet, let us admit our repeated violations of our covenant with God. Let us humbly ask for the power to obey Christ's words: "From now on, stop sinning!"

Monday after the Fourth Sunday of Lent

THEME

A Christian must respect the person of God within himself and within his neighbor.

EXPOSITION

The temple was the dwelling place of God. The things that were being sold in the temple were not for any profane use. They were to be used in the sacrifices of the temple and were the necessary items for the worship which the Jewish people gave to God. Our Lord reacted so strongly because selling and buying in the temple was an affront to Almighty God no matter what was sold or bought. Our Lord was insulted and angered by the lack of respect which this custom evidenced. He reacted strongly to this affront to the majesty and honor of God.

APPLICATION

Does this story have any application to us? I would suggest this one application. God dwells within us and within every human being. He dwells in a special way in every Christian since by baptism we were made temples of the Holy Spirit. Thus it should be clear that we must treat ourselves and others as the dwelling places of Almighty God.

Ask the Eucharistic Lord through this sacrifice to give you great respect and reverence for God Who dwells in you and in your neighbor. If you can spend these next three weeks striving to fulfill the theme of this morning's Mass—reverence for God Who dwells in you and in others, you will have prepared well for Easter.

Tuesday after the Fourth Sunday of Lent

THEME

The effort to know Christ is a never-ending one.

EXPOSITION

This morning's Gospel is indeed a complicated piece of work. The first and the second parts deal with the questions: "Who is Christ?" "Where does His learning come from?" The middle section discusses an attempt by the Pharisees to kill Him.

If we concentrate on the first and third parts, we realize that Christ certainly knew more than an ordinary human being. He possessed human and divine knowledge. The Pharisees and Scribes were satisfied with a superficial knowledge of Who Christ was and where He got His learning. The ordinary people of His day were not. They sought for deeper meanings, and we also have to probe more deeply into the reality which is Christ.

307

It is simple to say that Christ is God and man, that He has both divine and human knowledge. But these statements do not exhaust the reality of Christ. If we spent all our life studying Christ and trying to imitate Him, we would never come to the end of our quest.

One of the best ways we have of knowing and loving Christ is the Mass. That is why the closeness to Christ which we share through the Mass is so important. It is wonderful that you are here. Please make every effort to take advantage of the richness, the knowledge, and the love of Christ which is available to you through this sacrifice.

Wednesday after the Fourth Sunday of Lent

THEME

Today is a day to examine our faith and see how we are living it.

EXPOSITION

Wednesday in the fourth week of Lent was the day on which the ancient Church examined those preparing to be baptized to see how well they had learned the truths of the Faith. It is a day even now when baptism figures very much in the Mass. If you think back over the three readings of this Mass, you will see how a washing or a cleansing with water stands out quite prominently.

APPLICATION

Today let us scrutinize our own allegiance to Christ. Exactly how have we lived out the implications of our baptismal

308

promises? Is it too much to ask that this Mass become the occasion for a deep probing of our commitment to Christ? Here at Mass we have an opportunity to renew our act of faith in Christ and in His Church.

The three lessons should remind us that the waters of baptism have cleansed us and have given us a new spirit. This spirit teaches us, as it did the blind man in the Gospel, to get to the core of the matter. It helps us to see that Christ is the prophet and the Messiah. He is our salvation. If we follow this spirit, we will be able to say, "I do believe, Lord" and pay homage to Christ during this Mass.

Thursday after the Fourth Sunday of Lent

THEME

Christ always makes the difference.

EXPOSITION

The theme of today's Mass is the restoration of life. The first reading shows us how the prophet Elijah had to work so hard in restoring the boy to life. In the Gospel God's almighty power accomplishes the same thing with just a few words: "Young man, I bid you rise up."

In both instances, physical life is restored to the dead by the power of Almighty God. The stories differ only as regards the ease and facility with which the restoration is accomplished. Do not ask: "What is the difference?" but, "Who is the difference?" Christ is the difference between the two accounts. He always makes the difference.

309

At Mass today we have Christ Who can restore the life of the body, and, what is even more important, the life of the soul. If we are lucky enough to be living a full and active life with Christ, let us use this opportunity to thank Him for His care and guidance. If our life with Christ is not what it should be, now is the time to do something about it. It's never too late or too early to grow more Christlike.

Pray also at this Mass for those souls who are dead to Christ's life. Ask Him to restore His divine life in them as He once restored the life of the widow's son.

Friday after the Fourth Sunday of Lent

THEME

Christ's way is the best way for us.

EXPOSITION

Today's account contains so many wonderful insights into Christ and His relationship with Lazarus, Mary and Martha that we could never mention all of them. We will consider only one aspect of the story. Notice how truly Christ loved Lazarus, and yet He did not do the obvious thing. He procrastinated until it was too late, or so it seemed. He chose the time and circumstances for His miracle with great care.

APPLICATION

Christ loves us just as truly and as deeply as He loved Lazarus, Mary and Martha. His love is an effective love. It helps us and guides us, and yet it does not do the obvious thing. We have to believe in His love and allow Him to work out our destiny. He will use the best approach today with us as He did with Lazarus so long ago.

Christ's plan for our salvation may not be the one we think best. In fact, it probably will seem completely inadequate to us, but if we believe in Him, we will follow His plan. His way is always the best way for us.

Perhaps the words at the end of this morning's Gospel may help us. "Many of the Jews put their faith in Him" because of what He had done. Believe in Christ because of what He has done for Lazarus and all of us. At this Mass express that belief. Let Him know that you realize how deeply He loves you. Let Him know that you accept His plan for you with all its circumstances. Tell Him once again that His way is the best way for you.

Saturday after the Fourth Sunday of Lent

THEME

Christ, the light of the world, lights our way through the darkness of the next two weeks to the glory of Easter.

EXPOSITION

Christ's words to the crowds of the Jews, "I am the light of the world," set before us the theme which is very prominent in St. John's Gospel. He stresses the contrast between light and darkness, between good and evil, between Christ and the powers that oppose Him. To this theme of light St. John also adds one of unity. Christ and the Father are one, and the Father gives testimony to what Christ says and proves that it is true.

APPLICATION

In the Communion Hymn we will pray: "The Lord is my shepherd, I shall not want. In verdant pastures He gives me repose, beside restful waters He leads me." The Lord is our true shepherd. He, as our light, will guide us through the darkness of the next two weeks to the glorious feast of Easter. During this time we must be condemned with Christ, suffer and die with Him in order to rise with Him. Our position must be close to Jesus to the last and after.

Offer your Mass today so that you will stay close to Him. Ask Him for the strength and grace that you need to walk shoulder to shoulder with Him through His sufferings, passion and death to the glorious feast of Easter. After Easter, you must and will stay close to Christ because you will never want to walk in darkness again once you have enjoyed the light of Christ.

Monday after First Passion Sunday

THEME

Are you willing to gamble on a second chance to repent?

EXPOSITION

The people of the city of Nineveh believed the work of God and acted upon it. They proclaimed a fast and all of them, great and small, put on sackcloth. Even the king did penance for his sins.

They realized that God would forgive and hold back His blazing wrath once He saw that they had turned from their evil ways. Their sorrow and acts of mortification were sincere and effective. They were not play-acting in any way. God had given them a chance to repent and to make amends. They weren't going to miss the opportunity.

APPLICATION

Yesterday Christ told us in the Gospel that those who belong to God hear and keep His word. The Jewish people and the Pharisees were not able to find Christ when they wanted Him because of the hardness of their hearts. If we do not want to suffer the same frustration, then we not only have to hear the word of God but keep it. Like the Ninevites we must do penance for our evil ways.

We begin Passion Week on a note of sorrow for our sinful ways. If our thirst for Christ is big enough, we will find the way to come to Him. He will help to give us the strength to give up our evil habits. Are we ready to follow the Ninevites or will we wait for the next time around? There may never be a "next time around." I myself am not gambler enough to go against odds like that. Are you?

Tuesday after First Passion Sunday

THEME

Jesus, refusing to seek His own glory, lives and dies for the glory of the Father.

EXPOSITION

In the first lesson we see that the world, represented by the enemies of Daniel, hates him and tries to destroy him. But Daniel is not destroyed. God's glory shows forth in his miraculous escape from the lions while his enemies are destroyed. Daniel in the lions' den is an image of Christ, the suffering servant of God.

Jesus says in the Gospel that the world hates Him. Why? Because He is not of the world. If the world hated Christ, it will hate His followers also. Our Lord refused to adore the devil, the world or His own honor and glory. He lived and died for the glory of the Father.

APPLICATION

In our lives as Christians we must be prepared to suffer hatred and persecution. We will never really be popular with everyone. In fact, it is quite possible that we may be unpopular with most people because our lives contradict their way of life.

We must be courageous enough to speak about Christ openly, and to live our Christ-lives courageously. Notice that all the prayers of the Mass refer to the acquisition of eternal life. During Mass today turn your gaze to what really counts, your eternal life. In order to gain it, you should be willing to suffer whatever hatred and persecution the world can fling at you. Don't be deceived. It will be the hardest fight you ever entered, so keep in condition.

Wednesday after First Passion Sunday

THEME

Baptism makes us sheep in Christ's flock.

When the Pharisees asked Christ to tell them in plain words if He was the Messiah, He set them straight. He had told them repeatedly, and yet they did not believe because they were not his sheep. Our Lord also said that "the Father and I are one. . . . The Father is in Me, and I am in the Father."

APPLICATION

We are Christ's sheep. Do we hear His voice speaking to us today in the Gospel and through the other parts of this Mass? Do we realize that Christ speaks to us through His Church, through our daily lives, and by means of our consciences? Let us listen a little more carefully at Mass today and try to catch His voice.

As we go through the day, Christ will speak to us often and in many different ways. Let's not miss His voice because we think that He speaks to us only in church. He is where we are because He is in us and works through us. Think about that for a while and see if it does not change your outlook on life!

Our chief task in life is to be one with Christ and the Father; to live in them and let them live in us. The Eucharist can help us mightily in this endeavor. Make the best possible use of this Eucharistic sacrament and sacrifice to live in Christ and in the Father.

Thursday after First Passion Sunday

THEME
How to welcome Christ to our souls.

EXPOSITION

Today's story shows us how to welcome Christ. There is the Pharisees' way and the way of the sinful woman. The Pharisee gave Christ just the barest essentials of politeness. The sinful woman's greeting to Christ overflowed with sincere love. She is a model penitent. She had faith in God's mercy which gave her courage to approach Christ. She had sorrow which caused her to weep for her sins. Finally and most important of all she had love for God.

APPLICATION

Why is it that most of us think we are so good? We are proud and bullheaded, we lie and cheat, we gossip and ruin another's reputation, but all the while we appear so holy. That approach hasn't gotten us anywhere, has it? Of course not!

God hates insincerity and hypocrisy. We have tried the Pharisee's way and it has not worked. Why not try the other way? The sinful woman became a model penitent. Isn't it about time we joined her?

Friday after First Passion Sunday

THEME

Are we as blind as the Pharisees?

EXPOSITION

The chief priests and Pharisees did everything but the right thing. They refused even to think that Christ is Who He claimed to be—the Messiah, the Son of God. They were blind, and they did not know it. As St. Augustine says in his commentary on St. John, the Jews were so fearful of losing their temporal positions that they ignored the things of eternity. In doing this, they lost both.

Just a week before Good Friday, the Church reminds us that Christ died to save all of us from our sins. He died for all of us no matter where we are scattered throughout the world.

APPLICATION

Are we as blind as the chief priests and the Pharisees were? I don't mean in theory but in practice. We are very good in the theory department. We admit Who Christ is and what He did for us. The way we act often tells a different story. We act as if Christ had never come and saved us from sin. He died to restore us to a loving union with God, our Father. The only way His death can be cheated of achieving its goal is if we refuse to love God.

The Pharisees refused to love God because they were so fearful of losing their wealth and position. The same misfortune can happen to us if we become overly-attached to the wrong things. Is that happening to us? Let's not wait until we are as blind as the Pharisees were—because that will be too late! There is still time to straighten out our lives during this Lent. Don't waste it!

Saturday after First Passion Sunday

THEME

"Look, the world has run off after Him."

EXPOSITION

The attitude of the chief priests towards Lazarus is almost laughable. What a desperate and futile gesture it would have been to kill him. If Christ could bring Lazarus back from death once, He could do it again. He is the Lord of life. Yet He does not hold on to His life but willingly surrenders it in accordance with His Father's plan. He is the grain of wheat that dies and brings forth much fruit.

APPLICATION

The Pharisees were wrong in their attitude toward Lazarus. They were also wrong when they said, "Look, the world has run off after Him." It was not true then, as Good Friday showed. It is not true now. The world thinks that it can get along without Christ, and it can for a time. However, we can help in some small way to bring the world back to Christ and Christ to it. We must die to self if we are to accomplish such a purpose.

People believed in Christ because of Lazarus. What effect do we have on the people who know us? Do they come closer to Christ because of us or do they revolt at how we so-called "good Christians" speak and act? That is a good question to ask yourself during Holy Week, and the answer could make or break this Lent for you!

Monday of Holy Week

THEME

Christ and His Friends.

EXPOSITION

As we begin this holiest week of the year, we see Christ surrounded by His friends. Lazarus, living proof that Christ is Master of both life and death, was grateful for His new lease on life, and recognized His complete dependence on the Lord for its continuance. Martha was eager to serve Christ and provide for His every need. Mary, impulsive and filled with a great love, anointed Him for his burial. Judas objected strenuously to Mary's extravagance, but not for the charitable reason he gave. He wanted the money for his own use. He had been a friend, but lately the desire for money had begun to undermine the true friendship that he had with Christ.

APPLICATION

Love is shown by action. That sentiment has been repeated so often and in so many ways that it may no longer have any impact on us. There can be no doubt about its validity, however. Christ's friends proved their love for Christ by their actions. Judas was no longer one of that group. His actions and words showed only contempt for Christ's intelligence and common sense. Judas had been a true friend of Christ but he allowed their relationship to be destroyed by greed.

Our friendship with Christ is the real thing, I hope, but it cannot be ignored. It must not be subordinated to anything else, or it will die. Christ doesn't take any of us for granted. Let us not take Him and His friendship for granted either.

We need contact with Christ daily at Mass, in the sacraments and through our prayers. We must walk with Christ and see Him in our neighbors. Our friendship for Christ must be shown by our actions, for that is the way love speaks to the loved one. Speak to Him "loud and clear" this week!

319

Tuesday of Holy Week

Because of the reading of the Passion, I suggest that a short introduction to the Passion be given, stressing how Mark is so concise and realistic in his description. He highlights certain points such as the hatred of the Jewish leaders for Christ; the cowardice of the Apostles, especially Peter; the serenity of Jesus during all His sufferings; and the centurion's profession of faith.

If possible, the Passion should be read by three persons. I have done it with college students and also with eighth grade boys. Either way, it was impressive and relieved the boredom of such a long reading. The eighth grade boys were commentators for the school's First Friday Mass so they had some experience. Nonetheless they were not so exceptional that equally qualified students could not be found in almost any school. Such boys should be good readers who are not afraid to speak out. They should receive at least a modicum of practice in church.

Wednesday of Holy Week

(Once again we urge the three-part reading of the Passion and just a slight introduction to each of the three readings.)

The First Reading: The Prophet Isaiah shows us the loneliness of the Man of God, the sense of abandonment that He will feel. *The Second Reading:* The Prophet Isaiah gives us the Passion of the Old Testament, the description in prophecy of what Our Lord would suffer. Here we see the Man for

Others who takes upon Himself the sins of the people and atones for them.

The Third Reading: The Passion: Today we hear the Passion according to St. Luke which stresses Christ's mercy and forgiveness. Notice the mercy of Christ toward the slave whose ear was cut off; toward Peter who denied Him and received only a tender look of reproach; toward the good thief who was given Paradise; toward those who crucified Him.

Notice also the dignified silence of Christ throughout all of His sufferings and His passion; throughout the interrogations by the Chief Priests, by Herod and by Pilate. His actions spoke to everyone more forcefully and lovingly than any words He might have used.

During this Mass do your best to enter into the spirit of Christ, and try to realize the depths of His mercy. Anchor yourself to Christ with the firm conviction that He will always be merciful!

Holy Thursday

THEME

Today we honor the super-abundant generosity of God.

EXPOSITION

Today we thank Christ for the Eucharist, the priesthood and His example of charity in action. When we speak of the Eucharist, we must realize that it is a sacrament, a sacrifice and a presence.

The Eucharist is a sacrament. At the Last Supper Christ took bread and wine and pronounced the words we know so well. Immediately the bread and wine became His Body and Blood—the sacrament of the Eucharist which we receive in Communion.

The Eucharist is a sacrifice. Christ linked the Last Supper and the Crucifixion on Calvary so closely that every time the Mass is offered, the great sacrifice that took place on the first Good Friday is re-enacted.

Finally, *Christ gave us a presence*—His own person in the Blessed Sacrament. After this Mass we will march in procession with the Blessed Sacrament and then place it on the altar of reposition. Today, and tomorrow until the afternoon service, there will be people from the parish here adoring the presence of Christ in the Blessed Sacrament.

We also commemorate today the institution of the priesthood. Christ ordained the twelve Apostles so that they might teach, sanctify and rule His people.

Finally, when Christ washed the disciples' feet, He said to them and He says to us: "I have given you an example that as I have done, you also should do." Christ had told us that we must love our neighbor. Now He shows us how to do it.

APPLICATION

How are we to thank Christ the Lord for all these gifts? We can never hope to thank Him fully. The most we can do is to single out the greatest gift—the Eucharist—and try to express our appreciation concretely. We should grow in knowledge and in love of the Eucharist. How? Each of us must try even harder to comprehend the reality of the Eucharist by going to Mass more often, by more actively participating in it, by reading and studying about it.

Let's not take the Eucharist for granted. There is much that we do not know about it. We should read about it, perhaps starting with an article in a religious magazine. Let's not go out and buy eight or nine books and magazines. If we begin slowly and work at it consistently, we will make greater headway. When we have read something, let us think about it, pray over it and make it our own. We can then use our new outlook to offer the Mass better.

Some people say that they do not like the new Mass. This

very vocal minority does not realize that the changes which have been made in the Mass have brought us closer to the original. We can now see that the Eucharist is the sacrifice of Calvary, the repetition of the Last Supper, and the presence of Christ among us.

Today at Mass let us offer our hearts to Christ in return for all His gifts, and promise Him that we will grow in our understanding and love for the Eucharist. On Holy Thursday of all days we should make the greatest possible effort to mean what we say.

Good Friday

THEME

Our place at the foot of the Cross.

EXPOSITION

There is no Mass today but there is a beautiful four-part service. As you know, the first part contained the readings, and especially the Passion according to St. John. In the first Lesson God told us that He desires sincere, heartfelt penance, while in the second reading we were reminded that Good Friday is related to the ancient Passover of the Jews, our spiritual ancestors. In the Passion Christ proves Himself to be King and Master of His own fate. We also observe Mary's place in His sufferings and how the prophecies of the Old Testament are fulfilled.

Next we have the solemn prayers for the Church, the Pope, the faithful and for all classes of people. When the celebrant says "Let us pray," during these prayers, he means just that. Everyone here in church should pray for the intentions of the Church.

323

In the third part the Cross is venerated. The celebrant proclaims "Behold the wood of the Cross on which has hung the salvation of the world." We adore Christ and as a pledge of our love and in gratitude for His sufferings we kiss the Cross. Our kiss is not a Judas kiss, but a sincere declaration that His sufferings were not in vain.

Finally in the fourth part, we have the Communion service. The "Our Father" and the "I confess" serve as our preparation for Communion. We receive our Lord's Body and Blood which He sacrificed for us on that first Good Friday.

APPLICATION

Throughout this service and this day we should express many things—appreciation for what Christ did, sorrow for ignoring His Cross in the past, and determination to make better use of the graces He gained for us. In His sufferings, passion and death, Christ knew and loved each one of us as an individual, as a special someone. We were not just a face in the crowd or a number on a computer card.

During the remaining hours of Good Friday, seek to return Christ's love. Give Him your own warm personal love in return for His. In that way His Cross will become a sign of victory, not of defeat.

The Easter Vigil Service and the Masses on Easter morning

Each Mass, whether the Vigil Mass or one of the Masses on Easter morning should be linked most definitely with the Easter Vigil service. Three things should stand out quite prominently in the sermon. The Paschal Candle signifies for all the light of the risen Christ in the world. The blessing of the baptismal water should remind us of the graces of our

baptism. This can be brought out quite clearly by the renewal of baptismal vows.

Each person who offers Mass on Easter should have the
oportunity to renew his or her baptismal vows. This could
easily be the conclusion of the sermon. Finally the Eucharist
must be explained as the means by which we take our special
part in the banquet prepared for the baptized.

Easter Monday

THEME

Do we recognize Christ in the breaking of the bread at Mass?

EXPOSITION

The Masses of Easter Week complete the initiation of the
newly baptized. Peter, in the first lesson, preaches to the Gentiles and to us about Christ's mission and death, His Resurrection and its proofs.

In the Gospel Christ appears to the disciples on the road to
Emmaus. Christ's death was so real to them. His Resurrection
was not. They had heard rumors of His Resurrection. They
wanted to believe, but found it almost impossible. Christ
Himself had to show them why He underwent suffering and
death in order to enter into His kingdom.

What a Scripture lesson He gave those disciples! If only we
could have been there! They recognized Christ in the breaking of the bread at the meal that they shared with Him, and
then they believed. Notice the three elements in today's story;
the Scriptures, a meal, and a renewed faith.

At this Mass we have the Scriptures read to us and expounded in the homily. We share a meal with Christ. We discover once again the necessity and the means to a stronger faith. We do believe in Christ, but our belief often lacks depth and practical application. At Communion today as we break bread with Christ and our brothers and sisters, we should ask Him for a strong faith in His Resurrection and all that it implies.

In the Prayer after Communion the Church tells us to pray: "Lord give us the spirit of Your love and may these Easter Sacraments help us to be of one mind." We must be God's loving children united in one mind, convinced of Christ's Resurrection and willing to declare it to the whole world.

Tuesday of Easter Week

THEME

Suffering and death are swallowed up in the victory of the Resurrection.

EXPOSITION

In today's Gospel Christ appears to His disciples and goes to great lengths to convince them that He is not a ghost but truly risen. He calms them and settles all their doubts. As He did with the disciples on the way to Emmaus, He gives an explanation of the Scriptures, using Moses, the prophets and the Psalms to show how the Messiah had to suffer on His way to glory.

"Christ has truly risen, Alleluia!" This should be our greeting during Easter Week. When we say it, we must realize the true meaning of the Resurrection as Christ's victory over death and suffering. If we accept our sufferings in a Christlike manner, then they will lead us to glory.

In the Prayer of the Mass we acknowledge God as the source of all growth in the Church. At this season we are especially aware that He continually gives new children to His Church. His goodness and loving concern do not stop with our baptism, however, but extend to every moment of our existence.

God gives all His children the grace that they need to accept sufferings and disappointments. Ask God, Who is the source of all growth, to help you to grow in Christ—in the victorious risen Christ.

Wednesday of Easter Week

THEME

Our risen Savior takes care of all His disciples' needs.

EXPOSITION

St. John tells us about Christ's third appearance to His disciples. We see how Peter, still the man of action and the leader, helps the others find relief for their feelings of disappointment by a hard night's work. Once again the eyes of love recognize Christ first, and John tells Peter that it is the Lord.

What a magnetic pull Christ has on St. Peter! For the second time he leaps out of a boat to reach the Lord. When the others bring the boat to shore, Christ has prepared a breakfast for them. As they eat, they remember the Last Supper and how they abandoned Him. They are afraid; they hold back, but His love wins them over. The old familiarity returns.

APPLICATION

Our Lord takes care of His disciples' needs. They were hungry for food, but most of all they hungered for assurance of His love and of His forgiveness. What they wanted, He gave them with all His heart. He does the same for us at this and every Mass. He provides us with food for our journey. He gives us the assurance that our sins are forgiven if we are sorry, and that He loves us, no matter what we have done. That's what Easter should mean to us. Easter newness should continue to grow in us by every Mass and Communion. Make sure that it does!

Thursday of Easter Week

THEME

Find Christ in His sacraments and in His people.

EXPOSITION

Our Lord shows Himself to Mary and tells her that He will ascend to His Father. He gives her a message for His disciples. Mary, before all the others who were Christ's friends, was found worthy to see Him. Mary is the model of perfect sorrow for sins, and of an all-encompassing love of Christ. When Christ revealed Himself to her, she instinctively threw herself at His feet. Because Christ had a new mode of existence, He said to her, "Do not cling to Me."

Like Mary we are not to cling to Christ in His physical person. We must touch Him now by faith in the sacramental order, in the order of sacred signs which He himself established.

Christ is truly present among us during this sacrifice of the Mass and in the sacrament of the Eucharist. He is ours in the sacrament of penance. We must wipe away the cobwebs from our eyes and see Christ in these things; we must reach out and grasp Him under these sacred signs.

We touch Christ in our neighbors in whom He lives. Jesus only gradually manifested Himself to Mary. He will treat us in the same way. We should not dismiss so casily the idea that Christ dwells in everyone we meet. John alone recognized the man on the shore as Jesus. Mary alone and only gradually, saw that the man who looked like a gardener was the Lord.

Have you been as perceptive as John and Mary, or have you missed Christ in your neighbors? If they have been baptized, they are Jesus Christ.

Friday of Easter Week

THEME

We must be conscious of our mission to spread the good news of Christ's Resurrection.

EXPOSITION

The Gospels of Easter week certainly jump around from scene to scene and time to time. Today's Gospel tells us of Christ's last appearance to His disciples as recorded in

Matthew, Ch. 28. In this scene, Christ confers upon His apostles their mission to make disciples of all nations by baptizing them in the name of the Trinity and by teaching them all that He had taught. It is a mission as wide and universal as the world to which they are sent.

Christ assures and encourages them with his closing remarks: "And remember, I am with you always. Yes, even to the end of the world." Christ thus begins to act through others—using their hands, feet, bodies, to do His work. He will save the world in and through His followers.

APPLICATION

We, as followers of Christ in the 20th century, must be conscious of our duty to spread His word not only as individuals but also as members of His Church. Christ remains always with His Church. It is to the Church that He gives the universal mission to help all men believe in Him.

At Mass today ask Christ for the grace to follow His plan. In the Prayer of the Mass we ask that our actions reflect our belief. Repeat this request often. Also ask yourself: "Is there anything in my conduct which says that I am a risen, living Christian, an Easter Christian in the truest sense? If the answer is "Yes," then you are already a missionary to the 20th century. If the answer is "No," use this opportunity to make it "Yes."

Saturday of Easter Week

THEME

Mary, Peter and John show us how to love our risen Savior.

330

EXPOSITION

As we close this week, we glance back to the great fact of Christ's Resurrection. We have heard over and over again of His appearances. Today we hear the story of Mary, Peter and John at the tomb. Each had burning love for Christ. Each of them can teach us how to love Christ and serve Him even better than we are doing at present.

Mary had a strong impulsive love which made her want to be near her Lord even in death. Peter had a love which fell but came back even stronger. His was a love that would lead others to Christ. John possessed or was possessed by that purity of love which never knew failure or disappointment in the Beloved. Christ was everything to John.

APPLICATION

We believed in the Resurrection of Christ even before this Easter. The Masses of this week should have reinforced this belief. The Church has been teaching us our true worth even as she confirmed our faith in the Resurrection. She wants us to thank God for the great gift of baptism which gave us the life of Christ for the first time. She urges us to glory in the Resurrection.

The Church asks us to see in Mary, Peter and John examples of what we should be. Ask this trio of lovers to teach you through this Mass and Communion how to love Christ as they did. Surely one of the three—Mary, Peter or John—is the model of what we have sought this Easter week. Can we continue to follow their example?

The Vigil of the Ascension

THEME

Today we prepare for the great joy of Christ's final victory.

EXPOSITION

Today's Mass, unlike other vigils in the liturgy, has no mention of sadness, penance or mortification. It is a joyful vigil. Christ is reaching the climax of His mission when He will return to the Father, bringing with Him those whom He has saved.

In the Epistle, St. Paul quotes Psalm 68:18: "When he ascended on high, he took a host of captives and gave gifts to men" (Eph. 4:8). Paul interprets the phrase "he ascended" as a reference to Christ's ascension and "he gave gifts" as a reference to the descent of the Spirit. We are the captives whom Christ leads to heaven, captives of His loving concern for us exemplified by His passion, death, and Resurrection.

APPLICATION

It is good to pause before the great joy of tomorrow's feast to recollect our thoughts. Let us realize that only by living like Christ on earth can we share in His glory.

Christ did not come to His Ascension as a refuge from failure, but neither was He unmarked by the battles He had won. He carried on His body the scars that were only a small indication of what He suffered. Let us realize that suffering and persecution must also be the prelude to our sharing in Christ's glory.

Today is a fitting time to rededicate ourselves to a Christ-like career here on earth. Tomorrow we will lift our eyes toward the heaven to which Christ ascends. Why not jump the gun a little, and spend today thinking of heaven where Christ rules with His Father and our Father?

The Feast of the Ascension

THEME

Lift up your hearts to the Lord!

EXPOSITION

Today we celebrate the great feast of the Ascension—the commemoration of Christ's victory over suffering and death, sin and evil. Our eyes are lifted up to heaven where Christ has gone. We may view today's feast from two viewpoints, Christ's and our own. Christ tells the Father, "I have done all that you have told Me. All of mankind can be saved now if they cooperate with our loving plan."

We have our own viewpoint. We would love to have Christ present in His visible, human touchable form, but that is not possible. He is, however, present to us through His Spirit. By our acts of faith, hope and love we gain the right to follow Christ to heaven. We witness to Him on earth so that we may rejoice with Him in heaven.

APPLICATION

Make your day a joyful one. Offer your Mass and Communion so that all of us will one day join Christ in the glory of heaven. Ask for the grace to spend the time that comes before your ascension in a Christlike manner as a witness to the love, the goodness and the truth of Christ and His Church.

Smile, be happy, and when the priest says to you today: "Lift up your hearts," do just that! Lift up your hearts to the Lord! He is waiting to take your hearts and all of you to heavenly glory.

The Vigil of Pentecost

THEME

Today's vigil shouts to us "Get ready for the feast of the Holy Spirit."

EXPOSITION

Today some people think we no longer need vigils before great feasts. I disagree. We are so absorbed in day-to-day living that many times we forget about the birthdays and anniversaries of our closest relatives. In our culture, it is even easier to forget about religious holydays, except the two major feasts which have acquired an immense commercial significance.

Vigils remind us that something important is going to happen. They shout to us: "Get ready!" Today we prepare to celebrate the great outpouring of the Holy Spirit upon the followers of Christ.

APPLICATION

When the Holy Spirit came down upon those early Christians who had gathered around the Blessed Virgin Mary in the Cenacle, He filled them with an unquenchable love for Christ.

334

Inflamed by this love, they went out to talk about Christ, to live for Christ, and even to die for Christ. Offer this Mass as a preparation for tomorrow's feast. Ask the Holy Spirit to fill you with the same committed and intense love of Christ which He gave to the Apostles on the first Pentecost.

During the day, pick out five persons who aren't attractive and well-liked by the crowd at work, in school or around the neighborhood. Show them that the phrase "loving Christ in people and people in Christ" is more than eight words. While you are doing it, you will be showing the Holy Spirit that you are worthy of His gifts.

Monday after Pentecost

THEME

If one believes and is trying to live a good life, there will be no obstacle to the coming of the Holy Spirit.

EXPOSITION

The joy of Pentecost is prolonged for a whole week so that we will be able to digest, in a sense, the wonderful nourishment set before us by this feast. In the first lesson of today's Mass, Peter addresses Cornelius and his family. These Gentiles are the first non-Jews to hear the message of Christ.

When Peter finished, the Holy Spirit quickly showed His approval. He came down upon the Gentiles so that they were able to speak "in tongues" and to glorify God. Peter and all the Jews present realized that God had spoken, and so they baptized Cornelius and his family. In this way the Holy Spirit personally opened the Church to the non-Jewish people.

The Church stresses the importance of baptism in this lesson, in this Mass and throughout this whole week. This week is to be a furthering of the education of the newly-baptized. Today the Church declares that she is universal in membership and extension.

None of us would disagree, would we? Of course not, but the Holy Spirit seems to have better results with certain classes, races, or colors, doesn't He? No, He does not, and there is no obstacle to the coming of the Holy Spirit if one believes and is trying to lead a good life.

You are a believer and you must be trying to live a good life if you are here. Open your heart to the universal appeal of Christ and His Church. Don't discriminate. All are called and it's up to you to help them make the right reply.

Tuesday after Pentecost

THEME

Through confirmation the Holy Spirit helps us to live, to witness and to worship as mature apostolic Christians.

EXPOSITION

On this second day after Pentecost, the Church shows us the Holy Spirit strengthening those already baptized. He helps them to live as mature Christians. He has done this for us in confirmation. The Gospel shows us that following Christ means being one of His sheep. He is the shepherd; we are His sheep. We follow His voice and must go through Him if we are to "have life and have it to the full." Christ is the one and only Savior Whom we must all follow. The Holy Spirit helps us to do just that.

APPLICATION

In the Prayer of the Mass we ask the Lord to let the power of the Holy Spirit be with us, gently cleansing our hearts and guarding us against all danger. The Holy Spirit does this and more. Through confirmation He helps us to live, to witness, and to worship as mature apostolic Christians. In a sense this is in one sentence the essence of Vatican II's *Declaration on the Apostolate of the Laity.*

One sentence may capture the essence of the Declaration, but it will take a lifetime of effort to realize its full meaning. If you have not yet read this document on the laity, why not do so during this week? If you have read the Declaration, try to estimate how well you are implementing its contents. Either way Christ and His Spirit will bless such a Pentecostal undertaking.

During Mass stir up the graces of the Holy Spirit so that you will be able to live, to witness and to worship as a mature apostolic Christian. Let the refrain of the Alleluia echo throughout your whole day: "Come Holy Spirit, fill the hearts of Your faithful and enkindle in them the fire of Your love."

Ember Wednesday after Pentecost

THEME

Spring with its sudden burst of growth should remind us of the invisible growth of the Holy Spirit within us.

337

EXPOSITION

This is a joyful time of the year when the sun shines, the grass grows and the flowers and shrubs blossom again. The joyful signs of growth which are associated with spring point to the invisible interior growth within us of the Holy Spirit.

The first two readings show us some of the wonderful works done by the apostles—the things they said and the cures they achieved. The apostles spoke and acted in this way because they were filled with the Holy Spirit.

APPLICATION

The Holy Spirit was not invisible to the apostles. He was visible in the tongues of fire and in the wonders He accomplished through them. We are not so lucky today, or are we? Hasn't our age been called the Age of the Holy Spirit?

The Holy Spirit has spoken to us through Vatican II and the renewal it has sparked in the Church. What about the civil rights' movement, Vista, the Peace Corps and our missionary efforts in South America? What about the ecumenical movement and the involvement of the laity in the Church? All of these are indications that the Holy Spirit is active today.

Don't spend your time wishing that you lived in the first apostolic age. Be happy you are alive during *this* apostolic age. The Spirit of Christ seeks to become visible to a world which was never before so close to conversion as it is now. The world needs love and Christ's Spirit is willing. Can you bring the two together?

Thursday after Pentecost

THEME

The Church was on the move from the very beginning.

EXPOSITION

It was not too long after the Holy Spirit's pentecostal visit
that the Church moved out of the confines of Jerusalem and
went into Samaria. Philip talked about Christ and convinced
the people that Christ was the Messiah by the miracles which
he performed. Our Lord's words in the Gospel were literally
borne out by Philip, who was able to cure diseases and to
drive out devils. Philip shared with the Samaritans his great
message and they shared with him whatever they had.

APPLICATION

The Church was on the move right from the first moment of
its existence. It was not content to rest on its laurels, rejoicing because it possessed the truth and the message of Christ.
It was a missionary Church from the very beginning and it is
a missionary Church today.

Don't ever forget that you belong to such a Church. It is a
Church on the move. Are you a Christian on the move? You
possess the truth and the good news of Christ. Are you trying
every day to share these gifts with others? The only way to
understand and appreciate what you have is to share it with
another. A shared thought or experience means so much more
than a solitary one.

Seek in these moments with Christ during His sacrifice to
understand the implications of your membership in such a
missionary organization. Find here what you need to go out

339

and to live in the world as a person who has a mission from God through Christ and inspired by the Holy Spirit.

Ember Friday after Pentecost

THEME

Does everybody need somebody sometime or all the time?

EXPOSITION

The Ember Fridays of the year are characterized by a penetential note. Today's Mass mixes this note of penance with a joyful one. The Entrance Hymn especially makes us want to sing out in praise of the glories of this feast.

However, the Gospel has the message we should consider today. It tells us about the faith of the man who had been paralyzed for years, and about the cleverness of his friends who were determined that he would get to Christ. They believed that Christ could work a miracle and cure the man. They sought one cure and were given two; for the Lord gave the patient health of body and soul.

Jesus certainly saw the great sorrow in the heart of the man He cured. However, I think that Christ was moved to work the miracle partially because of the faith of the people who carried the man. Our Lord just had to be impressed with their determination and resourcefulness.

APPLICATION

We need the help of others if we are to live the Christian life to its fullest. We are not saved alone. We are saved in company with all humanity, especially the other members of

Christ's mystical body. We must work together if we are to achieve our goal as members of God's family.

Ask the Holy Spirit through every Mass and Communion for the Christian-family spirit. Work with the other members of this family because each of us needs help in following Christ. It is a great deal easier to be kind, honest, apostolic or any other Christlike quality if we have some company in the endeavor. "Everybody needs somebody sometime." The words of the song are true but they don't go far enough. Everybody needs somebody all the time.

Ember Saturday after Pentecost

Theme

And so this week after Pentecost ends today. Make sure its influence does not!

Exposition

Today we come to the last day of the Easter season. We have celebrated Our Lord's Resurrection and Ascension and the descent of the Holy Spirit upon the apostles. For the last week we have been following the lead of the Church in begging the Holy Spirit to stir up within us His grace to make us the type of Christians we should be.

Today's Mass rings with a feeling of love; the love of God in Christ which has been poured forth upon us by His Holy Spirit, and the love which we must have for one another. Love prompted Christ to cure Simon's mother-in-law and the others who were brought to Him. Love urged Him to preach the good news to the other towns in Judea.

341

We must be convinced of the love which God has for us. We must share this love with others. The Holy Spirit will guide us in showing the love of God to our world. The key word in that last sentence is "guide." It is our world and we have to work for its improvement.

This week should have taught us many things about the Holy Spirit and ourselves. We don't have all the answers yet, but we have a Spirit of love and understanding Who will help us in the search. Don't ignore the Spirit of Christ. Open yourself to His influence a little more each day. And so this week after Pentecost ends today. Make sure its influence does not!

Ferial Masses during the Week of the First Sunday after Pentecost

THEME

Our love for God is measured by the love we have for our neighbor.

EXPOSITION

Today's Mass is that of the first Sunday after Pentecost but it is never said on that Sunday because of the feast of the Holy Trinity. It is regretable that the beautiful prayers and readings from this Mass are not said on some Sunday when all the parish is gathered together for worship.

Today the Liturgy of the Word speaks of social justice. The love we have for God is measured by the love that we show to our neighbor. This is the essence of God's words to us through St. John's Epistle and through His Son's words about measuring and judging others as we want to be judged.

It is so very simple in these weeks after Pentecost to start to relax. We do not want to give up the fervor of the Easter season, but we do. One way of preventing such a surrender is a careful and prayerful consideration of this fact. We truly serve God when we serve our neighbor with Christ-like love.

Ask the Holy Spirit for guidance during these weeks after Pentecost. He will help you to know the value of true love— true love of God as shown in true love of neighbor. Pray that He will help you to be quick to love and forgive, slow to judge and accuse, and determined to see and serve Christ in others.